Political Leadership in Liberal and Democratic Theory

Political Leadership in Liberal and Democratic Theory

Edited by
Joseph Femia, András Körösényi
and Gabriella Slomp

imprint-academic.com

This Collection copyright © Joseph Femia, András Körösényi
and Gabriella Slomp, 2009

Individual chapters copyright © their Author, 2009

The moral rights of the contributors have been asserted
No part of this publication may be reproduced in any form
without permission, except for the quotation of brief passages
in criticism and discussion.

Published in the UK by Imprint Academic
PO Box 200, Exeter EX5 5YX, UK

Published in the USA by Imprint Academic
Philosophy Documentation Center
PO Box 7147, Charlottesville, VA 22906-7147, USA

ISBN 9 781845 401719 (cloth)
ISBN 9 781845 401726 (paperback)

A CIP catalogue record for this book is available from the
British Library and US Library of Congress

Contents

Introduction 1

Part I

John Horton
    Political Leadership and Contemporary Liberal Political Theory 11

Peter Lassman
    Political leadership, Judgement and the Sense of Reality 31

Gabriella Slomp
    The Janus Face of Leadership:
    The Demands of Normality and Exception 49

Part II

Joseph Femia
    Elites vs. the Popular Will: a False Dichotomy 67

András Körösényi
    Political Leadership: Classical vs. Leader Democracy 79

Jules Townshend
    Getting from Here to There: Marxism and the
    Paradoxes of Leadership. 101

Part III

Donald D. Searing & Marco R. Steenbergen
    Virtues and Vices of Liberal Democratic Leadership 125

Raia Prokhovnik
    Political Leadership and Sovereignty 151

Gábor G. Fodor
    The Two 'Faces' of Political Creativity:
    Two Paradigms of Political Leadership. 177

Index 193

Introduction

Leadership may be defined simply as the quality permitting one person to command others. Nevertheless, leadership is essentially based on consent rather than coercion. Ordering someone about at the point of a gun is not leadership, though leaders will normally impose coercive sanctions on those (presumably a minority) who refuse to accept their commands voluntarily.

The topic of leadership has stimulated two rival modes of approach. The classical approach focuses primarily on the personalities of 'great men', depicting them as unique and heroic figures capable of inspiring their disciples through sheer force of will. Examples would include Rousseau's Great Legislator or Nietzsche's 'superman'. Especially influential in modern social science has been Max Weber's 'ideal-type' of the charismatic leader, endowed with some extraordinary quality (real or imagined) that enables him (almost always a male) to mobilise human effort and transform the material world, for good or ill. Weber contrasted charismatic authority with two other types of domination: traditional (where obedience is based on custom and revered precedent) and 'rational-legal' (where compliance is based on legally established rules and procedures). Both these modes are stable and predictable structures of everyday life. By way of contrast, charismatic domination in its pure form is mercurial and transient, and the changes it inspires may or may not be desirable. Social scientists in the early twentieth century tended to see charismatic authority as a symptom of modernity. The decline of traditional practices and institutions, according to psychologists such as Freud and LeBon, had exposed the deep human craving to surrender to a hypnotic leader. In this literature, leaders were portrayed rather negatively, as self-absorbed and irrational theatrical figures who posed a threat to human liberty. The devotion they engendered (or would engender) in their followers was deemed to be a dangerous manifestation of mass psychic disorder. The subsequent rise of Mussolini and Hitler seemed to confirm such fears.

After World War II, the idea of charisma as a diabolical trait was set aside in the interests of a more sociological understanding of leadership. Weber was accused of underestimating the social significance of the charismatic leader as a symbol, catalyst, or message-bearer, embodying the values and hopes of the social group. Charisma, after all, depends on social recognition and must therefore reflect, in some intangible way, the culture and sensibilities of those who come to validate it. Whereas Weber stressed the revolutionary or disturbing aspects of charisma, it was now seen as instrumental in maintaining social order.[1] Leaders, according to this new approach, are hardly extraordinary. In the words of Cecil Gibb, 'leadership is not a quality which a man possesses; it is an interactional function of the personality and of the social situation'.[2] In fact, some studies indicated that leaders, far from being unusual, were often the group members closest to the statistical average whose very ordinariness allowed them to make innovations.[3] The focus now was on the needs and structures of the group and the surrounding situational context, and on the resulting dynamic between leaders and led. This approach to leadership was egalitarian in its assumptions and did manage to explain the type of 'leader' who claims only to be a 'mouth-piece' for his followers.

Not all leaders, however, simply mirror an existing consensus. Some attempt to create a new consensus—remote and majestic men and women, who are objects of fear and reverence. Even leaders dismissed as mere managers will, if they are effective, usually command a measure of devotion and possess certain human attributes beyond the normal: courage, intelligence, imagination, perseverance, and the like. Good leaders generally evince a rare combination of characteristics, which allows them to come to the right decision in a manner that transcends rationality. Starting with Machiavelli, many have tried to develop a science of leadership, but history suggests that leadership ability is akin to artistic talent, which can neither be reduced to a set of maxims nor acquired by reading books.

We may conclude that Weber's mysterious idea of 'charisma' still has something important to tell us about leadership. The relationship between a political leader and his/her followers is not just a matter of rational calculation. To the contrary, it expresses underlying psychic processes that challenge our cherished belief in fundamental human equality. This may help to explain why the great bulk of the scholarly literature on leadership is produced by sociologists, psychologists, and experts in

---

1 E.Shils, 'Charisma, Order and Status', *American Sociological Review* 30 (1965), pp. 199–213.
2 C. Gibb, 'The Principles and Traits of Leadership', *Journal of Abnormal and Social Psychology* 42 (1951), p.284.
3 E. Hollander, 'Conformity, Status and Idiosyncrasy Credit', *Psychology Review* 65 (1958), pp. 117–27.

business management; and why political theorists seem reluctant to speculate in any systematic way about—or even acknowledge—the role of political leadership in modern society. If, as the American Declaration of Independence informs us, 'all men are created equal', then political leadership, at least in its more proactive forms, represents a deviation from the ideal of personal autonomy. Leadership smacks of hierarchy, of exceptional individuals, of the primordial fact that there will always be rulers and ruled. For this reason, the idea of democracy will never sit easily alongside the need for leadership. Insofar as liberalism is associated with democracy, as well as individual rights and the rule of law, it too has an inherent antipathy to strong leadership. Indeed, the main purpose of liberal theory has been to justify *restrictions* on what leaders may do.

But the implicit egalitarianism of our political culture is not the only reason why theorists are loath to recognise or analyse the positive benefits of political leadership. After all, mediaeval Europe, despite its rigid hierarchical structures, saw earthly power-holders as mere functionaries, executing God's law in strict collaboration with the Church, and foreswearing any creative ambitions of their own. As the existing social and political order was seen as divinely ordained, infused with the purpose of preparing mankind for the 'life beyond', rulers were expected to demonstrate due humility. Even during the Renaissance, a period which valued individual achievement, the ubiquitous advice-books for monarchs were basically mediaeval in conception, describing ideal rulers who were paragons of piety and rectitude, and whose judgement was confined to the deductive application of eternal truths. Machiavelli, in his classic work *The Prince*, subverted this literature by dealing systematically with the requirements of leadership in the real world, where abstract universals rarely survive contact with unpropitious circumstances. Jettisoning all teleological baggage, abandoning the idea of an immutable universal order, he insisted that a virtuoso politician could decisively shape human events. For Machiavelli, politics was not the expression of a sacred plan, derived from Scripture; it was a struggle for power and advantage, in which the different protagonists were engaged in a never-ending game of political chess, with winners and losers. Success was enjoyed by those who aligned themselves with dexterous and ruthless leaders, masters of calculation and prediction.[4] Leadership, as Machiavelli made clear, becomes a political necessity only in a context of conflict and uncertainty, where choice often involves selecting the lesser of two evils. If politics is reduced to moral principles, or defined as the pursuit of some abstract

---

4   See J. Femia, *Machiavelli Revisited* (Cardiff: University of Wales Press, 2004), ch. 3.

ideal, then leadership, with its vicissitudes, may be perceived as a threat to the achievement of the 'good'.

For almost half a century now, mainstream liberal and democratic theory has seen its task as one of identifying truths about how we should live—truths inherent in our essential human nature and discoverable through rational analysis. The normative bias of analytical political philosophy, instigated by Rawls, and the 'deliberative' and 'participatory' bias of speculation about democracy, inspired mainly by Habermas, leave little scope for political leadership. Politics is understood as the executive instrument of some moral purpose, which imposes severe constraints on what political leaders can rightfully do. Making the moral prior to the political is the defining feature of what Bernard Williams calls 'political moralism', which he contrasts unfavourably with 'political realism'. The latter, says Williams, recognises a 'general truth' discovered by Goethe's Faust: in the beginning was the deed (not the word). That is to say, political theory will seem to make sense only by virtue of the historical situation in which it is presented, and which it will to some degree reflect. It follows that no political theory can by itself determine its own application.[5] On this understanding of the relationship between theory and practice—and it is an understanding that permeates this volume— the role of leadership is crucial.

Our starting point is that this neglect of leadership is a deficiency that needs to be explained and corrected.[6] Our overall aim is to dissect, discuss, and evaluate descriptive, analytical, and normative arguments

---

5   B. Williams, *In the Beginning was the Deed: Realism and Moralism in Political Argument*, edited and forwarded by G. Hawthorn (Princeton: Princeton University Press, 2005), pp. 1–17.

6   There has, however, been a significant literature on leadership as such in political *science* during the last three decades (e.g. J.M. Burns, *Leadership* (New York: Harper and Row, 1978); J. Blondel, *Political Leadership* (Sage, 1987); and R. Elgie, *Political Leadership in Liberal Democracies* (London: MacMillan, 1995). Moreover, empirical research in comparative politics and government reveals, though often indirectly, the growing importance of political leaders in liberal democracies (e.g. G.Sheffer (ed.), *Innovative Leaders in International Politics* (New York: State University of New York Press, 1993); R.L. Jacobs, R.Y. Shapiro, *Politicians Don't Pander. Political Manipulation and the Loss of Democratic Responsiveness* (Chicago and London: The University of Chicago Press, 2000); R.R. Aminzade et.al., *Silence and Voice in the Study of Contentious Politics* (Cambridge: Cambridge University Press, 2001)). The decline of political parties in the last decades (e.g. P. Mair, *Democracy Beyond Parties* (Irvine: University of California, Center for the Study of Democracy, 2005); J. Blondel, 'The Links Between Western European Parties and Their Supporters. The Role of personalization', *Occasional Papers N. 16/2005* (CIRCaP, University of Siena, 2005), pp. 1-27.) arguably mirrors the increasing personalization and Americanization of politics in Europe. Authors such as Bernard Manin (*The Principles of Representative Government*, Cambridge: Cambridge University Press, 1997) talk about a new epoch in the history of representative democracy, while Thomas Poguntke and Paul Webb (*The Presidentialization of Politics: A Comparative Study of Modern Democracies* (Oxford: Oxford University Press, 2005)) and their co-authors write about the 'presidentialization' of European Politics. We may conclude that *empirical* research, at least, deals adequately with the role of leaders in contemporary Europe and USA.

regarding the role and value of leadership in a liberal and democratic society. In carrying out this aim, the volume will show that there is a pessimistic or 'realist' strand of liberal and democratic thinking (e.g. Max Weber, Joseph Schumpeter, Isaiah Berlin, Judith Shklar) that does indeed underline the need for leadership, though it has been submerged in recent decades by the academic dominance of deontological liberalism and 'deliberative' or participatory democracy

* * *

The first section of the volume focuses on the issue of leadership in liberal theory. In *Political Leadership and Contemporary Liberal Political Theory* John Horton analyses what explanations might be given for the neglect of the problem of political leadership in the canonical texts of contemporary liberal theory—those by John Rawls, Ronald Dworkin, and Brian Barry in particular. In doing so Horton addresses a larger lacuna in liberal theory: the neglect of questions of political agency, collective action and power. He suggests that this neglect is primarily the result of a preoccupation with '*ideal theory*', and of a remarkable indifference to the relationship between ideal theory and political action. For Horton, the lack of concern with political agency distorts our understanding of politics and is symptomatic of the moralising of politics and of the desire 'to take politics out of politics'. As a result politics is limited to a relatively narrow range of issues, with most of the fundamental questions lying beyond political contestation. Its inherent individualism also makes liberal theory suspicious of collective action and power. Horton argues, however, that some strands of contemporary liberal theory, such as the 'liberalism of fear', identified by Judith Shklar, and the 'modus vivendi liberalism' defended by John Gray, are less idealizing in their approach, less demanding in their normative claims, and therefore more receptive to the problems of leadership.

While Horton analyses mainstream liberal theory, especially in its recent manifestations, Peter Lassman (in *Political leadership, Judgement and the Sense of Reality*) looks at those untypical authors within the context of twentieth century liberalism, namely Max Weber and Isaiah Berlin, who felt it necessary to tackle the problem of political leadership. Weber emphasizes supposed facts of modern political reality, such as (1) the 'fact' that politics is struggle, (2) the 'fact' of 'the rule of man over man' and (3) the 'fact' of value pluralism. According to Weber, these facts epitomise 'the disenchantment of the world' and lead us to the classical Platonic question of 'who should rule' and to the examination of the qualities of the good ruler. Lassman compares Weber's account with the one offered by Isaiah Berlin. It is noticed that both writers were concerned with the question of pluralism and shared similar views about the limitations of political knowledge. Lassman gives particular attention to the implicit normative judgements that these thinkers make about the quality of political leaders, focusing upon the problem of political judgement under conditions of uncertainty and value pluralism. The examples of Weber and Berlin demonstrate that the recognition of political leadership in modern states is not necessarily incompatible with the liberal outlook. In addition, Lassman argues that the examination of their work shows a remarkable mutation of the Platonic ideal of the philosopher ruler.

While Horton and Lassman write about leadership in general terms, Gabriella Slomp (*The Janus Face of Leadership: the Demands of Normality and Exception*) differentiates between leadership in two distinct political situations of liberal democracies: the state of normalcy and the state of emergency. Slomp argues that since the Thatcher/Reagan era a handful of liberal theorists have shown an interest in political leadership but that their analyses tend to contain a serious flaw, which she tries to bring to light by taking the work of Kenneth Ruscio as an example. Slomp contrasts Ruscio's discussion of leadership with that of Machiavelli, Hobbes, Locke and Schmitt, respectively, and claims that while the latter discuss the requirements of leadership when sovereignty is challenged, Ruscio, like most other liberal theorists, limits his argument to normal and peaceful times when all conflict is just 'disagreement among friends'. Slomp contends that any discussion of political leadership must address the challenges faced by liberal democratic leaders in *both* normal and exceptional times, and spell out their role in the process of establishing a state of emergency. She suggests that a theory of leadership that examines the duties and qualities of liberal democratic leaders only 'under normal circumstances' is not simply incomplete but also inadequate.

The second section of the volume concentrates on how different types of democratic theory deal with the idea of leadership. In *Elites vs. the Popular Will: a False Dichotomy*, Joseph Femia targets those radical idealists who believe that the purpose of democracy is to reflect some 'real' or 'true' will of the people, unsullied by elite influences, which are presumed to be self-serving, if not actually malign. Using empirical studies to examine how the mechanisms of radical democracy—referenda and small-scale participatory bodies—work in practice, he argues that manipulation by elites is impossible to avoid, given the dynamics of social interaction and the limitations of the mass public. In particular the chapter throws doubt on the assumptions of the 'deliberative democrats', who insist that rational debate will transform ignorant and selfish preferences into properly 'authentic' ones. Femia concludes by suggesting, perhaps counter-intuitively, that our present form of representative democracy, for all its faults, may be better at responding to people's genuine wants than the supposedly egalitarian alternatives, where *de facto* leadership would be exercised by self-appointed, unacknowledged, and therefore unaccountable elites.

While Femia's main argument is that political leadership, in some shape or form, is inevitable, no matter what schemes are devised to by-pass it, András Körösényi (*Political Leadership: Classical vs. Leader Democracy*) mounts a defence of political leadership as essential to good governance—or indeed any governance at all. The chapter proceeds by way of a systematic comparison between the 'classical' view of democracy as 'rule by the people', and what Körösényi, following Max Weber, calls 'leader democracy'. The latter is democratic only in the sense that the citizens choose their rulers, who may or may not be responsive to the perceived wishes of those who elect them. According to this model, the people may have grumbles and prejudices, and even vague preferences. But this doesn't amount to a *settled will* that could be implemented by politicians. Körösényi attempts to demonstrate that the classical model is based on empirically unrealistic and logically dubious premises. It is sometimes argued that, although leader democracy may be *descriptively accurate*, it nevertheless lacks *normative validity*, since it rejects (both in theory and in practice) the quasi-sacred value of political equality. Körösényi challenges this argument, asking why a value that is so far removed from reality should inform our understanding of democracy. If leader democracy provides responsible government, if it promotes security and prosperity, then it is morally superior to an 'alternative' that exists only in the realms of rhetoric and speculation.

Both Körösényi and Femia embrace 'political realism'—to use Williams's terminology. Marxism, with its vision of a totally transparent society, where the age-old distinction between rulers and ruled becomes redundant, would seem to be an example of the opposite approach: i.e. 'political moralism'. In *Getting from Here to There: Marxism and the Paradoxes of Leadership*, Jules Townshend shows us that any such description of Marxism would be a half-truth at best. Marx despised abstract moralism and thought that the glorious communist future was immanent in the historical process, in objective material conditions. He recognised that 'getting from here to there' required leadership, in the form of a vanguard party, but he thought that such leadership would simply amount to 'guidance', as the logic of history was unfolding before our very eyes. Once we reached the end of the journey, political leadership—certainly in any institutionalised form—would 'wither away'. The refusal of history (or the workers) to behave as Marx expected put his later disciples in a quandary. Either they adopted a 'top-down' approach (e.g. Lenin), where leadership shaded off into despotism, or they remained faithful to the idea 'self-emancipation' ('light-touch' leadership), and therefore ended up with no emancipation (in their sense) at all. Townshend suggests that the disarray of Marxism, with its many conflicting strands, can be largely explained by the historical refutation of Marx's teleology.

The third section of the volume explores the meaning, significance and role of political leadership in relation to concepts such as sovereignty, governance and regime building. In *Virtues and Vices of Liberal Democratic Leadership*, Donald D. Searing and Marco R. Steenbergen argue that leadership ought to be an essential component of any comprehensive normative theory of liberal democracy that addresses feasible as opposed to ideal models of democracy. They offer a tentative exploration of the virtues that are expected of leaders in liberal democracy, with the aim to ensure a normatively desirable but also efficient political leadership. They argue that good leaders are those who excel at the motivations and skills needed to protect and promote liberal democratic institutions and cultures. They refer to these skills as 'civic virtues' and explore their role in facilitating the principal functions of democratic leadership, namely regime building, governance, accountability and representation. This chapter can be interpreted as a complementary essay to William Galston's (1988) celebrated article on the virtues of liberal democratic citizenship; certainly Searing and Steenbergen expand on Galston's suggestions about leadership virtues and provide a novel analysis of plausible leadership vices. Searing's and Steenbergen's overall goal is to develop normatively informed concepts suitable for a dialogue between democratic theory and empirical research programs. They emphasize that leadership's virtues and vices are fundamentally psychological phenomena, even if of course they are practiced in institutional settings, and that the political theory of virtues and vices needs to be linked to relevant work in political psychology.

In *Political Leadership and Sovereignty* Raia Prokhovnik makes the case that clarifying the relation between leadership and sovereignty is central to understanding the role of political leadership in politics, and to comprehending and redressesing the neglect of political leadership in mainstream strands of democratic theory. As a first step, Prokhovnik analyses the 'three faces' of leadership and explains how the traditional ideas of political leadership are under threat, through the challenge to the identity of the state, through the challenge to the identity of the political process and through the challenge to the identity of international politics. For Prokhovnik the democratic tradition fails to integrate the concept of leadership into its theory and is unable to enhance our understanding of its meanings and functions. The mainstream notion of sovereignty as 'ruler sovereignty', and the traditional dichotomy between legal and political sovereignty, Prokhovnik contends, do not capture our political experiences and add little to the understanding and rethinking of political leadership. According to Prokhovnik, the effectiveness of political leadership in all its faces can be enhanced by recognizing the way in which 'the political property' of sovereignty operates. Prokhovhik explains how the political property of sovereignty that she outlines links with—and differs from— the dominant notion of political culture; finally, she emphasizes its strong normative dimension.

Whereas Searing and Steenbergen stress the link between the concepts of political leadership, regime building and representation, and Prokhovnik emphasizes the relationship between leadership and sovereignty, Gábor G. Fodor in *The Two Faces of Political Creativity: Two Paradigms of Political Leadership* makes it his business to clarify the relationship between leadership and governance via creativity. Against recent attempts by mainstream governance theory to undermine the *political* content of governance and to focus on the managerial, administrative, and technical facets of leadership, Fodor makes the case that creativity is the focal point of political leadership and that in turn political leadership is at the core of governance. Governance is for Fodor a political process that obtains momentum from the way in which political leaders exercise power creatively. He argues that the concept of political leadership as a creative force can be conceptualized as having two faces. On the one hand, political creativity can be said to have a hidden face, concerned with the organization of power and the conditions of governance; this concept, inspired by Tilo Schabert, emphasizes princely figures that have appeared at all times and in all places in human history. On the other hand, political creativity has an open face, is concerned with the exercise of power and the business of government; this concept, inspired by Frank Ankersmit, describes the nature of modern democracy as a problem of mediatization. The creativity thesis, Fodor argues, emphasizes the power component of governance and highlights the creative contribution by political leaders to the organization and operation of political power.

John Horton

Political Leadership and Contemporary Liberal Political Theory

> Thinking about politics creates a unique dilemma, for it seems inevitably to lead to thinking about thinking; and the more we think about thinking, the less we think about politics. Human thought has a natural tendency to narcissism, and narcissism disposes it to reflexivity. Like the uncomprehending pet spaniel who stares curiously at his master's pointing finger rather than the direction in which the gesture is intended to move him, we humans are often led to dwell introspectively on the processes of our own consciousness rather than gaze outward at the myriad objects that are its presumed targets.[1]

A proposal to discuss 'Political Leadership and Contemporary Liberal Political Theory' is likely to give rise to the quip, often associated with topics like 'business ethics', that it will only be a very brief discussion. And, indeed, probably the most immediately striking point that one notes if seeking to interrogate contemporary liberal theory with a view to exploring its ideas about or approach to political leadership is that it has virtually nothing of substance to say about it: contemporary liberal theorists appear to have shown almost no interest in the role, meaning, value or ethics of political leadership. One can scan the indexes, contents pages and texts of the canonical writings of contemporary liberal political theory — whether it be the work of Rawls, Dworkin, Brian Barry, Raz or pretty much any of the other leading liberal theorists of our time — in vain in search of any explicit reference to political leadership, let alone any serious theoretical discussion of it. At most, an actual political leader may occasionally be mentioned in passing, to illustrate some other point, but there is nothing about the role or significance of political leadership as

---

1   B. Barber, *A Passion for Democracy* (Princeton: Princeton University Press, 1998), p. 3.

such.[2] The issue simply does not figure in the writings of contemporary liberal political theorists as something relevant to their concerns or worthy of their attention. What I want to do here, therefore, is to take this lacuna as my point of departure for a rather general and speculative enquiry into what, if anything, this tells us about the character of contemporary liberal political theory and the conception of politics at work within it. In the course of this enquiry I shall also make a few unsystematic remarks about how the theorising of political leadership might be taken forward, but liberal political theory is my focus.

I

It may be appropriate to begin, though, by asking whether the lack of any concern with political leadership is of any particular significance; that is, whether it is something that is worthy of further enquiry. After all, it is not behoven of any single political theorist that he or she must discuss any particular aspect of political life, and no theorist can encompass everything (even assuming that we have some idea of what 'everything' might mean). All political theorists are inevitably selective in what they write about, reflecting to some extent the political and theoretical context as they understand it, their own sense of what is important or pressing, what happens to intrigue or challenge them, and on what they think they might having something worthwhile and distinctive to say. There is no reason to expect, therefore, that any single political theorist should be interested in the issue of political leadership. If liberal political theorists choose not to write about political leadership, why should this be seen as something that is particularly worthy of comment or analysis?

This response might well be sufficient were we concerned only with an individual theorist, or perhaps a proportion of theorists of a certain type or school. However, it seems less obviously so in this case, where we are dealing with pretty much the entirety of contemporary liberal political theory. If a particular, non-trivial issue is more or less absent from the entire literature of what is very much the dominant approach in contemporary political theory then that seems to provide at least a *prima facie* reason for regarding such an absence as systematic rather than merely incidental; indicative or symptomatic of something about the character of contemporary liberal theory or the outlook or assumptions of its practitioners quite generally, rather than simply the result of the miscellaneous interests and inclinations of individual political theorists. In short, the absence of any theoretical interest in questions of political leadership can

---

[2] See, for instance, J. Rawls, *Political Liberalism* (New York: Columbia University Press, 1993), pp. 249–54; B. Barry, *Why Social Justice Matters* (Cambridge: Polity Press, 2005), *passim*.

reasonably be interpreted as part of a pattern; and such patterns are especially liable to provoke curiosity, enquiry and some attempt at explanation. That, at least, is how I shall proceed.

Secondly, it might be asked, whether contemporary liberal political theory is unique, or even at all unusual, in its lack of attention to questions about political leadership. For, if political theory generally, either now or in the past, has shown little or no interest in political leadership then there would be no reason to think that the explanation has anything specifically to do with contemporary liberal theory. And, although there might still be a question worth asking, that question would more appropriately be about political theory in general.[3] It seems to me, though, that in fact contemporary liberal theory is to some significant degree unusual at least in the extent of its indifference to any questions about leadership; although the picture here is not entirely straightforward. In their different ways, both conservative political thought and Marxism appear to be considerably more concerned with questions about political leadership. That may be unsurprising in the case of conservatism, with its tendency towards elitism and hierarchy, sympathy for the notion of a governing class, sometimes associated with ideas such as *noblesse oblige*, and a historic fear of the power of the 'masses'. Additionally, inequality, a common currency of much conservative thought, provides naturally fertile ground in which ideas of leadership can take root without any embarrassment. More surprisingly, perhaps, leadership has also been the subject of serious discussion and debate within Marxism, in relation to questions such as the role of a vanguard party, the place of intellectuals in politics and the implications of false consciousness and the importance of an educative role for leaders. In fairness, though, it should also be acknowledged that liberals are not unique among contemporary political theorists in their neglect of leadership, as much the same can be said, for example, of their communitarian critics, and also of poststructuralists, whose Nietzschean credentials usually involve some denial of his thoroughgoing elitism; and in truth it cannot be said that questions of political leadership figure prominently in contemporary political theory, although of course, a good deal of it is, or is shaped by, some form of liberalism, broadly interpreted. It should be accepted, therefore, that some of the strictures that follow are not limited to contemporary liberal theory, but apply to some degree to contemporary political theory more generally.

---

3 For an interesting general discussion of the question of what political theory should be about, see: M. Freeden, 'What Should the "Political" in Political Theory Explore?', *Journal of Political Philosophy*, 13 (2005), pp. 112–34.

It is worth remarking that in earlier incarnations of liberalism, some liberal theorists at least, were much more interested in questions about political leadership. It was a topic of abiding importance, for example, to J.S. Mill, whose passionate advocacy of social and political freedom was combined with a serious desire to establish and maintain a leadership role for the best and most able minds, and with the social and political conditions that are necessary for such minds to flourish.[4] Moreover, with respect to political theory in general, from at least Plato onwards, through Machiavelli and numerous later thinkers, and encompassing such seminal twentieth century political theorists as Weber, Schmitt and the so-called 'elitist' theorists of democracy, like Pareto, Mosca and Schumpeter, leadership has been a significant issue within the canon of Western political thought, as it has been in many non-Western traditions, such as Confucianism.[5] So, while it is not an especially conspicuous concern within contemporary political theory generally, it is not the case that political theorists, either now or in the past, including an earlier generation of liberal thinkers, have all been equally indifferent to theorising about political leadership.

Finally, it can be asked whether political leadership is really so important in the modern world? This question, however, only has to be asked for the implausibility of anything other than an affirmative answer to be self-evident.[6] It is no doubt true that politics now, at least in polities with operative liberal democratic institutions, is not about personal rule in the way that it once was, for example, when monarchical or oligarchic government was the norm (although it is worth remembering that in much of the world, both today and in the past, any form of democracy has been something that only a minority of peoples have ever enjoyed). However, the relevance of political leadership is not limited to systems of more or less personal rule. Nor need we go all the way with Carnes Lord when he writes that: 'the theory of democracy tells us the people rule. In practice, we have leaders who rule the people in a manner not altogether different from the princes and potentates of times past'.[7] While that may be too strong, it remains true that even in a constitutional democracy and with the array of bureaucratic institutions of the modern state political leadership not only matters; it matters a good deal. Indeed, without reducing

---

4 For an interpretation of Mill that emphasises his elitism, see: M. Cowling, *Mill and Liberalism* (Cambridge: Cambridge University Press, 1963)
5 A useful survey of thinking about leadership can be found in T. Fuller (ed.), *Leading and Leadership* (Notre Dame: University of Notre Dame Press, 2000)
6 In support of this assertion, see J. M. Burns, *Leadership* (New York: Harper Collins, 1978)
7 C. Lord, *The Modern Prince: What Leaders Need to Know* (New Haven: Yale University Press, 2003), p. xi.

politics to personalities or denying the obviously fundamental causal significance of events, structures and processes, it seems scarcely credible to suggest that leadership is unimportant in modern democracies. For instance, can it be seriously be doubted that had the US and Britain had rather different political leaders from Bush and Blair in the early years of the twenty first century then this would have had significant implications for world history? And certainly some liberal theorists, either privately or in non-theoretical writings, or in their less cautious moments, and more or less tangentially to their theorising, let slip that leadership does matter, if only in their willingness to express their dismay about the quality of many political leaders.[8]

Moreover, it might be thought especially odd if liberal political theory were to hold that political leadership is unimportant. More than most modern political theories, liberalism assumes that human agency, in the sense of the capacity to make decisions and then act on them, has the potential to create and shape institutions and practices so as to manifest liberal principles and values. It is a fundamental commitment of liberalism that human beings are able to use their critical intelligence, powers of reason and argument and capacity for agency to mould and, where necessary, transform social institutions through rationally deployed political action. Without that possibility there would appear to be little practical point to liberal political theory, at least in the prescriptive form that is predominant in contemporary liberal theorising, and little basis for any optimism about the potential of human beings to bring about the kind of the progressive social and political change that is integral to such liberalism.

Therefore, none of these possible explanations, which were they successful would render the lack of concern with political leadership within contemporary liberal political theory more anodyne and less worthy of comment, has much plausibility. There do not appear to be any convincing reasons why political leadership should be of so little interest to contemporary liberal theorists. So, as they have not in fact shown any real interest in it, our initial puzzlement about this neglect and the desire to dig deeper into its causes and consequences remain unassuaged: the question of what, if anything, this lack of interest in political leadership reveals about contemporary liberal theory still appears to be one that is at least worth asking. For, as we have seen, this neglect is neither haphazard, nor justified by the unimportance political leadership in modern political circumstances, and while it does not figure especially prominently in contemporary political theory generally, this is itself to some extent a state of affairs that reflects the present hegemony of liberal theory. Moreover, this

---

8 Barry, *op cit, passim*.

neglect of political leadership has not always been a feature of political theory, including liberal political theory, in the past, and it is not neglected by all styles of political theory even now.

In what follows, therefore, my focus will be on two, related questions. First, why is liberal political theory so completely indifferent to the whole phenomenon of political leadership? As liberals rarely if ever directly comment on this neglect or seek to explain it themselves, the discussion of this question will inevitably be to some degree speculative and inferential. In any case, I am not interested in the actual motives of individual theorists, but in the kinds of consideration that could explain the broader pattern of neglect that has been identified. Secondly, I shall be concerned with what the explanation of this neglect of political leadership tells us about liberal political theory, and what light, if any, this aporia sheds on the character of contemporary liberal political theory and on its understanding of political life more generally. In particular, I shall be concerned with whether this neglect reflects what could be regarded as still deeper failings on the part of contemporary liberal political theory. So, as mentioned earlier, although I shall say a little in passing about political leadership, my main focus of attention is on liberal political theory and the light that is thrown on it when we view it from this perspective, rather than on political leadership itself.

II

If one looks at what it is that preoccupies contemporary liberal political theorists, it is clear that at its core is quite a narrow range of ideas and questions. The ideas of social justice, rights, equality, freedom/autonomy and, more recently, democratic deliberation, and the various possible relations between them, form the mosaic of the vast majority of contemporary liberal theorising. How these ideas should be interpreted and justified, and working out how they can be woven into a coherent and systematic political theory, comprises a very large part of the substance of the corpus of the most prominent contemporary liberal theorists. These ideas, in turn, give rise to a great many complex, difficult and genuinely intriguing theoretical issues, which it is certainly worth political theorists exploring and seeking to clarify. In describing the range of concepts and concerns as 'narrow', therefore, I in no way mean to belittle either their importance or interest. And there is, it should hardly need saying, no reason why liberal political theorists should not be interested in these ideas. Rather, the question is, why *only* these concerns, and not other important issues, such as political leadership? Moreover, it is not just the content of contemporary liberal theory that is in question, but also its 'style'; the manner that is regarded as appropriate for addressing what it takes to be important.

A general feature of these ideas is that they are all normative, in that they are intended to express values or principles. For contemporary liberal theory is overwhelmingly concerned with articulating normative prescriptions, and with their justification and implications. True, a theorist like John Rawls also attaches considerable importance to what he calls questions of 'feasibility' and 'stability', but even the interpretation of these requirements has a strongly normative dimension, and he has been much criticised by otherwise broadly like-minded liberal theorists for allowing 'practical' considerations to play (what is perceived by these critics to be) such a relatively prominent role in the normative theory of his later work.[9] Generally, the purpose of political theory on this view is to formulate, explain, justify and order normative principles that are designed to function as the appropriate measure or standard against which political institutions and practices are to be judged: such principles are intended to provide an authoritative guide to how politics should be organised and conducted. The underlying concern is above all to explain how political coercion can be justified in a context of extensive moral disagreement and cultural diversity in a way that is consistent with liberal political principles. What is central within the narratives of contemporary liberal theory is normative political principles, with the coercive institutions and actions of the state being understood to be legitimate only in so far as they can be justified by such normative principles. *The* problem of political theory for contemporary liberal theorists is taken to be the identification and articulation of political principles that everyone has good reason to accept (whether or not they are in fact accepted). And one of the worries that haunt the more reflective liberal theorists is that there may be no satisfactory answer to the problem when it is formulated in this way.

Whether or not there is a theoretically convincing answer, however, in undertaking this task, liberal political theorists pay little attention to what is ordinarily thought of as the day-to-day 'stuff' of actual politics.[10] Liberal political principles are the theoretical constructions of what Rawls

9 See, for example: B. Barry, 'John Rawls and the Search for Stability', *Ethics*, 105 (1995), pp. 874–915.
10 I have written more fully about what is becoming known as the realist critique of liberal theory in J. Horton, 'Realism, Liberal Moralism and a Political Theory of Modus Vivendi', *European Journal of Political Theory*, forthcoming. See also: B. Honig, *Political Theory and the Displacement of Politics* (Ithaca: Yale University Press, 1993); Glen Newey, *After Politics: The Rejection of Politics in Contemporary Liberal Philosophy* (Houndmills, Basingstoke: Palgrave, 2001); Bernard Williams, *In the Beginning was the Deed* (Princeton, NJ: Princeton University Press, 2005), chs. 1 & 5; Raymond Geuss, *Philosophy and Real Politics* (Princeton, NJ: Princeton University Press, 2008); and W. Galston, 'Realism in Political Theory', *European Journal of Political Theory*, forthcoming.

calls 'ideal theory', and all other questions are consigned to a nether world of non-ideal theory or partial compliance theory.[11] This means, as Glen Newey observes, that:

> Most political philosophers are currently not providing very much philosophical reflection on politics—at least not on politics as it is. The central concern of political philosophy since the publication of *A Theory of Justice* has been to arrive at a set of ideal prescriptions rather than attempting to provide a descriptive account of politics as it non-ideally exists.[12]

If one's knowledge of politics were derived exclusively from the writings of contemporary liberal political theorists one would likely be left almost entirely unaware of the nature of some of the most basic political institutions and practices of political life in liberal democratic states, including for instance the importance of such mundane but ubiquitous phenomena as political parties and pressure groups, and although the right to vote is on every list of basic liberal rights, comparatively little attention is given to elections. Liberal theorists also have surprisingly little to say about representation, and what that means and how it should work. Similarly, through ideal conceptions of public reason or democratic deliberation, the political process is typically characterised in a way that makes it sound much more like a well conducted and unusually polite academic seminar, rather than the rough and tumble processes of negotiation, bargaining and compromise that is typical of democratic politics. And, while it would be unfair to suggest that most liberal political theory is other than inspired by some genuine political concern, it often moves very rapidly away from that concern, as theorists write increasingly about each other's work. In this way theory becomes insular and feeds off itself, not merely in the range of views that are discussed but in the topics that are addressed. In short, there is a tendency for the whole activity to become introverted and, at its worst, even narcissistic.

The fundamental conception of politics implied within contemporary liberal theory (for it is rarely made explicit) is one that sees the point of politics as essentially the application of suitably philosophically justified, moral principles. Basic principles of social justice are supposed to determine the distribution of rights, opportunities and resources in society. The political is subservient to the moral; and while this does not mean that there is no place at all for democratic political decision-making within the liberal picture, its scope is significantly circumscribed by liberal principles, being limited to areas where outcomes are underdetermined by the

---

11 J. Rawls, *A Theory of Justice*, *revised* edition, (Oxford: Oxford University Press, 1999), pp. 7–8.
12 Newey, *op cit*, p. 15.

principles of justice. There is, unavoidably, some room for differences of opinion about how exactly the fundamental principles should be interpreted and implemented, to take account of local circumstances and an inevitable measure of indeterminacy of application that is common to virtually all abstract principles. However, even within that restricted scope, the kinds of reason for political decisions that many liberal theorists allow is still further limited. Politically relevant opinions, to be legitimate, must ultimately be capable of being expressed in a way that meets demanding standards of public reason, and typically must not, for example, be based on simple self-interest or other inappropriate concerns, such as a desire to promote one's own moral values at the expense of those of other people.[13] To a significant degree, therefore, politics is taken to be the handmaiden of a highly moralised liberal political theory.

Political leadership on this account scarcely seems to exist, implicitly amounting to little more than a *deus ex machina* for bringing about and implementing a political order that is consistent with liberal principles. There is little, if any, attempt by liberal political theorists to explain what this might involve, or to consider how political leadership might function, for example, to mediate potential tensions between liberal values and democratic institutions. Political theory is about normative prescription, about setting the rules within which the legitimate goals of political action may be pursued, while the 'how' of effecting what are deemed to be desirable changes belongs to the province of political science, or to the policy sciences more generally.[14] Thus, as we have seen, liberal political theory pays relatively little attention to politics as it actually exists and as is practiced in liberal democratic states. Indeed, interestingly, this way of conceiving political theory tends to have the consequence of making it directly rivalrous to the aims and purposes of those people actively engaged in political action. For many of those people are also motivated by a desire to bring about their cherished values and to realise their own ideas of a just political order, which may not coincide at all closely with the conceptions of liberal theorists. Arguably, this locates liberal political theory within the terrain of conflicting political ideologies. However, by locating fundamental political principles outside the political process, liberal political theory seeks to usurp this position by claiming for itself a sta-

---

13 See J. Rawls, 'The Idea of Public Reason Revisited', *The University of Chicago Law Review*, 64 (1997), pp. 765–807. I have criticised Rawls's conception of public reason in J. Horton, 'Rawls, Public Reason and the Limits of Liberal Justification', *Contemporary Political Theory*, 2 (2003), pp. 5–23.
14 I do not mean to imply that some legitimate division of labour between the political theorist and the social scientist is inappropriate; only that there are also important theoretical questions to be asked.

tus distinct from and superior to such ideological conflict. While many (although not all) of them would hesitate to express the matter in this way, political theorists are conceived as 'experts' in normative argument, and it is therefore for them to determine appropriate principles of justice, and these principles, in turn, set out the normative parameters within which legitimate politics is to be conducted. What is left to politics is not nothing; but it is largely derivative and of modest consequence. It appears that one major reason why liberal theorists see no real role for political leadership is because they have already abrogated a crucial aspect of that role to themselves: it is the business of political theorists to tell us what is right in politics and what kind of political order we should be seeking.

Admittedly, the foregoing is to some extent unavoidably a considerable simplification of contemporary liberal theory, which is much richer and more complex and sophisticated in many respects than the above characterisation may make it sound. But, even if there is an element of distortion in the picture of liberal political theory that I have just drawn, I would maintain that at worst it simply exaggerates features that are undeniably present; and in relation to political leadership, I think that it is sufficiently accurate not seriously to mislead. As liberals themselves show no interest in political leadership, it is perhaps not that surprising that the 'implicit account' of it that can be elicited from their work lacks the subtlety and sophistication that is often in abundance elsewhere. On the basis of their writings, it seems to be something that liberals have not given much thought to, or if they have thought about it, have deemed it as obviously unworthy of any serious theoretical reflection. And, what emerges is, in my view, an extremely limited and shallow, and surprisingly mechanical and instrumental, conception of political leadership. It is a conception that the idealisations of liberal theory leave etiolated, and emptied of most of the complexities and difficulties of political leadership. In particular, liberal theorists idealise out of the picture the circumstances and various constraints—economic and cultural, as well as political—within which effective political leadership has to be exercised in the context of 'real' democratic politics.

III

What, then, is the wider significance of this neglect of political leadership within liberal political theory? Why does this matter? What does it tell us about liberal theory? No doubt there is much that could be said about these questions, but there are, I shall suggest, three interconnected implications of this liberal indifference to political leadership that are particularly worthy of attention.

The first, and probably the most important, is this strand of liberalism's lack of any developed theory, or even remotely adequate conception, of political agency. For, liberal political theory's idealising assumptions and narrow focus on a small range of normative political principles mean that it has nothing of interest to say about how effective political agency is to be understood, and is thus indifferent to the problems and issues that confront the exercise of leadership—a fundamental form of political agency even in a modern democracy. In this regard, the neglect of political leadership is but a symptom of deeper features of liberal thought. The most important of these are its individualist ontology and its embarrassment in the face of political power. Its inherent individualism makes liberal theory suspicious of collective agency understood as anything other than the aggregated actions of individuals. Yet, effective political action in the modern world is almost invariably collective in a stronger sense. This does not mean that individuals are unimportant, nor need it involve metaphysically suspect notions such as a 'group mind', but political action typically involves the formation of a collective will, distinct from the individual wills of the people who comprise it.[15] One reason for this is that effective political action requires political power, and political power invariably requires mobilisation of support in a way that to some degree necessarily subjugates individual wills.

Contemporary liberal theorists, however, are notoriously shy about engaging with the challenges posed by political power, at least as something other than simply what has to be controlled in its exercise by liberal principles. It fits uneasily with their exclusive focus on the normative, and with the strongly idealising tendency even within that focus. Thus, it tends to erase awkward questions about power from its discourse, notwithstanding the fact that bringing about the changes that liberalism advocates most certainly requires the exercise of a considerable measure of political power. Political power, of course, is also integral to political leadership, and political leaders always have to be sensitive not only to how it is used, but how it is generated and sustained. Indeed, this crucial nexus between power, leadership and political action is almost entirely neglected within contemporary liberal theory. That there are potentially interesting theoretical issues to be explored here, for example about political styles for effecting change can be seen from a work like George Klosko's *Jacobins and Utopians*.[16]

---

15 For some serious philosophical work on the metaphysics and powers of agency of social groups and collectivities, see: K. Graham, *Practical Reasoning in a Social World: How we act together* (Cambridge: Cambridge University Press, 2002).

16 G. Klosko, *Jacobins and Utopians: The Political Theory of Fundamental Moral Reform* (Notre Dame: University of Notre Dame Press, 2003).

Ultimately, it is hard to resist the conclusion that the implicit conception of political agency embodied within liberal political theory is so distressingly naïve and simplistic that it scarcely amounts to a conception of *political* agency at all. For, on this view, political agency is simply a matter of realising the political principles that liberal theorists claim to justify, and it seems to amount to little more than the idea that people should be persuaded by the arguments of liberal political theorists, and then act accordingly. But it has nothing at all to say, for example, about how this can be made to happen, or, for example, about whether, and if so on what terms, force or subterfuge can be part of legitimate political strategies in pursuit of liberal ends. And the whole issue of the role of the emotions and rhetoric within persuasive political discourse is similarly disdained. There seems to be a naïve faith in notions of 'reasonableness' or the effectiveness of a suitably constrained process of 'democratic deliberation' to bring about the desired political changes. Generally, liberal theorists are silent about how to act when the arguments for particular liberal principles are politically ineffective and about the political difficulties leaders face, given for example the realities of electoral politics, when liberal principles cannot command sufficient support. At best, such questions are consigned to the realm of non-ideal theory, and then ignored.[17]

Even within its broadly individualist framework, that there are interesting theoretical questions that could be asked in this context can be seen, for example, in some of the work of Bernard Williams. Thus, among many interesting questions, he asks: 'What sort of person do we want and need to be politicians?' And as he immediately goes on to remark that such a question 'is importantly different from the question of what the correct answers are to moral problems which present themselves within political activity'.[18] I am not here concerned to pursue the details of Williams' discussion in response to this question, thoughtful and insightful though they often are, and which mostly explore aspects of the so-called problem of 'dirty hands'. But what is of relevance is how Williams' question acknowledges and opens up the space to ask a question that most liberal political theory simply passes over in silence. Politicians are, like all of us, flawed and fallible human beings who, at least if they become political leaders, and particularly if they obtain high office, are sometimes likely to have to act quickly, decisively and effectively in highly pressurised and unpromising circumstances. They will often have to deal with people and groups, who are, at least from a liberal perspective (and occasionally from

---

17 J. Rawls, *Justice as Fairness: A Restatement* (Cambridge, Mass: Harvard University Press, 2001), p. 13.
18 B. Williams, *Moral Luck* (Cambridge: Cambridge University Press, 1981), p. 54.

pretty much any perspective), 'unreasonable' and politically myopic and ruthless, who may engage in political blackmail and have the capacity to do some serious harm. But they may, nonetheless, sometimes have to be appeased, and undeserving groups may be given preference to more deserving ones, if the success of other, important political aims is not to be put in jeopardy. Moreover, leaders will often have obligations to their supporters, and these will carry weight whether or not they accord with liberal principles, not least because continuing in power may depend upon retaining their support. And this need not be merely a matter of political horse trading, important though that is likely to remain in any world that we can realistically envisage, but also raises questions about what it means to be a representative within a liberal democratic polity. More generally, it might be asked, how far we really do want our political leaders to be 'principled', attractive though that quality may superficially appear, rather than pragmatic and willing to compromise, even at some serious cost to their own deepest convictions, and even if those convictions are impeccably liberal. It is easy to cast the unbending politician of liberal principle as a moral hero, but perhaps such a position is not merely likely to be too often ineffective, but sometimes also *politically* irresponsible.

Where liberal theory is simply blank about such questions, Williams encourages us to think about the kinds of qualities that we want and need decent, but also effective, political leaders to have, and about how those qualities relate to the political system and the wider economic and cultural context in which political leaders have no option but to operate. Does the political system select for the kind of people we want, and if not what are the likely implications for the quality and character of political leaders, and indeed for political life more generally? For instance, what sort of people can we reasonably expect to enter politics and to flourish in the sort of tabloid culture that is now very much the stock in trade of political journalism in Britain? What kind of politicians (and political culture) can we expect if there is no room for lively political debate and contestation because every disagreement is presented as a 'row', 'squabble' or 'split'? These questions, and many more like them, challenge us to think about politics in a way that has legitimate claims to be no less 'theoretical' than liberal theory, but which is much more concretely 'situated' within political life as it is. And one might also think in this context of the work that has been done in relation to political leaders on the idea of moral capital.[19] But my point in raising these questions at this point is not to try to answer them, but simply to recognise their importance. If we are

---

19 J. Kane, *The Politics of Moral Capital* (Cambridge: Cambridge University Press, 2001).

to engage seriously with the problems of political agency, part of that engagement will have to involve a consideration of the many facets of the role of leaders and leadership

Secondly, the neglect of political leadership, because it is a manifestation of the underestimation of its importance, is also likely to lead to a devaluation of politicians and political leaders. Political leadership is on any account a difficult and precarious art, fraught with difficulties on all sides; yet again, though, one would get no sense at all of this from contemporary liberal political theory. If we view politics exclusively from the perspective of liberal political theory, then it seems to me that it is almost guaranteed that we will be deeply disappointed by almost all of our political leaders, and very likely disillusioned with politics itself. This is not to suggest that we should all be like Voltaire's Pangloss, cheerfully believing that we live in the best of all possible words, and blind to the more than ample evidence to the contrary. Some modest measure of cynicism about politics and a pair of less than rose-coloured spectacles through which to look at politicians are no doubt highly desirable if we are not to fall prey to the various dangers that an excessively reverential and respectful attitude towards political leaders can give rise. However, these are surely not the most pressing dangers that face us in the West, at least at the present time, it being very many decades since most people had an excess of faith in, or dereference towards, their political leaders. Rather, the principal risks are those associated with a general dismissiveness towards politics, a withdrawal from democratic processes, and an ultimately corrupting cynicism and mistrust towards political leaders of all stripes.

The sources of the widespread disdain felt towards politicians are no doubt many and various; and it would be fanciful in the extreme to apportion much of a causal role in this popular perception to the work of liberal political theorists. However, the failure of liberal theory to show any interest in the difficulties and dilemmas of political leadership, and the inclination of contemporary theorists to encourage the assessment of political leaders solely in relation to the rather high-minded and politically naïve ideals of liberal theory is of piece with this general mistrust and hostility towards political leaders. Even when political leaders do receive sympathetic mention, such as Martin Luther King, his frankly emotional story telling is approved only because it could be (somewhat unconvincingly) translated into an appropriate form of public reason.[20] Moreover, the tendency to move seamlessly in this way between a real historical figure and the requirements of ideal theory betrays some confusion. For, it entirely neglects the fact that the conditions under which King

---

20 Rawls, *op cit* (n.2), pp. 249–51.

was speaking were a very long way from those of ideal theory. In the context of the widespread racism in many southern states, for instance, what would be the relevance of ideal theory? Would it be appropriate to require King to ensure that his political speech was consistent with the demands of public reason when almost all the rest of political speech was not? Moreover, it seems unlikely that he would have inspired so many people who would otherwise have remained defeated and despairing if he had eschewed his passionate and emotional (and also deeply Christian) rhetoric.

Because politics as we know it is so distant from the idealised conception of what it should be within contemporary liberal theory, the gap is likely to be filled with disillusion and despair towards politics and contempt for politicians. In a very real sense, anything recognisable as ordinary politics drops out of view, and political theory tends to become ever more academic, in both the literal and colloquial senses of that term. Liberal political theory turns increasingly in on itself, becoming a technical, edificatory and practically disengaged discourse that is exclusively practised by and of interest only to other political theorists. At best, it becomes no more than an inappropriate stick that can be used to beat political leaders who fail to live up to the rigours of ideal liberal theory, while completely ignoring the inconvenient fact that actual political leaders have to practice their art in the all too imperfect real world, not that of ideal theory.

Finally, it may be appropriate to say something more about the light that the lack of concern with leadership throws more directly on the relationship between liberal political theory and democracy. Although of course all contemporary liberals find a place in their theories for democratic decision-making, it is far from original to remark that democracy is also a source of unease for many of them.[21] It is only fair to say that the tensions between liberalism and democracy have a history as long as that of liberalism itself. It seems, though, that one of the principal motivations behind the various theories of justice that have dominated liberal political theory over the last four decades has been a desire significantly to circumscribe the role of politics, in the form of democratic decision-making, especially in so far as this is understood to be about such things as majority voting, pragmatic coalition building and trade-offs between competing interest groups. Particularly in relation to political and personal liberties, but also with regard to questions of distributive justice, liberals are worried by what they perceive as the illiberal tendencies of 'popular'

---

21 See, for example, B. Barber, *The Conquest of Politics: Liberal Philosophy in Democratic Times* (Princeton: Princeton University Press, 1988).

politics, and pressure to alight on the lowest common denominator when it comes to legislation and policy-making. Correspondingly, they have been concerned to try to limit the legitimate scope for popular influence in such matters: if political leaders are not much to be trusted to make these decisions, this is in part because neither is the citizenry.

One can see this very clearly in the case of Rawls, as he seeks to place fundamental political principles outside the normal processes of democratic politics. The two principles of justice frame and set the limits within which legitimate democratic politics should take place. They are not supposed to be amenable to change through democratic politics, no matter how large a majority may wish to reform them, or what the material benefits from doing so might be, and would thus be more secure than even the most firmly entrenched constitutional provisions. As we saw earlier, they are rather conceived as being in an important sense outside or beyond politics. As Rawls writes on the very first page of *A Theory of Justice*:

> Each person possesses an inviolability founded on justice that even the welfare of society as whole cannot override. For this reason justice denies that the loss of freedom for some is made right by a greater good shared by others. It does not allow that the sacrifices imposed on a few are outweighed by the larger sum of advantages enjoyed by the many. Therefore in a just society the liberties of equal citizenship are taken as settled; the rights secured by justice are not subject to political bargaining…[22]

Nor is Rawls unusual in this regard. The desire to constrain the influence of politicians and ordinary people on democratic politics is, perhaps, still stronger in the work of Ronald Dworkin—who, like several leading American liberal theorists, has a legal training—where judges are more to be trusted to make fundamental political decisions than are elected politicians or ordinary citizens.[23]

The explanation of this suspicion of popular opinion, majority votes and elected politicians is fairly easy to relate to some aspects of the earlier argument. The focus on normative political principles, and on the role of political theory in articulating them, inevitably means that the scope for democratic decision-making must be limited by the political principles justified by liberal political theorists. But neither popular opinion nor politicians can be relied upon to restrain themselves in the requisite ways. The issue is not, of course, that such worries are without foundation; democracies can behave illiberally, and liberal values are often likely to be under attack from some quarter or other. However, what is at issue is that these liberal theorists seek to combat these dangers not *through* politics,

---

22 Rawls, *op cit* (n. 11), pp. 3–4.
23 R. Dworkin, *A Matter of Principle* (Cambridge, Mass: Harvard University Press, 1985), Ch. 1.

but by somehow depoliticising a whole range of fundamental questions about how a society should be governed. In a world without any wise leaders modelled after Rousseau's legislator, an unelected constitutional court, composed of politically unaccountable judges, so far as possible free to resist the vicissitudes of democratic politics, is the closest that we can realistically get (even if that is not very close) to having virtuous liberal political theorists as guardians of the political order. While one might try to interpret the role of such judges as involving a kind of leadership, in truth this seems rather strained, especially if we are thinking in terms of *political* leadership, and harder still to see them as instances of *democratic* political leadership. In truth, the model is not one of political leadership but judicial adjudication on the basis of the 'correct' constitutional principles that have already been decided; not, of course, politically, but by liberal political theorists.

But, this is all a fantasy: the actual operation of the Supreme Court in the U.S. is, as one would expect, highly political. There is no way that anything can be placed permanently 'outside' politics. But the consequence of this way of thinking is that questions about the relationship between democracy, liberalism and political leadership that should be of interest to liberal political theorists are simply never properly raised. For example, there are theoretically challenging and practically important issues surrounding the concepts of representation and accountability. Both are obviously crucial to any theory of representative democracy, but they also connect with the role of political leaders. And, as none of the prevailing contemporary liberal political theories envisage any system of government other than some form of representative democracy, such questions surely ought to be an integral part of a liberal political theory. What is the proper relationship between representatives and those they represent? How is it possible for one person to represent a large number of other people? What is it that political leaders are representing? What kind of democratic political structures best fit with an adequate theory of representation? What are the normative requirements and constraints on any adequate theory of democratic representation? How far is it consistent with their representative function and their accountability to those they represent for political leaders to act independently and contrary to the clear and explicit views and wishes of those whom they represent? It is not that political theorists have not discussed these questions; but that liberal theorists have not discussed them in the context of developing their own political theories.[24]

---

24 For an interesting discussion of issues around representation, see: H. Pitkin, *The Concept of Representation* (Berkley: University of California Press, 1972).

IV

My primary purpose in this discussion has been to explore contemporary liberal political theory, if only in general terms and in an admittedly rather speculative spirit, from the unusual perspective of what it has to say, or, more accurately, what it does not say about political leadership, and to consider some of the implications of that neglect. In at least one respect, therefore, I am only too aware of having succumbed to the very fault with which I have charged liberalism. For, I too have had relatively little to say constructively about political leadership, and have been reflecting on theory, rather than theorising about politics. However, in arguing that the neglect of political leadership by the dominant strand of contemporary liberal political theory is not without damaging consequences to both liberalism and our understanding of politics, I have also tried to indicate at least some the ways in which thinking about political leadership theoretically is both possible and desirable. In doing so, I have also tentatively suggested some questions about leadership that should be of interest to political theorists, even if I have made no effort to answer them.

However, lest this all appear far too negative and even hostile towards liberalism *per se*, which is not my intention, let me also briefly suggest that there are some less prominent strands in contemporary liberal theory more receptive to the strictures that I have advanced here. What Judith Shklar has called 'the liberalism of fear' is no less 'theoretical' in its concerns than the dominant form of contemporary liberal theorising, but it is markedly less idealising in its approach, and also much less demanding normatively.[25] For the liberalism of fear—and one could say much the same of all more sceptically inclined forms of liberalism, such as John Gray's 'modus vivendi liberalism'[26]—focuses primarily on the risks and dangers that confront us both without politics and from politics itself. These risks and dangers are both universal, in the sense that the costs of the absence of an effective political authority and the threats from one that is all too effective are omnipresent in the human condition, but also particular and circumstantial in the specific form that they take. This means that, as Bernard Williams puts it:

> What [the liberalism of fear] offers or suggests in any given situation depends on that situation: it depends in particular on the politics of that situation. The liberalism of fear, once more like its natural counterpart, *The Prince*, does not displace politics, but is understood only

---

25 J. Shklar, 'The Liberalism of Fear' in N Rosenblum (ed.), *Liberalism and the Moral Self* (Cambridge, MS: Harvard University Press, 1989).
26 J. Gray, *Two Faces of Liberalism* (Cambridge: Polity Press, 2000).

in the presence of politics, and as addressing its listeners in the face of their politics.[27]

Williams' mention of *The Prince* neatly connects the liberalism of fear with questions of political leadership. For, the understanding of politics afforded by the liberalism of fear is one that gives a place to the realities of political life, of which leadership, as I have argued, is an important feature. From this perspective, rather than deleting political leadership from the agenda of liberal political theory, we accept its inevitability and centrality in political life, and begin to open up both conceptual and normative questions to which it gives rise. How exactly should we conceive of the role of political leaders within a modern democracy? How ought we elaborate the idea that political leaders should be sufficiently empowered to do what they need to do, while being sufficiently limited and accountable not to be too easily tempted to try what we not want them to do? What kinds of qualities make for better or worse political leaders in a democracy? What pressures are at work in modern democracies that either facilitate or undermine effective political leadership? These are pretty obvious question to ask, and simply asking them is, of course, only the first step. Moreover, in seeking to answer them perhaps we should not expect anything like a general theory of political leadership. But this kind of liberal theorising is at least receptive to the development of theoretical ideas about political leadership, and enables us to begin to see why and how a serious theoretical discussion of it matters.

Along with other of its critics, I believe that any adequate liberal political theory needs to be much more attentive to the realities of politics as it is practiced than has typically been true of its leading contemporary advocates.[28] Political leadership is one such aspect of politics to which it would pay liberal theorists to give much more attention. Normative arguments about political ideals and principles of justice are important, but their place in politics is limited, and they should not exhaust the enterprise of political theory. Political theorists should be interested in a much wider range of issues, including issues that are much closer to politics on the ground. At best, liberal principles have to be enacted through political processes. Political leaders will have an important role in such processes, but those processes also constrain their capacity for political action in a multitude of ways. Probably the most important of such constraints in societies with broadly liberal democratic constitutions are the realities of democratic politics itself. Ultimately, political leaders have to achieve some measure of popular support if they are to be effective, and if they are

---

27 Williams, *op cit* (n. 10), p. 59.
28 See the works cited in n. 10.

to be in a position to exercise political power on a significant stage they have to do such banal things as win elections. But real elections are not conducted in the realm of ideal theory: electorates are not composed of ideal liberal citizens and electoral debates do not even remotely approximate to models of public reason. These are the conditions of politics, even under favourable circumstances, yet faced with such realities the kind of liberal political theory explored earlier prefers to talk about the world as it would like it to be. It is not that the world cannot be changed for the better, but doing so has to begin by taking account of the way the world is, and making realistic judgements about what is politically possible, and this includes giving serious thought to political agency and the place of political leadership.

As an alternative to an over-idealised liberal theory, I have very tentatively gestured in the direction of a somewhat different and much less prominent strand of liberal theorising, certainly contemporary in its relevance, but perhaps also harking back to an earlier liberalism, which might help to enable us to begin that task. This more modest and sceptical brand of liberalism at the very least invites us to take questions of political leadership seriously. Moreover, I also believe that our understanding of political leadership would be advanced through the meticulous and rigorous attention that liberal political theorists at their best would bring to it. For, what philosophical literature on leadership there is, is often not particularly profound or illuminating when it comes to political leadership,[29] and writings on leadership by politicians are too often little more than exercises in self-congratulation.[30] The bottom line is that political leadership matters, and it is worthy of some serious consideration by contemporary liberal political theorists. The key question that this poses for the predominant strand of liberal theory is how far its style of theorising can accommodate an engagement with the complexities of political leadership, and whether such an engagement will leave the fundamentals of contemporary liberal theory untouched? My own view, as should be clear by now, is that liberal political theory would benefit, in this regard and many others, from some significant recasting in the direction of a more sceptical and less idealised form of liberalism.[31]

---

29 For instance, C. Hodgkinson, *The Philosophy of Leadership* (Oxford: Basil Blackwell, 1983).
30 A good (i.e. bad) example of the genre is R. Giuliani, *Leadership* (London: Time Warner Book Group, 2002).
31 An earlier version of this paper was presented to the panel, 'Political Leadership: A Missing Element in Democratic Theory' at the ECPR Joint Sessions in Helsinki in May 2007. I am grateful for the helpful discussion the paper received on that occasion, to the comments of two anonymous referees for Imprint Academic, and in particular for the helpful suggestions of Joe Femia.

Peter Lassman

Political Leadership, Judgement, and the Sense of Reality

1. Introduction

Political leadership has been a neglected topic in contemporary political theory and political philosophy especially in its dominant liberal democratic mode.[1] The egalitarian bias of this kind of theorising has probably had some influence here with a resulting general distrust of any claims made for the unavoidable reality of political leadership in the modern state. Ideas of, for example, the centrality of charismatic leaders in modern democratic states would, presumably, appear to be too much of a surrender to a view of the political domain as being under the influence of irrational and, even worse, dark and unpredictable forces. The idea that political leaders are able to shape the course of events in an unpredictable manner can be taken as an example of the irreducible freedom of action that defies explanation in political scientific terms. The fact of political leadership can be taken to imply the high degree of contingency that eludes the conceptual net of much political science and philosophy.

It is also often argued that leadership in a democratic society must have something anti-democratic about it or that leadership is a necessary evil. In addition, ideas of leadership come into conflict with the idea that the liberal democratic state aims to replace the rule of men with the rule of law.[2] Perhaps the continuing existence of political leadership in modern democratic states and the high visibility of political leaders are some of those 'uncomfortable facts' that confront both political philosophers and political scientists. Nevertheless, it is worth noting that intimations of the

---

1 For example, there is no entry for 'leadership' in the index of, John S. Dryzek et al (eds.), *The Oxford Handbook for Political Theory* (Oxford University Press, 2006).
2 András Körösényi, 'Political Representation in Leader Democracy', *Government and Opposition*, Vol. 40, No. 3 (Summer 2005) pp. 358–78.

significance of political leadership appear even in what would appear to be the most unlikely places. For example, it is more than a little surprising to find that John Rawls's version of political liberalism contains an implicit recognition of the central role of political leaders at critical moments in political history. It is quite clear that Rawls, despite his central claim to steer by the star of public reason alone in order to avoid the charge that his own theory is itself no more than another 'comprehensive doctrine', has his own view of which particular leaders are his political heroes. Martin Luther King and Abraham Lincoln are two of the political heroes who clearly complement the contribution of his philosophical hero Kant in his own intellectual development.

What is it that Rawls finds admirable in Lincoln and King? One relevant fact is that they both stood up during periods of deep moral and political conflict for the values and ideals that Rawls himself believes are, or ought to be, the outcome of the free use of public reason. Lincoln's condemnation of slavery was, Rawls implies, an act of real political leadership in its refusal to accept the conventional 'communitarian' justification of that institution that was on offer at the time. Lincoln's achievement was, in Rawlsian terms, to set in motion a reconsideration of our considered convictions and principles on this controversial topic.

Similarly, Rawls takes his cue for the correct understanding of constitutional government from Lincoln. The significance of Abraham Lincoln among Rawls's political heroes is clear. One might almost say that this is an example of uncritical hero worship. Lincoln, it seems, can do no wrong. Even his Proclamation of a National Fast Day in 1861, Two Proclamations of Thanksgiving in 1863 and 1864, as well as the prophetic Second Inaugural interpretation of the civil war as a sign of divine retribution are, Rawls argues, not to be considered as violations of public reason 'correctly understood'. Martin Luther King appears in the text of 'Political Liberalism' in a similar way as a political leader whose Civil Rights campaigns Rawls enthusiastically endorses. However, in doing so Rawls gets himself into a convoluted argument the intention of which is to show that a controversial political leader such as King is acceptable because, after all things are considered, he did not really 'go against the ideal of public reason' that Rawls himself endorses.[3] Whatever the merits of Rawls's account of the role of public reason in political life it is clear that the recognition of the significance of political leaders such as Lincoln and King within a text which in other respects aims for a high level of philosophical abstraction reveals something about the implicit intellectual and moral

---

3   John Rawls, *Political Liberalism* (New York: Columbia University Press, 1996), p. 254.

commitments that underpin his theory as well as the convenient silences that persist within it.

It is not only liberal political philosophers who have failed to attend to the problem of leadership. This fact is also true of most of their critics and especially for those on the left or what counts as the left in a post-Marxian age. Curiously influenced by Carl Schmitt, many leftist critics of liberal political philosophy have made the activity of politics and the work of politicians of secondary importance in their search for an essence of 'the political'. The elevation of 'the political' over mere 'politics' reinforces the tendency to pay little if any attention to the activity of politics, which must include the consideration of the performance of political leaders.[4]

Earlier liberal political thinkers were not so averse to a direct consideration of the nature of political leadership. The examples of Max Weber and Isaiah Berlin are indicative of the fact that recognition of the role of political leadership in modern states is not necessarily incompatible with a liberal outlook.[5] Furthermore, examination of their work, it is argued here, shows a remarkable mutation of the Platonic ideal of the philosopher ruler. In both Berlin and Weber we can observe a shared view that if politics takes place in 'the right way' there ought to be a marked similarity between the virtues that we ought to expect of the good or successful political leader and the virtues of the enlightened political theorist or philosopher.

1. Max Weber

(1) Politics and Leadership

In sharp contrast with most contemporary Anglo-American political theory Max Weber offers an account of politics in which the idea of leadership occupies a central place. In so doing Weber was more in tune with the central tradition of political theory from Plato to Marx which had placed the question of who should rule and what the qualities of the good ruler ought to be at the heart of its inquiries than much of modern political philosophy with its central concern to justify items of public policy. Weber's approach to concept-formation was cautious and pragmatic. For example, he appreciated that defining the meaning of 'politics' is a difficult and in some ways pointless task. To begin with Weber points out that it is an extremely broad term due, in part, to the fact that it embraces 'ev-

---

4   See, for example, Chantal Mouffe, *On the Political* (London :Routledge, 2005).
5   I do not want to enter here into the question of whether Weber can be truly called a 'Liberal'. I think for the moment that it is best to say that he can be called , as was Tocqueville, a 'liberal of a strange kind'.

ery kind of independent *leadership* activity'.⁶ In fact Weber, following his generally nominalistic approach refers to at least four distinct ways of thinking about politics that resemble more recent attempts to distinguish between 'politics' and 'the political'. The incorporation of Weber into a canon of sociological theory has led to a concentration upon the structural features of his account of forms of rule at the expense of an almost total neglect of what he thought was of central importance. The key to understanding the nature of politics is to recognise that it is an activity. It is a marked feature of Weber's writings that he constantly describes politics as an activity and, in particular, uses verbs such as that of 'striving' for power. What is of interest to him is primarily an explication of what political agents are doing when they act politically. Given his intellectual commitments it ought to come as no surprise that Weber was concerned with the meaning of the activity of leading from both the standpoint of the leader and the external observer. Therefore it is the activity of political leaders that is central for an understanding of politics. In other words, the interest, or lack of it, in leadership is a reflection of a deeper theoretical attitude towards politics.⁷

Politics can refer to rule and leadership as well as to the act of politicking. Weber points out that it can also refer, for example, to policy making. The policy of a bank on foreign exchange, the policy of a trade union during a strike, or the efforts of a wife to guide her husband could all be described as being political in some sense. However, Weber focuses his concept of politics upon political leadership. He was convinced that an understanding of modern politics must focus upon the practice of leadership. This is not to be conceived in narrow terms as being simply focussed upon particular individuals. The activity of leaders is inseparable from the struggle for power a major part of which is the struggle to exercise influence on leaders. The most important context for the exercise of modern political leadership is in the activity of the state. This is taken to be the most significant form of modern political association. The political leaders who count in Weber's eyes are all those bound up in the struggle for power in the modern state. This includes the leaders of governments, the leaders of political parties, the leaders of trade unions, and the leaders of states.

The matter would be fairly straightforward and relatively uncontroversial if Weber stopped there. As far as Weber was concerned the reason why it was not helpful to use the concept of politics in too broad a sense

---

6   Max Weber, *Political Writings*, eds. P. Lassman and R. Spiers (Cambridge: Cambridge University Press, 1994), p. 309.
7   Kari Palonen, *The Struggle with Time* (Hamburg: Lit, 2006).

was that to do so would mean avoiding its specifically dangerous and unpleasant aspects. To put it very simply Weber reminds us over and over again that there are certain 'facts' that have to be appreciated in order to understand the nature of modern politics. The first is that 'politics is struggle'. The topoi of struggle, conflict, and selection as well as those of leadership and policymaking are central guiding ideas that structure Weber's vision of political and social reality.

In addition, there are two other 'facts' of modern political reality that must be recognised. One is 'the fact' of the coercive power of the state and the other is the fact of plural and conflicting values. Both are, of course, also the two central 'facts' that shape the central concerns of contemporary political liberalism.[8] While Weber and contemporary political liberals share a remarkably similar view of the political predicament their disagnoses are quite different. It is here that the marked difference in the attention paid to questions of leadership becomes most apparent. Quite simply, political leadership as a problem and a fact is largely absent in the work of modern liberal political theory while clearly it is of central concern for Weber. As far as Weber was concerned, any attempt at serious thought about politics that does not take account of the reality of political leadership is bound to produce, to misquote John Rawls, an 'unrealistic utopia'. It seems that it would not be too much of an exaggeration to say that what is revealed in the contrasting amount of attention paid to questions of leadership is a deep philosophical disagreement about the nature of politics.

Political leadership is of central importance for Weber as a consequence of his recognition of the unprecedented concentration of power in the form of the modern western state. The state, as is well known, is in Weber's formulation that 'human community which (successfully) lays claim to the *monopoly of legitimate physical violence* within a certain territory'. Furthermore, politics means 'the striving for a share of power or influence on the distribution of power, whether it be between states or between groups of people contained within a single state'. In addition, 'anyone engaged in politics is striving for power, either power as a means to attain other goals (which may be ideal or selfish), or power 'for its own sake', which is to say, in order to enjoy the feeling of prestige given by power'.[9] It is in the way in which violence is bound up with the operation of political power that problems that are peculiar to political leadership arise. The state is ultimately to be understood as a relationship of rule (Herrschaft) of men over men.

8   John Rawls, *Political Liberalism*.
9   Weber, *Political Writings*, pp. 310–11.

Although he has not generally been considered, at least in the Anglo-American world, to be a central member of the canon of political theory, Weber is, curiously, in tune with the traditional concern of political philosophy with the question of who ought to rule and why. However, he introduces an additional element that makes a clean break with that tradition. This is the argument that the modern condition is best characterised in terms of its 'disenchantment'. As with much contemporary liberal theory Weber saw the modern political predicament as a fateful combination of two other factors; one being the eclipse of commitment to formerly held beliefs and ideas that had provided grounds for the legitimation of claims to lead and to rule. This, in turn, deepened the conflict of plural values, the 'war of the gods'. At the same time, 'the ultimate, most sublime values have withdrawn from public life'.[10] The interesting contrast with contemporary liberal and deliberative democratic theory is that Weber's response to the 'facts of coercion' and disenchanted value pluralism was not to search for some ground, hypothetical or real, for agreement between citizens. Such agreement, if it could be found, would only be a temporary truce in the constant struggle of values and interests and, hence, could only have a very thin character. The modern state is not the ancient polis (not the real polis, of course, but the imagined one).

This interpretation of the modern political condition is one in which questions of political leadership become of immense importance. In effect, Weber seems to be claiming that it is the quality of political leadership that can make a crucial contribution to the construction of social stability, if anything can. Effective political leadership offers the best, possibly the only, way of coping with the realities of modern political life. But, given his account of disenchantment how is it possible for such leadership to be able to make any successful claims for its legitimacy? Furthermore, does not this stress on the importance of leadership devalue the claims of democracy and the liberal value of liberty that Weber also wanted to defend?

Although he failed to arrive at a satisfactory resolution for these dilemmas the case of Max Weber is interesting and informative for the problems that it raises. The centrality of leadership and especially of charismatic leadership in Weber's work has produced accusations of 'decisionism'. This is often a veiled way of implying a link with Carl Schmitt and preparation of the ground for the Nazi regime.[11] These

---

10   Max Weber, 'Science as a Vocation' in 'Max Weber's "Science as a Vocation"', P. Lassman, I. Velody and H. Martins (eds.) (London: Unwin Hyman, 1989), p. 30.
11   For example, Wolfgang Mommsen, *Max Weber and German Politics 1890-1920* (Chicago: University of Chicago Press, 1984) and Jürgen Habermas, 'Discussion of Value-Freedom and

charges have been subsequently withdrawn or modified. However, they do point to a difficult question. What are the normative implications of taking Weber's advice seriously and putting leadership back into the centre of our reflections on modern politics?

(2) Caesarism, Demagogues, and Democracy

The concept of Caesarism occupies a central place in Max Weber's writings on politics. The term was in common usage in Weber's time in, for example, the debate about the status as statesmen of such figures as Bismarck and Napoleon. In order to appreciate Weber's use of the term it is necessary to recognise the way in which he modified the conventional terms of the contemporary debate and introduced a new and challenging way of thinking about the relationship and tension between forms of political leadership and parliamentary democratic government. His theoretical innovation was to argue that the most politically responsible way in which a modern mass democracy could function would have to be through the harnessing of Caesarism with parliamentary government. The novelty of this approach is clear when it is remembered that Caesarism had usually, and still often is, thought of as the enemy of representative or parliamentary government.[12] Weber's innovation was to think of Caesarism in terms that distinguished it from its Bonapartist and Bismarckian forms. It was normal in the nineteenth and early twentieth centuries to think of Caesarism as a repressive outcome of the collapse of democracy and as a form of military dictatorship. In Weber's usage the term now referred to a more normal form of rule that is not necessarily the outcome of a crisis. Nor is Caesarism necessarily tied to the restriction of civil liberties and, indeed, when allied with a strong parliament that can defend them.

The radical nature of Weber's conceptual innovation is easily overlooked. However, comparison with the sources upon which he relied shows that although much of what he says about, for example, the nature of mass political parties and parliamentary government is no more than a summary of their conclusions, he does depart from them on this crucial point. It was generally assumed by most of his contemporaries that the new form of mass democracy and mass political party with its Caesarist leader was seriously undermining the autonomy of parliaments. Weber, on the contrary, put forward a more complex and, from a modern liberal standpoint, more troubling argument.

Objectivity', in O. Stammer (ed.) *Max Weber and Sociology Today* (Oxford: Basil Blackwell, 1971).

12 See, Peter Baehr, 'Max Weber and the Avatars of Caesarism', *Dictatorship in History and Theory*, eds. Peter Baehr and Melvin Richter (Cambridge: Cambridge University Press, 2004).

In a series of newspaper articles written in 1917 that offer a diagnosis of the political situation in Germany Weber puts forward an account of modern political reality that has implications that go far beyond the immediate context. The claim that the religious prophet and the political demagogue are the two figures who play a central role in Weber's political and social thought contains a great deal of truth.[13] It is clear that for Weber the widespread influence of the political demagogue is an inevitable consequence of democratisation. However, Weber's idea of the demagogue is not the popular and dismissive one. Weber does not deny that demagogy in 'the bad sense' exists but what interests him more is the way in which the successful political leader in a modern democracy has to be a demagogue.

The genuine political leader is selected not by bureaucratic means but through political struggle because, as has been stressed, 'all politics is essentially struggle'.[14] The struggle that Weber is referring to is one that is carried on through the 'craft of demagogy' rather than, for example, the control and manipulation of the means of administration. Weber's formula is that 'democracy and demagogy belong together'. The modern situation is such that 'active democratisation of the masses means that the political leader is no longer declared a candidate because a circle of notables has recognised his proven ability, and then becomes leader because he comes to the fore in parliament, but rather because he uses the means of *mass* demagogy to gain the confidence of the masses and their belief in his person, and thereby gains power. Essentially this means that the selection of the leader has shifted in the direction of *Caesarism*. Indeed every democracy has this tendency'.[15]

The problem, however, is that the plebiscitary selection of leaders exists in a state of tension with the parliamentary principle. Again Weber points out that 'every kind of direct *election by the people* of the bearer of supreme power, and beyond this every kind of position of political power which in fact rests on the trust of the masses rather than that of parliaments ... lies on the road towards these "pure" form of Caesarist acclamation'.[16] Weber gives the American presidency as an example of what he has in mind.

Central to Weber's understanding of the predicament of modern democratic government is the idea that there is a deep tension between the Caesarist and the parliamentary method of selecting political leaders. However, Weber did not lend his support to the current opposition to the

---

13   Wilhelm Hennis, *Max Weber. Essays in Reconstruction* (London: Allen and Unwin, 1988), p. 183.
14   Max Weber, *Political Writings*, p. 219.
15   *Ibid.*, pp. 220-21.
16   *Ibid.*, p. 221.

institution of parliament in either its Leftist or Rightist versions. Weber did not achieve a final and satisfactory resolution in his struggle with this problem. Nevertheless, he resolutely held on to the idea that a parliament was an ideal counterweight to the necessary and unavoidable role of the Caesarist principle. A parliament can function to maintain stability, and control the power of a Caesarist leader. It can preserve legal safeguards against such a leader. Parliament, as is often pointed out, was not valued for its own sake by Weber, for its possession of any particular qualities as such other than these and in particular its role as a an arena in which leaders could prove their political abilities and, in the last instance, act as peaceful way of *'eliminating* the Caesarist dictator when he has *lost* the trust of the masses'. Nevertheless, in his last published work on this topic Weber did opt for granting more power to a directly elected head of state than we would be led to expect from his earlier statements. In an article published in 1919 Weber advocated the introduction of a directly elected President. Among the reasons that he gives are the following: such a figure would signify the unity of the state at a time of political breakdown; the directly elected head of state would not be hampered by the shifting coalitions and alliances in parliament; and, above all, 'a popularly elected president ... as the possessor of a delaying veto and the power to dissolve parliament and to consult the people, is a palladium of genuine democracy, which does not mean impotent self-abandonment to cliques but subordination to leaders one has chosen for oneself'.[17]

There is one other important factor that ought not to be lost sight of when trying to make sense of Weber's account of political leadership. Weber, unlike most modern liberal theorists, attributed a positive value to political leadership as such. Political and especially Caesarist leadership is valued because of its dynamic and innovatory character. The alternative form of political regime would be a form of 'passive democratisation', which would lead to a form of 'uncontrolled bureaucratic rule'. This is, of course, one of the arguments that Weber put forward against socialism that also applies to its modern surrogate, radical democracy.

The problem of leadership is central for Weber's diagnosis of the political crisis confronting modern democratic societies. Leadership is an unavoidable feature of modern politics. This is made clear, as much as anything, by the fact that Weber defines politics in terms of leadership. But what is leadership? And what are the qualities that a leader ought to possess? Weber spent a great amount of energy trying to work out the best institutional form for the relationship between political leaders, democratic arrangements, and legitimacy. However, the most important and

---

17   Ibid., p. 308.

innovatory part of his account is his consideration of the nature of political leadership under the conditions of a disenchanted modernity and the necessary personal characteristics that are required to make a successful political leader.

In his discussion of the foundations of the different types of legitimate rule Weber makes it clear that what most interests him is that form of rule that functions 'by virtue of devotion to the purely personal "charisma" of the "leader" on the part of those who obey him'.[18] It is noticeable that in his writing that is primarily addressed to an academic audience Weber subsumes the concept of the Caesarist leader under the general heading of charismatic rule. The idea of charisma is closely connected by Weber to the concept of a calling or vocation (Beruf). Devotion to a charismatic political leader 'means that the leader is personally regarded as someone who is inwardly "called" to the task of leading men, and that the led submit to him, not because of custom or statute, but because they believe in him'. Although leadership has existed at all times and places Weber insists that the figure of the political leader has specifically Western origins. Political leadership is traced back to the 'free "demagogue"', who grew from the soil of the city-state, a unique creation of the West and the Mediterranean culture in particular, and then in the figure of the parliamentary "party leader" who also sprang from the soil of the constitutional state, another institution indigenous only to the West'.[19]

The transformation of politics in Western states brought about by, among other factors, the development of the modern political party 'machine' has produced a form of plebiscitarian democracy. Followers of a party expect that the personality of the party leader will have a demagogic effect in the struggle for votes. Indeed, Weber argues that there is a clear distinction to be made between the satisfaction to be gained by party workers who out of conviction are devoted to a party leader, 'the dictator of the electoral battlefield', who possesses charisma rather than to 'the abstract programme of a party composed of mediocrities'. There is, however, a problem here. The dominance of the plebiscitarian form of democracy implies the 'spiritual proletarianisation' of the party following. This is the price that has to be paid for the emergence of this kind of state and party. The stark choice is between 'a leadership democracy with a "machine" and democracy without a leader, which means rule by the "professional politician" who has no vocation, the type of man who lacks precisely those inner, charismatic qualities which make a leader'.[20]

---

18 Ibid., p. 312.
19 Ibid., p. 313.
20 Ibid., p. 351.

It is clear that Weber's diagnosis of the fate of politics in the modern Western state puts an enormous weight of responsibility upon the shoulders of political leaders. It follows from his account of disenchantment and value pluralism that the sources for the necessary strength of character would have to be found from within. A genuine political leader would have to be someone who 'lived for' rather than 'off' politics. He (or she) would have to have an inner calling or vocation (Beruf). This, as Weber allows, must lead to the consideration of ethical questions. The political leader under modern conditions with its unprecedented and vast concentration of power has a special responsibility imposed upon him.

Weber's account of leadership is particularly interesting and controversial because he does not fall into the trap of offering a description of the formal properties of the institutions of leadership. Instead, he explores the question of the meaning of leadership. It is at this point that Weber enters into a discussion that oversteps the boundaries of any appearance of offering a morally neutral account. It is here that, perhaps more explicitly than elsewhere in his work, Weber is implicitly referring to an older tradition of practical philosophy and in this particular context, what he has to say clearly has echoes of the Platonic idea of the 'Philosopher Ruler'. I am not suggesting that Weber wanted rule by philosophers. That would be absurd. However, what Weber does suggest is that the political leader ought to possess certain virtues. He argues that the political leader ought to be guided by a passion, a sense of responsibility, and judgement. The problem, of course, is as in the case of Plato's just man, to strike the necessary balance in his soul. The Weberian political leader must have a sense of moral purpose and the ability to take responsibility for their actions. However, the most important virtue for the political leader is to have a sense of judgement. An adequate sense of judgement requires an understanding of the nature of political reality, of what can and cannot be achieved under given circumstances. Judgement is a craft or skill that is essential for the practice of political leadership and government. But because 'the decisive means of politics is the use of violence' the practice of judgement is of crucial importance. Although the political leader is operating in a distinct reality, it is striking that the virtues that Weber ascribes to him are similar to those that he ascribes to the scholar or scientist. To put it briefly, the most important virtue of scholarship and science (Wissenschaft) is to produce clarity of thought. In helping us to understand the meaning of our actions and ideas it clarifies our sense of reality. The political leader in Weber's view must have the commitment, clarity of vision, and sense of judgement that also characterises the scholar who has a genuine calling or vocation.

2. Isaiah Berlin

(1) Two Concepts of Leadership

Although the problem of leadership is almost completely absent from the work of contemporary political liberalism there seems to be no reason why liberals who are not committed to the current obsession with the search for agreement over principles of justice acceptable in principle to all are prevented from paying some attention to this topic. Isaiah Berlin is an interesting example of a liberal thinker who did reflect upon the nature of political leadership in modern politics. In fact consideration of the quality of political leadership is extremely important for Berlin for two reasons. The first is that a consideration of the nature of political leadership plays a central role in his struggle against what he sees as the deficiencies of a deterministic social scientific view of history. The second is that an understanding of leadership can act as an antidote to the widespread failure to appreciate what he understands as the 'sense of reality' appropriate for successful political conduct.

Berlin proposes a distinction between two types of leadership. He argues that 'there are two kinds of political greatness, incompatible with, and indeed sometimes opposed to, each other'.[21] Clearly reflecting his famous use of his distinction between intellectual hedgehogs and foxes Berlin argues that we can observe those political leaders who combine a simplicity of vision with an intense and even fanatical idealism and, in contrast, those leaders who are aware of the 'infinite complexity of the life which surrounds them' but, nevertheless, are able to see some kind of intelligible coherent pattern.[22]

Leaders of the first type are 'larger than life'. They see life in terms of simple contrasts between good and evil, their own cause and the evil misguided opposition to it. They resemble Weber's charismatic leader s insofar as they 'attract their followers by the intensity and purity of their mind, by their fearless and unbending character, by the simplicity and nobility of the central principle to which they dedicate all that they have, by the very fact that they impose some pattern so clear, so uncomplicated, upon the manifold diversity of life, that other men, smaller, more troubled and more fearful, weaker, at times subtler and more intelligent than the leaders, feel liberated and vastly strengthened by the very directness and sincerity with which the unadorned central doctrine is presented to them'.[23] Needless to say such doctrines are described by Berlin as often

---

21 Isaiah Berlin, *The Power of Ideas* (London: Chatto and Windus, 2000), p. 186.
22 Isaiah Berlin, *The Hedgehog and the Fox* (London : Weidenfeld and Nicholson, 1953).
23 *Ibid.*, p. 186.

being utopian in character. Examples of such leaders are Garibaldi, Napoleon, de Gaulle, Trotsky, and, at the extreme, Hitler and Stalin. Often leaders of this type, who are prone to offer utopian solutions, tend to stand apart from the people with whose destinies they are engaged. They are guilty of creating a myth and, if not completely believing it themselves, do identify with it.

The second type of leader is one who is characterised by an awareness of 'the smallest oscillations, the infinite variety of the social and political elements in which they live'. Such individuals are able to create an integrated and coherent picture from the variety of instances but, at the same time, to be flexible and responsive to the contingency of social and political life. As examples of such individuals Berlin mentions Abraham Lincoln, Franklin Roosevelt, and Chaim Weizmann.

Berlin's attention to the role of political leaders is also a reflection of his philosophy of history and his view of the nature of political knowledge. The idea that political leaders can shape and change the course of history is a clear example of Berlin's opposition to all forms of determinism in history and politics. Berlin's examples of the most impressive and successful political leadership of the twentieth century are to be found in essays on Chaim Weizmann, Winston Churchill, and Franklin D. Roosevelt. Each of these statesmen represents a form of political greatness. Berlin's argument is that a true understanding of their careers defies the conventions of normal political science. It has been suggested as well that it offers a corrective to some versions of the received view of Berlin's work. Berlin's ideas on value pluralism and his contribution to the Liberal tradition have received most recent attention. What has escaped notice by most commentators on Berlin is his account of the way in which the survival of liberal institutions and values requires at crucial moments the intervention of political leaders whose conduct and virtues step outside the boundaries of liberal society.[24]

Berlin was not prepared to accept that political theorists ought to be embarrassed by their recognition of the greatness of political leaders. Indeed, the acceptance of the causal power of political greatness in history was one aspect of Berlin's assault upon determinism and positivism in social science. He rejected the idea put forward by 'social theorists of various schools' that 'greatness is a romantic illusion- a vulgar notion exploited by politicians or propagandists, and one which a deeper study of the facts will always dispel'.[25] This 'deflationist' attitude can only be

---

24 Ryan Patrick Hanley, 'Political Science and Political Understanding: Isaiah Berlin on the Nature of Political Inquiry', *American Political Science Review*, vol. 98, no. 2 (2004), p. 333.
25 Isaiah Berlin, *Personal Impressions* (London: The Hogarth Press, 1980), p. 32.

refuted, Berlin argues, by experiencing at first hand an example of true greatness. What does Berlin mean by political greatness? He tells us that it is not a specifically moral attribute nor is it a private virtue.

> A great man need not be morally good, or upright, or kind, or sensitive, or delightful, or possess artistic or scientific talent. To call someone a great man is to claim that he has intentionally taken (or perhaps could have taken) a large step, one far beyond the normal capacities of men, in satisfying, or materially affecting, central human interests.[26]

Political leaders of this type must seem able to have dramatic transformative powers. This, of course, runs deliberately counter to any more structuralist account of history in which the role of great individuals is devalued. In Berlin's view, whatever the historical truth may turn out to be, the decisive importance of political leadership is one fact that is given powerful support by the history of our own time. In elaborating this account there are two examples of political leaders who, in Berlin's view, stand out in the twentieth century and each represents one side of this distinction. Winston Churchill is his example of a political hedgehog and Chaim Weizmann is the example of a political fox.

Winston Churchill represents the type of political leader who is possessed by a 'single, central, organising principle' and a 'historical imagination so strong, so comprehensive, as to encase the whole of the present and the whole of the future in framework of a rich and multicoloured past'. Churchill is presented as a kind of historicist. His wartime speeches possessed an archaism that produced the required degree of solemnity. Similarly Churchill's idea of history was to regard it as an epic in which heroes and villains 'acquired their stature not merely — or indeed at all — from the importance of the events in which they are involved, but from their own intrinsic human size upon the stage of human history'.[27] Churchill, in Berlin's account, is a fascinating example of a leader perceived as a political hedgehog. His strength, of being guided by an all-embracing vision during the war years, was to become a weakness during more normal times because of its inability to sense the complexity of changing circumstances.

If Berlin contrasts Churchill the political hedgehog with Weizmann the political fox there are other contrasts in Berlin's essays, such as with Franklin D. Roosevelt, but it is the discussion of these two figures that stands out in an intensity that is based to a large degree on personal contact. Apart from the comparison with Churchill Berlin draws out the distinctiveness of Weizmann's claim to greatness by comparing him with

26 *Ibid.*, p. 32.
27 *Ibid.*, p. 10.

another leader of the Zionist movement and political hedgehog, Theodor Herzl.

If there are political leaders who can be categorised as being either hedgehogs or foxes then Berlin believed that both were necessary. However, it is the fox with whom he is most sympathetic. For example, Berlin's contrast between Herzl and Weizmann is meant to bear this out. Herzl according to Berlin belongs to the class of political leaders who 'stand, in a sense, outside the the movements which idolise them; they are felt to be embodiments of greater virtues—and more mysterious ones—than their followers can emulate: they lead their armies to glory or to destruction, not by taking account of the obstacles in their path but by ignoring them; ... such leaders tend to be somewhat inhuman—because instead of understanding the details of the lives and characters of their own and other peoples, they oversimplify, they create a radiant myth with which they identify themselves, and which their followers bear in their hearts'.[28] Herzl's achievement was made possible because he constructed an ideal which bore only a remote connection with the facts of the situation but it enabled him to dramatise his task so that he had all of the necessary appearance of a man of destiny. Weizmann appears to Berlin as the complete opposite to this type of leader. He 'indulged in no fantasies, he was not a fanatic or a romantic or a national leader of fable'. Weizmann maintained 'a sense of proportion, understood things as they were, was never deluded by forms or words or ideals into forgetting the social and economic and human realities which he desired to create, and which could easily be lost, or at any rate damaged and compromised, by fanatical emphasis upon the outer framework to which Herzl, for instance, paid such passionate attention'.[29]

(2) *The Sense of Reality*

Berlin's account of the relative merits of the two types of political leader rests upon a vision of the nature of political reality. In brief, Berlin's argument is that it is those statesmen or political leaders who understand that reality who succeed while those who do not are bound to fail. Indeed, 'there is a sense, seldom denied even by the most biased historians, in which the difference between practical and Utopian statesmen is that the first are said to "understand", while the second are said not to "understand", the nature of the human material with which they deal'.[30]

---

28 Berlin, *The Power of Ideas*, p. 187.
29 *Ibid.*, p. 190.
30 Berlin, *The Power of Ideas*, p. 138.

Clearly, for Berlin, a correct understanding of the theory and practice of political leadership is inseparable from an appreciation of the limits, or, indeed, the failure of any kind of claim made for an understanding of political or social reality that is modelled on the example of the natural sciences. For example, Lenin is an example of a political leader who was guided by a belief in a science of history analogous to natural science and applied his understanding of the situation with a single-minded purpose. The result of such policies is always to fail to achieve the desired end and to become a victim of the law of unintended consequences. In contrast political leaders such as Bismarck, Lincoln, and Roosevelt were much more successful in achieving something close to their intended objective.

Successful statesmen and political leaders are to be understood as artists rather than as scientists. They understand the medium in which they are working rather than trying to impose an inappropriate and external standard. Berlin is insistent that successful political leadership defies easy explanation by both themselves and by external observers and analysts. We seem to have no alternative to the use of such terms as 'imagination', 'political genius', 'sense of history', and 'unerring judgement' which are, of course, terms that are completely outside of the range of social scientific discourse.

One unifying theme that runs throughout Berlin's reflections on the nature of political leadership is the fear of the harm that is most likely to result from bold, often revolutionary, schemes of change. Berlin names the Puritans, Robespierre, Lenin, Hitler, and Stalin as leading examples of political leaders who 'in a literal sense' knew not what they did, nor did they care.[31] On the other hand he argues that we are bound to have more trust in leaders such as Napoleon, Cavour, Lincoln, Lloyd George, and Franklin Roosevelt. They exhibit an understanding of the nature of the material that they are working with. Although the bias seems to be against the bold reformer or revolutionary Berlin claims that this is not meant to be a contrast between radicalism and conservatism. The basic point is that the conditions for the existence of successful political leadership are conditioned by the limits of our knowledge of social and political reality. The unavailability of predictive political knowledge means that those who place excessive faith in laws and methods derived from the alien field of natural science and attempt to apply them in a mechanical fashion are bound to be utopian.

At deeper level Berlin's ideas about the nature of leadership were fashioned by his reflections upon the political crises of the twentieth century.

---

31 Isaiah Berlin, *The Sense of Reality: Studies in Ideas and their History* (London: Chatto and Windus), p. 51.

The target that he was aiming at was totalitarianism in all of its forms. The experience of totalitarianism in the twentieth century represents a complete reversal of the governing political philosophical ideas of the eighteenth and nineteenth centuries. The idea that 'human society grew in a discoverable direction, governed by laws; that the borderline that divides science from Utopia, effectiveness from ineffectiveness in every sphere of life, was discoverable by reason and observation and could be plotted less or more precisely; that, in short, there was a clock, its movement followed discoverable rules, and it could not be put back'. All of this was undermined by three examples of a new type of leader; Lenin, Stalin, and Hitler. Berlin, using a phrase that is reminiscent of Hannah Arendt, asserts that the 'banisters upon which the system-builders of the nineteenth century have taught us to lean have proved unequal to the pressure that was put upon them'.[32] Berlin sees the difficulty of modern political leadership to be derived to a large degree, in a manner similar to Weber, from the 'disenchanted' character of the modern world. Political leaders operating under such novel conditions must somehow constantly struggle to justify themselves in the face of scepticism about the claims of legitimating myths. For Berlin there is 'no substitute for the sense of reality'.[33]

Conclusion

Weber and Berlin are two examples of political thinkers who were both Liberal in their philosophical inclinations and able to recognise the importance of political leadership. One possible reason for this is that both were, at various times in their lives, deeply involved in the political events of their own time. Both reached similar conclusions. Political leaders are essential and unavoidable features of the modern democratic state. Political leaders, if they are to be successful, must have an insight or understanding of reality that, unsurprisingly perhaps, corresponds to their own view of the limits of political knowledge. There are, however, two problems. The first is that the emphasis upon the creative power of leadership tends to have the effect of devaluing the role of followers. Obviously there can only be leaders if there are also followers. Both Weber and Berlin tend to relegate followers to a secondary or passive role. The second problem is that, in their accounts of the difficult and at times tragic character of leadership, they both fail to explore its normative implications. At times, for example, we are given the impression that any kind of leadership is acceptable as long as it works. There is no particular good that the leader ought to seek. As long as the leader has his/her own vision to steer by that

---

32 *Ibid.*, p. 11.
33 *Ibid.*, p. 35.

is enough. Of course, this may well be a consequence of accepting the ideas of disenchantment and value pluralism. Nevertheless, if we ask what the legitimate aims of political leadership ought to be we are inevitably led back to those questions that have been the traditional concerns of political thinkers, including those moderns who have not shown very much interest in leadership. That is to say, with questions of justice in the polis. Focussing upon political leadership might be one way of respecting normative concerns while recognising the constraints of realism.[34]

---

[34] Raymond Geuss, *Philosophy and Real Politics* (Princeton: Princeton University Press, 2008).

Gabriella Slomp[1]

The Janus Face of Leadership
The Demands of Normality and Exception

I. Introduction

In his work on constitutions Aristotle engages with three contexts: the world of experience, the interpretation by society of that experience, and the 'theoretization' of past writers. This triple engagement, according to Eric Voegelin;[2] captures the core of the Aristotelian method of enquiry. If we follow Aristotle in our study of leadership, and consider the three different contexts of experience, self-interpretation, and conceptualisation, we may notice that there has always been some discrepancy between, on the one hand, the prominence of political leaders in the experience and perception of people living in democracies and, on the other hand, the attention paid to the concept of leadership by theorists of democracy. In other words, whereas people living in democracies have always felt that leaders 'matter', theorists of democracy instead have shown little interest in the investigation of leadership and have often suggested that the democratic principle of 'rule of law' is incompatible with the notion of 'leadership'.

The compatibility between 'rule of law' and 'leadership' was keenly debated among the philosophers of Ancient Greece. The concept of leadership was mainly explored and supported by anti-democratic writers. To those of his contemporaries who claimed that the 'kingship of the law' was above any king, Heraclitus famously replied that 'the law can very well command to obey one man'.[3]

The most influential early insights into the concept of leadership were arguably provided by Plato in the *Republic* where he addresses the ques-

---

[1] I should like to thank Chris Brown, Vittorio Bufacchi, Tony Lang, William Walker and especially András Körösényi for very perceptive comments on an earlier draft.
[2] Eric Voegelin, *The New Science of Politics* (Chicago: University of Chicago Press, 1952).
[3] Heractitus, fragment no. 111 in Burnet, *Early Greek Philosophy* quoted also by K.R. Popper, *The Open Society and its Enemies* (London: Routledge, & Kegan Paul, 1945), Vol. I, p. 206.

tion 'who should rule?' Plato's complex and challenging reply can be seen as the origin of three distinct narratives in western political thought.

Firstly, it can be argued that Plato's question launched the western investigation into the concept of sovereignty, of its function and of its location.[4] Secondly, Plato's enquiry and his ensuing reflections on the education and training of 'guardians' fostered theoretical interest in the personal characteristics and virtues of rulers and prompted work on the education of leaders. Machiavelli's *Prince* is commonly regarded as the masterpiece of this tradition; even if Plato and Machiavelli ascribed very different characteristics to true leaders, their approach to this issue exhibited the same mode of thinking: leaders are necessary and should have certain specific personal qualities that can be enhanced with education or training. Thirdly, Plato's claim that the Philosopher-King should lead because of his access to the world of Forms can be seen to have pioneered the search for the 'objective', 'essential', or 'existential' characteristics that would entitle some (be they the 'wisest', 'the master race', the 'hero' or the 'proletariat') to rule over the rest; this line of inquiry inspired a wider investigation into the philosophy of history.

Although closely related, these three lines of enquiry were often developed separately and even in opposition to one another. For example, only the second narrative—which examines the personal characteristics of leaders—took leadership as its main focus. This tradition produced a *genre* of writings that was very popular in the sixteenth century but that became to some extent sidelined when the first narrative—which discussed sovereignty and its location—captured the imagination of western political thinkers. This sovereignty-based line of enquiry increasingly focused on institutions rather than leaders, and hence theoretical attention was shifted away from the personal characteristics and education of kings and princes. Nonetheless, important reflections on leadership continued and can be found not only in anti-democratic works but also in the political writings of philosophers such as Immanuel Kant who regarded enlightened leaders as an important component of mankind's progress towards perpetual peace.

In the twentieth century, the impact of leaders such as Hitler, Stalin and Mussolini on domestic and international politics gave rise to widespread

---

4 Not everybody agrees that the concept of sovereignty dates back to the Greeks. While 'primordialists' find precursors in ancient writers such as Plato, Aristotle, Polybius, Dionysius of Halicarnassus, Ulpian, Augustine, Dante, Ockham, Marsilius and Machiavelli, 'modernists' instead claim that sovereignty is a modern phenomenon linked to the birth and growth of the nation state; as such, state sovereignty was born in the 17th century and was first theorized by Jean Bodin and Thomas Hobbes. I have discussed this in G. Slomp, 'On Sovereignty', Trevor Salmon and Mark Imber (eds.) *Issues In International Relations* (Abingdon and New York: Routledge, 2008), second edition, pp. 33–45.

The Janus Face of Leadership

hostility to the notion of leadership—this hostility pervades Karl Popper's *The Open Society and its Enemies*, published in 1945. In the chapter entitled 'The Principle of Leadership', Popper challenges the very question that Plato posited, namely 'who should rule?', and argues that the format of such a query inevitably forces one to provide answers of the type that Plato gave. In his words:

> It is my conviction that by expressing the problem of politics in the form 'Who should rule?' or 'Whose will should be supreme?, etc., Plato created a lasting confusion in political philosophy. ... It is clear that once the question 'Who should rule?' is asked, it is hard to avoid some such reply as 'the best' or 'the wisest' or 'the born leader' or 'he who masters the art of ruling' (or perhaps, 'The General Will' or 'The master Race' or 'The industrial Workers' or ' The People'). But such a reply, convincing as it sounds—for who would advocate the rule of 'the worst' or 'the greatest fool' or 'the born slave'?—is ... quite useless.[5]

Popper does not deny that leaders are necessary in contemporary democracies and he admits that only a relatively small number of people can be actively involved in government. Popper also concedes that the power of leaders can never be as absolute as some claim, insofar as 'even the most powerful tyrant depends upon his secret police, his henchmen and his hangmen. This dependence means that his power, great as it may be, is not unchecked, and that he has to make concessions'.[6] Popper's concern, however, is to stress that individuals involved in government inevitably acquire a great amount of power, influence, and control over the others; for him, the advantage of democratic government is that 'we can get rid [of bad leaders] without bloodshed ... that is to say, the social institutions provide means by which the rulers may be dismissed by the ruled'.[7] Based on these considerations, Popper suggests that the correct way to address the problem of leadership in a democracy is not by asking 'who should rule?' but by asking 'how can we organize political institutions so as to minimize the damage that bad rulers can cause?'[8]

According to Popper, rather than speculating on the qualities of leaders and scouting out the people who would best fit the post, we should strive to refine the institutional means by which we may control the individuals who occupy positions of power. Popper writes:

> I am inclined to think that rulers have rarely been above the average, either morally or intellectually, and often below it. And I think that it is reasonable to adopt in politics the principle of preparing for the

5 Karl Popper *The Open Society*, p. 120.
6 *Ibid.*.
7 *Ibid.*.
8 *Ibid.*, p. 121.

worst, as well as we can, though we should, of course, at the same time try to obtain the best. It appears to me madness to base all our political efforts upon the faint hope that we shall be successful in obtaining excellent, or even competent, rulers.[9]

In short, a democracy for Popper is one where leadership is seen as a necessary evil and where a system of checks and balances enables its citizens to constrain and possibly remove leaders through peaceful means, such as general elections.

Popper's great suspicion of leaders may be understood as natural given some of the paradigmatic leaders of his time: Hitler, Stalin and Mussolini. Towards the end of the Twentieth Century, however, the experience of peaceful liberal democracies under the leadership of less threatening yet still highly influential individuals, such as Reagan and Thatcher, prompted a number of writers to reconsider the notion of leadership and to investigate its role in liberal democracies. Works such as Dennis F. Thompson's *Political Ethics and Public Office*,[10] Carnes Lord's *The Modern Prince: what Leaders need to know now*[11] and Kenneth Ruscio's *The Leadership Dilemma in Modern Democracy*[12] are examples of a growing interest in leadership in liberal democracies; this can be interpreted as a revival of the second narrative that, as mentioned above, runs through the history of western political thought.

It is hoped this brief sketch provides an adequate background for the chapter, the aim of which is to reflect on the questions and concerns that a contemporary theory of leadership in liberal democracies ought to address. I will take as my point of departure Ruscio's stimulating work on leadership. Ruscio observes that his work could be criticised for assuming a specific notion of liberal democracy. In this chapter, I level a wider charge against Ruscio: he addresses only one of the three narratives in western political thought that I sketched above.

Although Plato's and Machiavelli's works on leadership contributed significantly to the tradition concerned with the education and training of leaders, these two authors, unlike Ruscio, addressed the other two narratives in the history of political thought, namely the one engaged with the issue of sovereignty and the one exploring the wider foundations of the political.

---

9   *Ibid.*., pp. 122–3.
10   Dennis F. Thompson, *Political Ethics and Public Office* (Cambridge, Massachusetts and London: Harvard University Press, 1987).
11   Carnes Lord, *The Modern Prince: what Leaders need to Know Now* (New Haven and London: Yale University Press, 2003).
12   Kenneth Ruscio, *The Leadership Dilemma in Modern Democracy* (Cheltenham, UK and Northampton MA: Edward Elgar, 2004).

Indeed, Plato's concept of guardianship is a component of a full-fledged theory of politics; similarly, Machiavelli's theory of leadership in the *Prince* is part of wider reflections on politics and history. The engagement with issues of sovereignty and with the foundations of the political enabled Machiavelli to advance a theory of leadership which considered the characteristics and duties of leaders in both normal times and in times of emergency, in domestic and foreign politics, and the role of leaders in the crucial process of establishing whether a situation is normal or in need of emergency measures.

This chapter suggests that a contemporary investigation into leadership in liberal democracies cannot limit itself to engage with only one of the three narratives that run through the history of western political thought; following Plato and Machiavelli, it must address the concerns raised by all three discourses. Especially in the contemporary world where the Westphalian notion of sovereignty has undergone irreversible changes and is being continuously redefined, where the location of the 'the political' is constantly shifting, any discussion of leadership must address the challenges faced by democratic leaders in both normal and exceptional times, and spell out their role in the process of establishing a state of emergency. The chapter suggests that a theory of leadership which examines the duties and qualities of democratic leaders only 'under normal circumstances' is not simply incomplete but also inadequate.

II. The Return of the Prince

A great merit of Ruscio's *The Leadership Dilemma* is that this work urges us to give leadership a central role in the debate on democracies. In his introduction, Ruscio writes:

> The theory of democracy does not treat leaders kindly. [...] Fear of leadership is a basic justification for democratic forms of government. Yet it is impossible to imagine a strong, healthy democracy without leaders. A central objective of this study is to recover those elements of democratic thought that acknowledge the indispensable, fundamental, and positive contribution of leaders.[13]

For Ruscio, the dilemma of leadership in a democracy 'is the process of constraining rulers because we fear them, even if we empower them to lead society in its collective pursuit of its noblest and most ambitious aspirations'.[14] Ruscio points out that 'making the case for a particular kind of leadership requires first making the case for a particular kind of democ-

---

13   Ruscio, *The Leadership Dilemma*, p. ix
14   *Ibid..*, p. x.

racy'[15] and emphasises that his aim is to advance a theory of leadership that is in accord with his own understanding of liberalism. Ruscio singles out the main responsibilities that liberal democratic leaders have and argues that the fostering of public reason and mutual trust are necessary for the form of liberal democratic leadership that he is proposing. The main responsibility that Ruscio ascribes to liberal democratic leaders is the promotion of the public interest above private interest.

The notions of public reason and public trust and the possibility of a common good are the three core premises of Ruscio's theory and are thereby also important conditions for evaluating it, and for accepting or rejecting it.

The notion of public reason grounds Ruscio's arguments on how to manage domestic conflict and on how to create the right conditions for collective action which, in turn, leaders must be able to incite and direct. To Rawls's question of how equal and free citizens divided by religious and moral disagreement can coexist and cooperate, Ruscio replies that 'they must reason publicly' and that they 'must understand if not always endorse the positions of those they live with'. Leaders have the same duties as ordinary citizens (indeed, Ruscio comments, that "their obligation is greater'), and 'they must also create the conditions that allow for public deliberation'.[16]

Ruscio appeals to the notion of public trust in order to resolve the tension between the opposite claims of the 'political imperative' of public accountability of public officials and the 'managerial imperative' of discretion and flexibility that the administrative tasks of government require. Ruscio then elucidates the meaning, significance and scope that such trust must take for his theory of leadership to hold.

The real possibility of attaining the common good and the rejection of the view that such notion is too elusive to define and unrealistic to attain, provide the basis for Ruscio's claim that leaders have an obligation that goes beyond the accommodation of separate and competing interests. They must lead in the wider sense of the world, providing direction, purpose and motivation.

Having granted that some may question his theory of leadership because it is linked to a specific notion of democracy and to a particular understanding of liberalism, Ruscio proceeds with the aim of showing that his theory takes seriously a number of claims made by Machiavelli, Locke, Montesquieu, Hamilton, Madison, Jay, Jefferson and Rawls.

---

15   Ibid.., p. ix.
16   Ibid.., p. xi.

For our purposes, it is worth noticing that Ruscio maintains that he shares some concerns with Machiavelli and Locke, and indeed that he adopts some of their ideas. For instance, Ruscio stresses the crucial role played by conflict in Machiavelli's discourse. He points out that although Machiavelli's measures are inevitably linked to his particular historical context, his achievement was to realise that the core task of leadership is conflict resolution. Ruscio claims that this is at the core of his own conception of leadership because 'modern politics accepts disorder and conflict as inevitable and leaders as an inevitable part of that response'.[17] Regarding Locke, Ruscio claims that the Lockean notion of 'prerogative' is a forerunner of his own 'managerial principle' which allows leaders some discretion in the complex business of governing a modern democracy.

To recap, then, this section has looked at Ruscio's proposal of a notion of leadership that is aimed at resolving disagreements and at giving direction to a democracy in accord with the liberal principles of public reason, trust and common good. Ruscio's leader is constrained by the 'political principle' of accountability but is nonetheless able to act efficiently thanks to the 'managerial principle' of discretion. Ruscio acknowledges that critics of liberalism may dislike his theory and does not deny that even liberals may have problems with it. He contends, however, that if we accept his premises (the triad of public reason, trust and common good) and his goal (the handling of conflict), then his theory of leadership can be validly deduced.

III. Machiavelli and the Disorder of Romagna

As seen above, Ruscio maintains that his theory of leadership addresses the problem of conflict in modern liberal democracies; in particular, Ruscio claims to be very sympathetic to Machiavelli's concern with domestic conflict. Ruscio emphasises that Machiavelli's specific (and often unpalatable) advice to princes is simply the product of different historical times. My aim in this section is to challenge Ruscio's claim and to suggest that the conflict examined by Ruscio and Machiavelli respectively is different in kind.

Conflict is indeed essential to Machiavelli's argument on leadership. For sure, the fact that Machiavelli was writing in the sixteenth century can explain the extreme measures that he recommends in order to overcome conflict. Indeed, one does not need to be a committed contextualist to notice that, as much as some contemporary Italian leaders might want to follow Machiavelli's handbook, they would not be able to stage anything like the massacre at Senigallia, the execution of Rimirro d'Orco, or the

---

[17] *Ibid..*, p. 12.

tragic dinner party at Fermo described in the *Prince*. Nevertheless, it is important not to write off the brutality of these incidents as being the mere product of different times. I would argue that the ruthlessness of the Machiavellian is not a quirk of history but the result of a type of conflict that Ruscio does not consider. In order to support this claim, it is worth examining some of the more extreme cases of brutality that Machiavelli describes.

The massacre at Senigallia took place in December 1502. There were two important events in the lead-up to this massacre: the rebellion at Urbino and the uprising of Romagna. These major political problems induced Duke Valentine (alias Cesare Borgia) to deceive the unsuspecting leaders of the Orsini family into accepting his invitation to Senigallia, where 'they were at his mercy' and where they were killed.[18] As a result of this massacre, Borgia 'had control of all the Romagna and the Duchy of Urbino' and, moreover, he 'won over the Romagna and acquired the support of its population, who were beginning to enjoy a new prosperity'.[19]

The historical background provided by Machiavelli for the execution of Rimirro d'Orco is similar to that of Senigallia. There was disorder in Romagna. It is worth quoting Machiavelli's account in full:

> [S]ince it would be sensible to imitate Cesare [Borgia]'s actions, I want to amplify what I have just said. Once the duke had subdued the Romagna, he found it had been under the control of weak nobles, who had rather exploited than governed their subjects and had rather been the source of conflict than of order, with the result the whole province was full of robbers, bandits and every other type of criminal. So he decided it was necessary if he was going to make the province peaceful and obedient to his commands, to give it good government. He put Mr Remiro d'Orco, a man both cruel and efficient, in charge, and gave him absolute power. D'Orco in short order established peace and unity, and acquired immense authority. At that point, the Duke decided such unchecked power was no longer necessary, for he feared the people might come to hate it. So he established a civil court in the center of the province, placing an excellent judge in charge of it, and requiring every city to appoint a lawyer to represent it before the court. Since he knew the harsh measures of the past had given rise to some enmity towards him, in order to purge the ill-will of the people and win them completely over to him, he wanted to make clear that, if there had been any cruelty, he was not responsible for it, and that his hard-hearted minister should be blamed. He saw his opportunity and exploited it. One morning, in the town square of Cesena, he had

---

18   Niccolo Machiavelli, *The Prince*, ed. and trans. David Wootton (Indianapolis/Cambridge: Hackett Publishing, 1995), p. 24.
19   *Ibid.*.

Remiro d'Orco's corpse laid out in two pieces, with a chopping board and a bloody knife besides it.[20]

In the *Prince*, Machiavelli insists that having 'surveyed all the actions of the Duke… [He] cannot find anything to criticize',[21] because Borgia's aim was to establish order and good government in the region and he was successful in laying down a 'sound foundation'.

From these examples and others, we can see that Machiavelli is examining extreme violence in extreme situations of conflict, when political power and sovereignty over a city or region are at stake. Needless to say, Machiavelli does not only consider times of emergency; for example, in the *Discourses* Machiavelli discusses the demands and requirements of leadership in normal, peaceful times. In the *Prince*, however, Machiavelli concentrates on 'new principalities' that are prone to experiencing times of exceptional political upheaval, times when there is fierce competition for political power and when disorder follows.

In other words, we could say that that the type of conflict that Machiavelli discusses in the *Prince* is the one that emerges when leadership faces the problem of sovereignty. This, I suggest, is the basic difference between the accounts of Machiavelli and Ruscio. This difference should not be obscured by the specific measures that Machiavelli describes and recommends, which are indeed linked to his own period of history.

Thus, whereas in the *Prince* Machiavelli considers exceptional conflict (namely, times when leadership faces the problem of sovereignty), in his work Ruscio exclusively examines unexceptional times, times when sovereignty is unproblematic and unchallenged, when all conflict is in fact disagreement among friends.

IV. Hobbes and the Danger of Democratic Leaders

In the writings of Thomas Hobbes, one can find a series of insightful reflections on leadership that ultimately reinforce the threat that serious conflict poses to Ruscio's theory. Indeed Hobbes, to a greater extent than Plato and Machiavelli, focuses on the impact that leadership may have on sovereignty and highlights the dangers of democratic leadership. Hobbes's argument can be broken down into the following four elements: Firstly, Hobbes argues that the sovereign power of a political association is the same, whether the government is democratic, oligarchic or monar-

---

20   *Ibid..*, pp. 24–5.
21   *Ibid..*, p. 26.

chic: 'the power in all forms, if they be perfect enough to protect ... is the same'.[22]

Secondly, Hobbes rejects the view that 'governors' may gain from damaging their subjects; he writes:

> But a man may here object that the condition of subjects is very miserable, as being obnoxious to the lusts and other irregular passions of him or them that have so unlimited a power in their hands. And commonly they that live under a monarch think it the fault of monarchy; and they that live under the government of democracy, or other sovereign assembly, attribute all the inconvenience to that form of Commonwealth.[23]

Thirdly, Hobbes points out that in fostering the common good 'sovereign governors' advance their own self-interest:

> the greatest pressure of sovereign governors proceedeth, not from any delight or profit they can expect in the damage weakening of their subjects, in whose vigour consisteth their own strength and glory, but in the restiveness of themselves that, unwillingly contributing to their own defence, make it necessary for their governors to draw from them what they can in time of peace that they may have means on any emergent occasion, or sudden need, to resist or take advantage on their enemies.[24]

Fourthly, Hobbes adds an important qualification to the original claim that governors' self-interest coincides with the public interest: he emphasizes the difference between a king and a democratic leader:

> The difference between these three kinds of Commonwealth [monarchic, democratic and aristocratic] consisteth, not in the difference of power, but in the difference of convenience or aptitude to produce the peace and security of the people; for which end they were instituted. And to compare monarchy with the other two, we may observe: first, that whosoever beareth the person of the people, or is one of that assembly that bears it, beareth also his own natural person. And though he be careful in his politic person to procure the common interest, yet he is more, or no less, careful to procure the private good of himself, his family, kindred and friends; and for the most part, if the public interest chance to cross the private, he prefers the private: for the passions of men are commonly more potent than their reason. From whence it follows that where the public and private interest are most closely united, there is the public most advanced. Now in monarchy the private interest is the same with the public. The riches, power, and honour of a monarch arise only from the riches, strength, and reputation of his subjects. For no king can be rich, nor glorious, nor secure, whose subjects are either poor, or contemptible, or too

---

22 Thomas Hobbes, *Leviathan*, ed. Edwin Curley (Indianapolis/Cambridge: Hackett Publishing, 1994), p. 117.
23 *Ibid.*.
24 *Ibid.*., pp. 117–18.

weak through want, or dissension, to maintain a war against their enemies; whereas in a democracy, or aristocracy, the public prosperity confers not so much to the private fortune of one that is corrupt, or ambitious, as doth many times a perfidious advice, a treacherous action, or a civil war.[25]

This quotation shows us why Hobbes maintains that democracies are more unstable than monarchies and oligarchies: although the sovereign power is the same in all forms of government, and although the long-term interest of all leaders lies with the public interest, more often than not shortsightedness and ambition, according to Hobbes, prevent democratic leaders from pursuing the common good; this in turn makes of democracy the least stable form of government and the one most liable to collapse into civil war.

This view, expressed by Hobbes in all his political writings, is supported by his account of the English Civil War offered in *Behemoth*. In Hobbes's narration, the civil war was fostered and ultimately caused by democratic leaders: bad teachers, bad preachers, and bad parliamentarians all manipulated people's fears, exploited popular ignorance, took advantage of human greed and exploited people's reluctance to pay their taxes to the king. For Hobbes, this is a prime example of the potential impact of leadership on state sovereignty: it can undermine the unity and security of a political association.

Whereas Machiavelli concentrated on the personal traits and characteristics that can enable princes to attain and maintain political order, Hobbes focused on the passions that can induce democratic leaders to compromise and finally destroy internal peace. Machiavelli saw Cesare Borgia's ambition as a tool to solve conflict and bring governance in Romagna, while Hobbes sees ambition as the common denominator of all democratic leaders and as the ultimate source of division and conflict within democracies. Machiavelli focused on the ability of leaders to cope with emergency situations; Hobbes instead focused on the tendency of democratic leaders to give rise to emergency situations.[26]

Hobbes would agree with Ruscio that good leaders are guided by the principles of the common good and public reason. Indeed, as pointed out by David Gauthier, Hobbes was one of the first writers to contribute to the development of the western concept of 'public reason'. However, Hobbes's theory poses a twofold challenge to Ruscio: from a Hobbesian perspective, a theory of leadership is seriously incomplete if, on the one hand, it does not dwell on the role of leaders in handling major conflict,

---

25 *Ibid.*, p. 120.
26 In his discussion of 'commonwealth by acquisition', Hobbes does acknowledge that kings and leaders can bring peace to a region and create order.

namely conflict that arises when sovereignty is challenged, and, on the other hand, it does not consider the motivations of individuals who become democratic leaders. For Hobbes, democratic leaders are the most ambitious people in a political association; moreover, unlike hereditary kings, democratic leaders attain their position by winning public support and this is often obtained neither by furthering the public good nor by developing public reason but by appealing to the strongest passions and the most widespread opinions of the majority.

Hence, not unlike Plato and Machiavelli, Hobbes appreciated the crucial importance of leadership and its impact on state sovereignty. He was critical of democracy because he believed that such a form of government would attract the most ambitious individuals to compete for power and would induce them to sacrifice the long-term common good to the whims, wrong opinions and shortsightedness of their supporters.

V. 'Emergency', 'Prerogative' and the Unpredictability of Politics

Finally, I would like to consider briefly Carl Schmitt's contribution to the narrative on leadership and John Locke's notion of prerogative.

Leadership is the focus of Schmitt's work on *Dictatorship*,[27] where commissarial and sovereign dictatorships are discussed. By 'commissarial dictatorship' Schmitt intends a transitional dictatorship that, in an emergency, suspends temporarily the constitution for the sake of protecting it; by 'sovereign dictatorship', instead, Schmitt means a dictatorship that abrogates the existing constitution with the aim to introduce a different one. Schmitt stresses that a commissarial dictatorship is different from arbitrary despotism or tyranny.[28] According to Schmitt, both commissarial and sovereign dictatorship have precedents in the works of Machiavelli, Bodin and Hobbes. Schmitt suggests that in Machiavelli's *Discourses* and in the *Prince* there are elements of both forms of dictatorship. Also in Bodin's work, Schmitt finds a precedent of 'commissarial dictatorship', namely a form of dictatorship that—in the case of exception- has the power to suspend temporarily the constitution with the aim to protect it. In *The Crisis of Parliamentary Democracy* Schmitt writes:

> The usual definition of sovereignty today rests on Bodin's recognition that it will always be necessary to make exceptions to the general rule

---

27 Carl Schmitt, *Die Diktatur, Von den Anfaengen des modernen Souveranitaetsgedankens bis zum proltarischen Klassenkampf* (Munchen-Leibniz: Dunker &Humblot, 1964). In this essay all references are to the Italian translation: *La dittatura. Dalle origini dell' idea moderna di sovranita' alla lotta di classe operaia* (Roma-Bari: Laterza, 1975).
28 Schmitt, *La dittatura*, p. 9.

in concrete circumstances and that the sovereign is whoever decides what constitutes an exception.[29]

In *Die Diktatur*, Schmitt singles out Chapter Eight, of Book One of *Six livres de la Republique* as the place where Bodin provides us with a 'definition of commissarial dictatorship':

> Bodin has not only the merit of having given us the concept of sovereignty, but also of having discovered the link between the problem of sovereignty and the problem of dictatorship and of having provided us with a definition that even today must be regarded as fundamental.[30]

For Schmitt, Bodin, whom he calls an 'otherwise moderate political writer', has made an important contribution to the understanding of emergencies and such understanding motivated Bodin's opposition to the division of power and his preference for monarchy as a form of government.

According to Schmitt, emergencies require urgent decisions and urgent decisions rule out committees and consultations. Indeed, as Tom Sorell points out: 'A leader exercising his judgment and implementing whatever measures seem appropriate in time of national peril seems better to him than rule by committee or constitution'.[31] Sorell convincingly argues that Schmitt is often approving of Hobbes's commitment to decisionism and (in spite of describing the Leviathan as a *machina machinarum*) to some form of personal leadership.

On the one hand, Schmitt contends that by promoting the rule of law and an impersonal legal system, liberal democracies disable themselves when it comes to the case of exception. On the other hand, Schmitt suggests that systems of checks and balances only serve as a mask which disguises the real concentration of power within liberal democracies. He claims that in a case of exceptional danger, coming from inside or outside the state, be it the partisan or any other lethal challenge, the location of supreme sovereign power becomes unambiguous; it becomes obvious that the sovereign power is undivided and personal because ' sovereign is he who decides on the exception'.[32]

Thus Schmitt, to an even greater extent than Machiavelli and Hobbes, focuses on the relationship between leadership and sovereignty and develops the two concepts so that they coincide in the case of emergency.

---

29 Carl Schmitt, *The Crisis of Parliamentary Democrac*, (Cambridge, Massachusetts: MIT Press, 1985), p. 43.
30 Schmitt, *La Dittatura*, p. 36.
31 Tom Sorell, 'Schmitt, Hobbes and the Politics of Emergency', *Filozofski Vestnik*, 24:2 (2003), 223–41, p. 223 reprinted in Tomaz Mastnak (ed.), *Behemoth* (Exeter: Imprint Academic, 2009).
32 Carl Schmitt, *Political Theology* (Baskerville: MIT Press, 1985), p. 5.

Although there are many differences between Machiavelli, Bodin, Hobbes and Schmitt, they arguably share the same ideology of emergency, namely the view that it is in a crisis that one grasps the function and essence of the political. More forcibly than anyone else, Schmitt stresses the importance of focusing on emergencies arising from conflict over sovereignty in order to get an insight into the role and significance of political leadership in any form of government, including democracies.

There are of course serious limitations to the ideology of emergency that runs through Machiavelli's *Prince* and *Discourses*, Bodin's *Six books on the Republic*, Hobbes's *Leviathan* and *Behemoth*, and especially the political theory of Carl Schmitt: this essay is not the place to explore them. It is worth reminding ourselves, however, that even John Locke—who rejected the ideology of emergency—addressed the problem raised by exceptional circumstances with his concept of 'prerogative'. Ruscio claims that Locke's 'prerogative' is merely a precedent of his 'managerial principle' that allows leaders some flexibility in the administration of their tasks; against Ruscio's reading, it can be argued with some credibility that Locke's concept of 'prerogative' gives leaders the licence to face exceptional situations with exceptional measures and is in fact a precedent for Schmitt 'case of exception'.[33] Writes Locke:

> The good of the society requires that several things should be left to the discretion of him that has the executive power (...). This power to act according to discretion for the public good, without the prescription of the law and sometimes even against it, is that which is called prerogative.[34]

Locke stresses that good government and prerogative go hand in hand and that

> prerogative can be nothing but the people's permitting their rulers to do several things of their own free choice where the law was silent, and sometimes too against the direct letter of the law, for the public good and their acquiescing in it when so done.[35]

Locke challenges the notion that rulers can have 'excessive prerogative' in so far as 'prerogative is nothing but the power of doing public good without a rule';[36] he remarks:

---

33 For the debate on whether the Lockean concept of prerogative can be interpreted as a precedent of Schmitt' concept of exception, see for example Iain Hampsher-Monk and Keith Zimmerman, 'Liberal Constitutionalism and Schmitt's critique', *History of Political Thought*, 28:4 (2007) 678–96.
34 John Locke, *Two Treatises of Government* (New York: Dent Dutton, 1978), p. 199.
35 Ibid.., p. 201.
36 Ibid.., p. 202.

> For as a good prince, who is mindful of the trust put in his hands and careful of the good of his people, cannot have too much prerogative—that is power to do good, so a weak and ill prince, who would claim that power his predecessors exercised, without the direction of the law, as a prerogative belonging to him by right of his office, which he may exercise at his pleasure to make or promote an interest distinct from that of the public, gives the people an occasion to claim their right and limit that power, which, whilst it was exercised for the good, they were content should be tacitly allowed.[37]

In the concluding section of Chapter IV of the Second Treatise we read:

> The old question will be asked in this matter of prerogative, "But who shall be judge when this power is made a right use of?" I answer: between an executive power in being, with such prerogative, and a legislative that depends upon his will for their convening, there can be no judge on earth. As there can be none between the legislative and the people, should either the executive or the legislative, when they have got the power in their hands, design, or go about to enslave or destroy them, the people have no other remedy in this, as in all other cases where they have no judge on earth, but to appeal to Heaven[38]

In Locke's opinion, no earthly judge, no institution, no system of law can be appealed to in order to establish whether prerogative has been abused. If the majority of the people, however, feel that such abuses have taken place, then they can take the matter into their hands. Such an action is according to Locke justifiable by the law given to man by God according to which

> it being out of a man's power so to submit himself to another as to give him a liberty to destroy him; God and nature never allowing a man so to abandon himself as to neglect his own preservation. And therefore, although the people cannot be judge, so as to have, by the constitution of that society, any superior power to determine and give effective sentence in the case, yet they have reserved the ultimate determination to themselves which belongs to all mankind, where there lies no appeal on earth, by a law antecedent and paramount to all positive laws of men... Nor let anyone think this lays a perpetual foundation for disorder; for this operates not till the inconvenience is so great that the majority feel it, and are weary of it, and find a necessity to have it amended'.[39]

To conclude, even though resisting the ideology of emergency that runs through the works of Machiavelli, Hobbes and Schmitt, John Locke puts forward a concept of prerogative that enables leaders to suspend the rule of law whenever it is deemed necessary. Although Locke was aware of the dangers of prerogative powers, he maintained that the pursuit of the com-

---

37 *Ibid..*, p. 201.
38 *Ibid..*, p. 203.
39 *Ibid..*

mon good often requires exceptional measures. From this perspective, the concept of prerogative is Locke's answer to the concerns raised by writers such as Machiavelli and Hobbes and anticipates Schmitt's speculations on the 'case of exception'.

Although Lockean prerogative does contain also the 'managerial principle' put forward by Ruscio in *The Democracy Dilemma*—namely the principle that acknowledges discretion and flexibility to leaders in their administrative tasks of government—it cannot be reduced to it. Rather, following András Körösényi, 'it can be argued that Locke's prerogative refers to the wider phenomenon of the unpredictable and contingent nature of politics and government in general and includes the exceptional case'.[40]

VI. Leaders and the Politics of Normal and Exceptional Times

It is now time to gather the loose threads of the preceding argument and to attempt to draw some conclusions. At the beginning of this essay, I suggested that Plato's question 'who should rule?' began the western investigation into political sovereignty, sparked discussions on the education and training of leaders, and fostered the search for a meta-theory that justifies why some individuals or groups should rule over others. Recent work on political leadership such as that of Kenneth Ruscio can be interpreted as a revival of the second of these three narratives, which focuses on leaders. As mentioned above, this approach fell out of favour in the seventeenth century when the attention of western political scholars turned to investigating the concept of impersonal state sovereignty.

In Section II, I tried to summarise broadly Ruscio's theory of democratic leadership and his contention that if we accept his premises (the triad of public reason, trust and common good) and his goal (the handling of conflict), his theory of leadership follows. I highlighted Ruscio's double claim that, like Machiavelli's *Prince*, his theory puts conflict at the centre of the debate on leadership and that the differences on this issue between Machiavelli and himself can be explained contextually, namely by looking at the historical differences between their times of writing. I also stressed Ruscio's contention that his 'managerial principle' allows leaders some administrative discretion, and that Ruscio finds a forerunner for this principle in Locke's concept of 'prerogative'.

In Section III, I focused on examples of conflict examined by Machiavelli and claimed that at the core of Machiavelli's theory is the analysis of the way in which leaders can address and solve sovereignty-related conflict. Indeed Machiavelli's theory of leadership stands

---

40 András Körösényi, private correspondence (June 2009).

out vis-à-vis handbooks for princes of the same period because Machiavelli was concerned with sovereignty, even if the actual word does not occur in his writings. If my reading is correct, Machiavelli made an immense contribution not only to the tradition on the education and training of leaders, but to the study of how leadership affects sovereignty.

Hence, the theory of leadership that Machiavelli put forward in the *Prince* can be seen as a component of a wider reflection on political institutions undergoing both normal and exceptional times. This engagement with issues of sovereignty and with the problem of politics allowed Machiavelli to advance a theory of leadership which considered the characteristics and duties of leaders in normal situations and situations of emergency, in domestic and foreign politics, and indeed in the crucial process of establishing whether a situation is normal or requires emergency measures.

In Section IV, I tried to show how Hobbes, like Machiavelli and Plato before him, was concerned with the impact of leadership on sovereignty: whereas Machiavelli stresses the positive role of leaders in emergency situations, Hobbes emphasises the negative impact that democratic leaders can have on security and their possible contribution to the weakening of internal and external sovereignty. I highlighted the personal characteristics that, according to Hobbes, democratic leaders must have in order to win the support of the majority and how these characteristics are unlikely to foster the pursuit of the common good and the development of public reason.

In section V, I singled out Carl Schmitt as someone who clearly recognized in the works of Machiavelli, Hobbes and Bodin the attempt to study the crucial role of leaders in an emergency, namely when sovereignty is at stake. I also argued that Locke's concept of 'prerogative' can be interpreted as a forerunner of Schmitt's 'case of exception'.

It is time to locate Ruscio's work on the map I have sketched and to try to draw some general reflections. For a start, it may be noted that the conflict examined by Machiavelli, Hobbes and Schmitt on the one hand and Ruscio on the other is of a different type; unlike Machiavelli, Ruscio assumes that the problem of sovereignty of a given democracy is solved. It seems to me that Ruscio only considers what can be termed as 'disagreement among friends' who do not question their belonging to the same political association nor do they doubt the foundations of that association. Their passions may be high and their disagreement may be highly felt, but what they seem to disagree about are issues such as the amount of public spending that should go to education or housing, the policy on the environment and so forth. This, I would contend, is the tacit and crucial assumption of Ruscio's discourse on leadership and the precondition for accepting it. Whereas Machiavelli's *Prince*, Hobbes's *Leviathan*, and Schmitt *Diktatur* study the role of leadership in exceptional times, namely when domestic sovereignty is endangered, Ruscio limits himself to consider the quarrels and disagreements of liberal democracies in unexceptional circumstances when state security is not in question.

One may try to reply that Machiavelli, Hobbes and Schmitt are voices of an ideology of emergency that must be resisted because it has been traditionally used to challenge human rights, namely the very building block of liberal democracies. Although this is true, if it accepted that exceptional situations are inevitable in politics, a theory of leadership that concentrates exclusively on 'normal times' leaves many questions unanswered. What happens, one wonders, when Ruscio's leaders need to face the problem of internal or external enemy, in the form, for example, of domestic or international terrorism? In an emergency situation, can a Ruscian leader be bound by the principles of 'public reason' and 'public trust'? Is it not possible that the common good of a liberal democracy requires sometimes measures such as the suppression or withdrawal of relevant information? What role has the leader of liberal democracies in handling emergency situations and above all, in naming the emergency? Is a Ruscian leader institutionally constrained in the process of naming an emergency? These, I suggest, are the questions that a full-fledged theory of leadership in a liberal democracy needs to answer; it cannot ignore the crucial issues of sovereignty and security.

To conclude, we may first note that a theory of leadership such as Schmitt's that focuses entirely on emergency situations and 'exceptional times' is unacceptable to the liberal mind. By the same token, however, a theory of leadership that ignores such situations and concentrates exclusively on 'normal times' is incomplete and ultimately inadequate to answer the apprehension that liberals have regarding the power of leaders. I believe that Locke's principle of 'prerogative' cannot be reduced to a managerial principle but is an acknowledgement that exceptional times are unavoidable in politics and that they require exceptional measures. According to Locke, leaders can declare exceptional situations and handle them outside the machinery of democracy. This power is the sort that worried Karl Popper in 1945 and what still worries many liberals today.

Joseph Femia

Elites vs. the Popular Will
A False Dichotomy

> The voice of the people is but an echo. The output of an echo chamber bears an inevitable and invariable relation to the input ... the people's verdict can be no more than a selective reflection from the alternatives and outlooks presented to them.
>
> V.O. Key, *The Responsible Electorate*

In *The Terms of Democracy*, Michael Saward bluntly states that 'direct democracy is more democratic than representative democracy' because 'the people get more of what they want, rather than what representatives or others want them to want'.[1] I intend to dispute this claim, primarily by demonstrating that direct democracy is actually quite dysfunctional as a mechanism for reflecting what Saward refers to as 'the felt wishes of the citizenry'.[2] Direct democracy takes two forms: (a) referenda, which are applicable in even the largest political units, and (b) deliberative assemblies that require face-to-face interaction among ordinary citizens. Different pathologies afflict each form. Referenda campaigns, as we shall see, involve a process of will-formation, giving disproportionate power to special interests with access to the means of public communication. Public communication rarely changes people's values, but it can induce people to hold *causal* or *factual* beliefs that are both inaccurate and conducive to the interests of the senders of the message. Put another way, the 'felt wishes of the citizenry' (vague, perhaps based on prejudice) may be replaced by induced preferences whose clarity is the product of doubtful information. In the case of deliberative assemblies, we shall see how social psychological research underlines the existence of pathologies that stem from the dynamics of social interaction: (i) conformity, (ii) group-think, and (iii) the 'group deficit' phenomenon. Radical democrats systematically ignore this body of evidence, which indicates that the pres-

---

[1] M. Saward, *The Terms of Democracy* (Cambridge: Polity Press, 1998), p. 83.
[2] *Ibid.*, p. 84.

sure of face-to-face deliberation may cause participants to endorse views which are neither rational nor truly reflective of their initial wishes. The paper concludes with a defence of representative democracy as a sound, if not ideal, mechanism for fostering responsiveness to 'the felt wishes of the citizenry'.

Radical democrats have been boosted, in recent years, by the revival of the idea of 'deliberative democracy', or decision-making by discussion among free and equal citizens. Largely under the influence of Habermas, the idea that democracy revolves around the transformation rather than simply the aggregation of preferences has become almost an axiom of contemporary democratic theory. It is assumed that preferences will adapt to reason, and that 'authentic' preferences are formed during the political process rather than prior to it. As Joshua Cohen puts it, 'outcomes are democratically legitimate only if they could be the object of a free and reasoned agreement among equals'.[3] Of course, the elevation of popular deliberation into a public or civic virtue originated in Athens in the fifth century B.C. Pericles, in his eulogy of Athenian democracy, said that 'instead of looking on discussion as a stumbling block in the way of action, we think it an indispensable preliminary to any wise action at all'.[4] Yet Athenian democracy was also the birthplace of the tendency to dismiss public discussion as sophistry or demagoguery. Plato was far from alone in distrusting clever speakers who could manipulate the responses of more gullible citizens.

Platonic doubts about the reasoning capacities of ordinary mortals long ago ceased to be fashionable. Underlying mainstream approaches to contemporary democratic theory is the image of an idealised citizen, free from prejudice, devoted to the common interest, and perfectly capable of arriving at rationally informed preferences. To the extent that one thinks this model conforms to reality, one will advocate public discussion as the surest route to a rationally motivated consensus. Deliberation, because it aims to inform our collective decisions with 'reasoned' argument, is considered normatively superior to the simple aggregation of preferences or interests that characterises liberal representative democracy. Being optimistic about the qualities, or potential qualities, of their fellow human beings, champions of deliberation never allow that the cognitive standards of the democratic process could actually *suffer* from the effects of public communication. It is never even suggested that people holding true beliefs about the world might acquire false beliefs as the result of

---

3   J. Cohen, 'Procedure and Substance in Deliberative Democracy', in S. Benhabib (ed.), *Democracy and Difference* (Princeton: Princeton University Press, 1996), pp. 99–100.
4   Quoted in the Introduction to J. Elster (ed.), *Deliberative Democracy* (Cambridge: Cambridge University Press, 1998), p. 1.

deliberation. What I wish to argue here is that a certain degree of Platonic scepticism may be in order.

Our mode of proceeding will be to look at empirical evidence on the nature of political preferences and why they may change. It is an oddity of the recent fashion for radical or deliberative democracy that most of its advocates betray little, if any, interest in the findings of political science and social psychology, even though these findings tend to undermine their most cherished assumptions about popular beliefs and attitudes.[5]

Referenda and Public Opinion

Even the most cynical critic of democratic deliberation is obliged to admit that citizens are not passive receivers of media communication. They possess a variety of interests, values, and experiences that may greatly affect their willingness to accept, or resist, certain types of messages. Zaller calls these 'political predispositions', the critical intervening variable between the communications people encounter in the mass media, on one side, and their statements of political preferences, on the other.[6] These predispositions are at least in part a distillation of a person's lifetime experiences, including childhood socialisation and direct involvement with the raw ingredients of policy issues, such as earning a living or paying taxes. While they primarily depend on socio-economic location, inherited and acquired personality traits may also help to shape these predispositions. In a minority of the population, they may be knitted together to form a coherent ideological framework, from which systematic and predictable policy preferences may flow. But survey studies consistently show that only the most politically aware citizens pay enough attention to political discourse to recognise the ideological implications of different policies – to learn 'what goes with what'. Those who are less aware, less ideologically attuned, may find it difficult to ascertain which attitudes or policy preferences are conventionally appropriate to their value-system or partisan orientation, and are therefore unlikely to develop 'attitude constraint' across issues. That is to say, an informed observer is likely to surmise that ordinary people harbour inconsistent beliefs, or – in some cases – no discernible beliefs at all. In 1964, Philip Converse famously

---

5   In the past decade or so, however, a number of deliberative democrats have evinced a concern for feasibility. Questions of social complexity and institutional design do receive some attention. See, for example, S. Elstub, *Towards a Deliberative and Associational Democracy* (Edinburgh: Edinburgh University Press, 2008). Nevertheless, realistic engagement with empirical reality is always limited by their aspiration to achieve the lofty procedural ideals that unite all deliberative theorists.

6   J.R. Zaller, *The Nature and Origins of Mass Opinion* (Cambridge: Cambridge University Press, 1992), p. 22.

concluded, after studying mass belief systems, that large portions of the electorate 'simply do not have meaningful beliefs, even on issues that have formed the basis for intense political controversy among elites for substantial periods of time'.[7] Much more recently, George Bishop has supported this conclusion, arguing that on many policy issues ordinary Americans are too ignorant of relevant information to hold meaningful opinions, and that the survey instrument 'frequently generates the conceptual equivalent of an optical illusion'. Door-step answers given to survey interviewers often reflect random influences or information provided in the questions themselves, not independently held opinions.[8] Lack of strong opinions, resulting in almost random responses, is one way of explaining the attitudinal and ideological inconsistencies identified in the survey-based evidence.

Some political scientists have found this interpretation unpalatable. If the non-attitude thesis is correct, Christopher Achen complains, 'democratic theory loses its starting point'.[9] There is, however, an alternative explanation of the evidence which is less subversive of the democratic idea. Zaller claims that most people's political beliefs are characterised by a high degree of *ambivalence*, expressing different feelings towards different aspects of most issues. In the absence of a fixed attitude on most issues, they will answer questions on the basis of the particular considerations immediately salient to them — perception of the interviewer, recent viewing of a relevant news story, and so on.[10] Robert Erikson reinforces this point, noting that even 'sophisticated respondents are ambivalent about questions of public policy to the extent that they tend to give somewhat flexible answers to the same policy questions when asked more than once'. Hence survey responses can easily be swayed by 'the subtle aspects of question wording'.[11] But being internally conflicted about an issue, or answering a survey question on it off the top of one's head, does not mean that a respondent is apathetic about the issue, or unwilling to engage with it, or even confused about it. Indeed, it suggests that ordinary citizens are, for the most part, thoughtful and open to persuasion.

Using intuition rather than survey evidence, Antonio Gramsci — the great Italian Marxist thinker — reached a similar conclusion about the

---

7 P. Converse, 'The Nature of Belief Systems in Mass Publics', in D. Apter (ed.), *Ideology and Discontent* (New York: Free Press, 1964), p. 245.
8 G. Bishop, *The Illusion of Public Opinion: Fact and Artifact in American Public Opinion Polls* (Lanham, MD.: Rowman and Littlefield, 2005), pp. xvi, 17.
9 C.H. Achen, 'Mass Political Attitudes and the Survey Response', *American Political Science Review*, 69 (1975), p. 1227.
10 Zaller, *The Nature and Origins of Mass Opinion*, pp. 91–2.
11 R.C. Erikson, 'Does Public Ignorance Matter?', *Critical Review*, 19 (2007), p. 28.

nature of mass opinion. He believed that individuals acquire some kind of spontaneous knowledge in their everyday life, a knowledge implicit in 'lived' experience. This knowledge successfully orients their everyday actions, though it may, and frequently does, conflict with the cognitive and evaluative framework imposed by the powers-that-be, through the myriad mechanisms of socialisation. The masses thus exhibited, to use Gramsci's term, a 'contradictory consciousness', only superficially in thrall to the prevailing 'bourgeois hegemony'.[12] If focussed on the inconsistencies in their thought-patterns, a dialogue with the masses could thus bear fruit for the Marxist cause.

But even assuming that ordinary citizens are receptive to competing arguments, this does not mean that public deliberation will achieve its intended 'rational' effects. Analysing the results of public opinion research, Zaller concludes that few people reason for themselves about politics.[13] Mass attitudes are a function of elite discourse — a point recognised by Gramsci, who stressed the role of the vanguard party in 'ironing out' the contradictions in working class consciousness. Communication takes place from the top down: elites, including policy elites, shape citizens' views on matters of public concern, either through persuasion or through sheer intensity of media exposure. As Adam Przeworski points out, deliberation in itself presupposes inequality of influence. If everyone had information of the same quality, and the same capacity to interpret this information, then deliberation as normally understood would be pointless. If beliefs are to be modified as the result of deliberation, it must be because: (a) individuals have unequal access to information, and/or (b) they see themselves as having unequal reasoning capacity. The mere existence of deliberation entails recognition of inequality, either of information or of the ability to process it.[14]

What are likely to be the effects of deliberation during a referendum campaign? To begin with, let us bear in mind that most referenda are initiated either by the state authorities (especially the case in Europe) or by big business interests and pressure groups (especially the case in the USA). Referenda rarely emanate 'from below', from the grassroots — even in those American states where 'popular initiative' is enshrined in the constitution. A referendum is normally held because the most influential or powerful groups in society are deeply divided on a salient issue, making it unwise to resolve those differences through the usual political channels.

---

12 For a discussion of Gramsci's concept of 'contradictory consciousness', see J.V. Femia, *Gramsci's Political Thought* (Oxford: the Clarendon Press, 1987), pp. 42–5.
13 Zaller, *The Nature and Origins of Mass Opinion*, pp. 310–12.
14 A. Przeworski, 'Deliberation and Ideological Domination', in Elster (ed.), *Deliberative Democracy*, p. 145.

Despite their populist rhetoric, referendum campaigns are really battles between competing elites, who will try to convince the public that their (the public's) values will be best embodied by a particular policy position. This is basically an empirical question. The intention will not be to change people's 'political predispositions', but to change their 'technical' beliefs about the causal relations between policies and outcomes. The minority who are politically aware will respond to 'cues' from the elite about the ideological or partisan implications of a particular argument, and align themselves with the position most suited to their general political perspective. It is widely assumed that political awareness generates resistance to elite influence rather than susceptibility to it. According to Zaller, the available evidence indicates that this is at best a half truth. Citizens who are attentive to politics respond to new information on the basis of 'external cues concerning the implications of that information for their values and other predispositions'.[15] An American liberal, for example, will discount information from a conservative source, and *vice-versa*. Those who lack political awareness will not necessarily understand the cues, and will tend uncritically to accept whatever ideas they encounter. To put it simply, the politically aware are unlikely to change their initial preferences during the process of deliberation; the poorly informed, by contrast, will be susceptible to whatever messages or arguments are most insistent or supported by the most powerful forces.[16] In general, the more abstract the link between a predisposition and a related policy issue, the greater the amount or obscurity of knowledge necessary to perceive the linkage, the more complicated the chain of reasoning involved, the more likely it is that the politically apathetic majority will endorse causal beliefs that are either wrong or dubious, and that may even be harmful to their perceived interests.[17] The public deliberation that precedes referenda will transform preferences, but not necessarily through force of reason. Moreover, the widespread belief that referenda will diminish the power of elites is almost certainly inaccurate. To say that referenda give the people 'what they want' may be technically true (indeed, a tautology), but it ignores the logic of will-formation in mass publics.

---

15   Zaller, *The Nature and Origins of Mass Opinion*, p. 47.
16   The reference to 'powerful forces' does not mean that I subscribe to the Marxist view of an asymmetric power relationship based exclusively on class, or that I am positing a hierarchy of elite manipulation and passive reception in which the public is subject to a spectacle of symbolic production controlled by a privileged minority in its own interests. In a pluralistic society, power does not flow from property alone. Nor should it be assumed that the 'powerful forces' on any given issue will necessarily align themselves with 'reaction' rather than 'progress'.
17   Zaller, *The Nature and Origins of Mass Opinion*, p. 48.

Deliberative Assemblies and the Dynamics of Interaction

On the face of it, gathering ordinary citizens together in deliberative assemblies, such as the New England Town Meeting, and asking them to reach authoritative decisions might seem to be the most appropriate way of ascertaining the 'felt wishes' of the people. Participatory democracy is of course the 'holy grail' of the radical democrat. What is often overlooked, however, is how the dynamics of social interaction can lead people to change (or refuse to change) their opinions for reasons that have nothing to do with Habermas's 'ideal speech situation' of 'pure intersubjectivity', where communication is undistorted, as all participants are free and equal, and unconstrained by self-delusion or the manipulation of others.[18]

A common phenomenon in all social interaction is that of *conformity*. The desire to be like other people is a mental mechanism ingrained in us from earliest childhood, as we are taught that conformity brings safety and security. As far back as the 1830s, Alexis de Tocqueville revealed that mass democracy was especially vulnerable to the debilitating effects of this phenomenon, since — almost by definition — it worshipped the lowest common denominator.[19] However, he thought that the devolution of power to small deliberative bodies could solve the problem of conformity by encouraging 'active' citizenship and independent thought. Empirical evidence would seem to support the opposite conclusion. People in collective settings appear only too ready to conform to the majority in the group and to abandon their own personal beliefs and opinions. Study after study has shown this to be a 'near-universal phenomenon', probably related to the human need for self-evaluation.[20] Festinger's seminal theory concentrates on the social construction of reality. We all have beliefs about the world that guide our actions and help us to make sense of events. Since we have no objective means or agreed procedures for verifying our theories, we turn to other people for information about the truth or falsity of our beliefs. Festinger concluded that the validation function served by social comparisons would ensure that people will generally value uniformity in groups and will often behave so as to enforce it. This explains hostility towards deviants.[21] According to Deutsch and Gerard,

---

18 J. Habermas, 'Towards a Theory of Communicative Competence', *Inquiry*, 13 (1970), pp. 360–75, 371–72.
19 A. de Tocqueville, *Democracy in America*, trans. G. Lawrence, ed. J.P. Mayer (New York: Harper and Row, 1969).
20 R. Brown, *Group Processes: Dynamics Within and Between Groups* (Oxford: Blackwell, 1988), p. 91.
21 L. Festinger, 'Informal Social Communication', *Psychological Review*, 57 (1950), pp. 271–82; and L. Festinger, 'A Theory of Social Comparison Processes', *Human Relations*, 7 (1954), pp. 117–40.

however, people may conform not because they are relying on their confederates' judgements to define reality for them but rather to avoid the possibility of social ridicule, of being the 'odd one out'.[22] Yet another perspective is provided by Baumeister and Leary, who have gathered together empirical research which suggests that the 'need to belong' is a 'powerful, fundamental and extremely pervasive motivation', governing to a remarkable degree our emotional and even physical well-being.[23] Whatever the precise explanation, there is no doubt that we have a general propensity to change our attitudes and behaviour so as to bring them into line with others around us. Encouraging direct political interaction will surely exacerbate this tendency.

Another (related) phenomenon that should trouble radical democrats in what Janis has called 'group-think', or mutually reinforcing bias.[24] This is a danger that especially threatens deliberative bodies whose members share similar value-systems. Such similarity of outlook may cause decisions to be made rather quickly. Once the unit reaches a consensus on what to do, or which policy to support, it will — on this theory, which is supported by plenty of empirical evidence — insulate itself from inconvenient information and rarely search systematically through alternative policy options to assess their relative merits. A symptom of group-think is the illusion of unanimity and correctness. Doubters within the group are shamed into silence, and proponents of alternative opinions may be demonised as embodiments of whatever 'evil' is most despised in group rhetoric. Once the members converge on a normatively 'correct' point of view, their attachment to it will become dogmatic. The price of unanimity or harmony — the aim, after all, of deliberative democracy — may thus be bad decisions and half-baked policies. Those who were initially ambivalent join in the 'unanimous' consensus not because they have been convinced by rational argument but because of their unwillingness to challenge a policy that is 'obviously' correct. The imperatives of social interaction — immersion in the group experience and the spontaneous merging of separate frames of reference — rather than calm deliberation of alternatives cause the convergence of views. Group-think may plausibly be interpreted as just one example of the wider phenomenon of conformity. In a sense, however, it is distinctive, as it originates not so much in the desire to conform as in a kind of intellectual laziness, in the natural human tendency to 'jump to conclusions' and to ignore evidence or coun-

---

22 M. Deutsch and H.B. Gerard, 'A Study of Normative and Informational Social Influence Upon Individual Judgement', *Journal of Abnormal and Social Psychology*, 51 (1955), pp. 629–36.

23 R.F. Baumeister and M.R. Leary, 'The Need to Belong: Desire for Interpersonal Attachment as a Fundamental Human Motivation', *Psychological Bulletin*, 117 (1995), pp. 497–529.

24 I.L. Janis, *Victims of Groupthink* (Boston: Houghton Mifflin, 1972).

ter-arguments that threaten one's preconceptions or emanate from 'unpalatable' sources.

Finally, there is the 'group-deficit' phenomenon. Empirical evidence suggests that groups are seldom able to use their resources to the full; processes within the group will impede maximum attainment. One problem is that of coordination. In a deliberative assembly, for example, the interventions of the various speakers will often be disjoined from one another, making it hard to discern distinct patterns of argument. Exchange of opinions does not necessarily breed clarity. There is also the problem of social dynamics: discussion groups can get 'stuck' on unproductive chains of thought, and discoursers may feel inhibited from expressing unorthodox ideas out of shyness or embarrassment. Furthermore, studies indicate that individuals in group situations experience a decline in motivation and concentration. In deliberative forums, this slackening of effort, or 'social loafing', takes the form of day-dreaming, staring out the window, etc.[25] Eloquent or charismatic or highly motivated speakers can, in such circumstances, dominate the proceedings, no matter how silly or self-serving their arguments may be.

An obvious rejoinder to my arguments is that they are too pessimistic. At the very least, participation in collective decision-making can provide participants with new information, and surely knowledge is better than ignorance. A lack of relevant information, according to this viewpoint, can inhibit self-reflection, and ill-informed preferences are not completely 'authentic'. In particular, the give-and-take of debate enables individual participants to eliminate any inconsistencies between their policy-judgments, on the one hand, and their underlying values and beliefs, on the other — such consistency being another criterion of 'authentic' or 'autonomous' preferences. While these points cannot be dismissed, the suspicion lingers that deliberative democracy rests on an unrealistic assessment of the cognitive and psychological resources of the mass public. Pessimism may be the enemy of reform, but history teaches us that excessive optimism carries its own dangers. The deliberative model explicitly assumes that individuals have the basic capacity (and willingness) to argue with reasons, to recognise criteria of justification, to understand rules of evidence, to grasp rules of inference and deduction, and to reflect on their own presuppositions. Only these qualities could deliver 'the transformation of preferences through rational deliberation' — the defining characteristic of deliberative democracy.[26] Given our general knowledge of human motivation and behaviour, this model of discourse seems utopian.

---

25   See Brown, *Group Processes*, pp. 124–36, for a useful summary of the empirical evidence.
26   Elster, Introduction to *Deliberative Democracy*, p. 6.

Scoccia points out that some (perhaps most) people are simply bad at deliberating and consequently make more autonomous choices by acting on impulse, as doing so reflects their 'true selves' more accurately.[27] Deliberative democrats are typically what Oakeshott described as 'rationalists', for whom preferences grounded in custom or habit or instinct are somehow illegitimate. Cass Sunstein, a harsh critic of 'aggregative democracy', summarises this perspective well when he claims that individual attitudes should 'be regarded as nonautonomous insofar as they are reflexively adaptive to unjust background conditions', such as 'existing consumption patterns, social pressures, and governmental rules'.[28] Underlying this statement is a conception of the person as a free-floating chooser, detached from his or her social context, and driven by pure rationality. Perhaps in an ideal world, preferences would indeed be formed through rational deliberation—but the world we live in is not ideal. People's untutored preferences may be more 'authentic', more reflective of their core identity, than the preferences that might arise through a process of deliberation subject to strong conformity pressures, and dominated by those who are articulate and assertive. Deliberation as an ideal is defined by reasoned argumentation under fair procedures; deliberation as a practical activity is susceptible to distortions arising from subtle kinds of 'exogenous asymmetry'.[29]

So far from confronting these asymmetries, many (not all) deliberative democrats seem determined—paradoxically—to create more of them. Inputs into the deliberative process, it is said, must be 'reasonable', or congruent with standards of fairness that require participants to be free and equal. An inference commonly drawn from this proposition is that inputs deemed racist, sexist, or homophobic must be ruled out *a priori*.[30] If the 'will of the people' does not conform to a progressive liberal agenda, it may legitimately be ignored. Having started out as opponents of elitism, some deliberative democrats smuggle it in *via* the back door by introducing *ex ante* constraints on what the masses may or may not say in their 'free and equal' deliberations. It should be apparent that attempts to censor public discourse on the grounds of a specific sense of what is good or valuable stand in contradiction to the central project of collective self-determination. Perhaps we should see this desire to control the pre-

---

27 D. Scoccia, 'Paternalism and Respect for Autonomy', *Ethics*, 100 (1990), pp. 318–34.
28 C. Sunstein, 'Preferences and Politics', *Philosophy and Public Affairs*, 20 (1991), pp. 21, 11.
29 J. Knight and J. Johnson, 'Aggregation and Deliberation: On the Possibility of Democratic Legitimacy', *Political Theory*, 22 (1994), p. 278.
30 See, for example, D. Miller, 'Is Deliberative Democracy Unfair to Disadvantaged Groups?', in D. Miller, *Citizenship and National Identity* (Cambridge: Polity Press, 2000), pp. 142–60; and R. Blaug, *Democracy: Real and Ideal* (New York: SUNY Press, 1999), pp. 148-9.

sentation and characterisation of issues in the deliberative process as tacit recognition that a degree of elite *diktat* is necessary in all forms of democracy.

Conclusion

Notwithstanding surface appearances, the mechanisms of direct democracy do not prevent elite opinions from seeping into the consciousness of ordinary citizens. Nor can these mechanisms obviate the need for leadership, or turn emotional creatures with limited reasoning abilities into rational calculating machines. Deliberative and radical forms of democracy will indeed have the effect of transforming preferences, but usually for the wrong reasons. When all is said and done, the most effective method for responding to the 'felt wishes of the citizenry' may — for all its flaws — be representative democracy. We have seen that public feelings are typically unfocused and contradictory. As Joseph Schumpeter pointed out in 1942, without the help of survey evidence, the public has 'wishes and daydreams and grumbles', its 'likes and dislikes'. But this does not amount to 'effective volition'.[31] In order to arrive at coherent policy positions, our elected representatives must crystallise issues on our behalf, since the public has no fixed attitudes toward what it wants done, just a range of only partially consistent considerations. Politicians are seldom the passive instruments of majority opinion. They are 'initiators and persuaders'.[32] They play upon the contradictory ideas that are always present in people's minds, elevating the salience of some, while downgrading or ignoring others. To convince us, they will manipulate cherished symbols and sometimes indulge in phoney rhetoric. Those critics who denigrate this type of leadership as 'elitist' make the mistake of comparing it with an idealised image of the alternatives. This is sometimes referred to as the 'Nirvana fallacy' — finding existing reality unsatisfactory because it fails to measure up to some image of perfection. As a matter of fact, leadership permeates direct forms of democracy, though this leadership is usually covert and self-appointed. Since it exists outside formal channels, it is responsible to no one. At least the leadership exercised through representative forms of government is open and accountable. Of course, powerful groups can manipulate our representatives by the use of threats or incentives, and we must keep a watchful eye on the role of these special interests. But politicians need to win elections. In devising poli-

---

31 J.A. Schumpeter, *Capitalism, Socialism and Democracy*, 3rd edition (New York: Harper and Row, 1950), p. 261.
32 A. Körösényi, 'Political Leadership: Classical vs. Leader Democracy', p.....? in present volume.

cies, our rulers will want to pander to our 'political predispositions' — to the relatively constant values, prejudices, and basic interests of the majority. In the final analysis, the self-interest of our elected representatives is to please us. An unlikely alliance of radical democrats (like Saward) and anti-democrats (like Michels and Pareto) somehow contrives to overlook this rather obvious consequence of the electoral process.

András Körösényi

Political Leadership
Classical vs. Leader Democracy[1]

> Truly it is no small thing to have to rule others, since in ruling ourselves so many difficulties occur. As for commanding, which seems to be so sweet: considering the imbecility of human judgement and the difficulty of choice in new and doubtful things, I am strongly of this opinion, that it is much easier and pleasanter to follow than to guide, and that it is a great rest for the mind to have only to hold to a mapped-out path and to be answerable only for oneself.[2]

Leadership has a rather ambiguous status in democratic theory. One of the two traditions in democratic theory neglects almost completely the role of leadership in democratic government. In the classical view of democracy (as Schumpeter called it) democracy means the self-rule of the people. Consequently leadership is usually either ignored, or seen as a notion with some suspicious connotation. The idea that there is something inherently undemocratic about the mere fact of leadership has been widely shared both by believers and critics of democracy.[3] There is a good reason for that. Democracy defined as self-government of the people seems to exclude the role of leadership and of government by leaders. The greater the significance of leadership, the more democracy, as a system of rule of the people, is violated. Leadership contradicts both the self-rule of the people and the assumption of equality of citizens. Since assembly democracy, where this view has its origin, is not a feasible option of modern government, representation is to be used as a means to achieve self-government of the people. Danilo Zolo calls this adaptation theory, since it justifies political representation in terms of an adjustment or

---

1   The Hungarian Scientific Research Fund (OTKA) supported my research (T 049132).
2   Montaigne, *The Complete Essays of Montaigne*, trans. Donald M. Frame (Stanford, CA: Stanford University Press, 1965), p. 193.
3   John Plamenatz, *Democracy and Illusion* (London: Longman, 1973), p. 56. See also Jean Blondel, *Political Leadership* (London: Sage, 1987), pp. 44–7.

updating of the Athenian model. Zolo states, 'according to the "adaptation theory", the institutions of political representation *indirectly* fulfil the same functions, which were previously exercised by direct democracy in the context of the *polis*'.[4] The adaptation theory of representation aims to ensure the necessary adjustment of democracy as self-rule to the circumstances of large-scale societies. In the modern version of classical democracy it is the people, the electorate, who decide the political issues and who then choose representatives to ensure that their decisions are carried out. The people choose them in order that they should produce results according to their wills. The adaptation theory is a manifestation of what Joseph Schumpeter referred to five decades earlier as the classical theory of democracy. He defined this approach in the following terms: 'the democratic method is that institutional arrangement for arriving at political decisions which realizes the common good by making the people itself decide issues through the election of individuals who are to assemble in order to carry out its will'.[5]

John Plamenatz, as well as Carole Pateman and David Held criticize Schumpeter for his invention of the concept of the *classical theory of democracy*, arguing that no classical author of political theory supported this doctrine.[6] But Plamenatz admits that there is a loose image or idea of democracy, shared both by believers of it and of those who attack it. Plamenatz states, '[t]hese believers think of it as a system in which the people decide what they want done about the larger issues that face the community and choose deputies to put their decisions into effect. Where there is a democracy, according to this idea of it, there is a will of the people, and the business of the government is to carry it out'.[7] Plamenatz suggests, that this idea is much better called *popular* than *classical*. It is to be found much more in political rhetoric such as in the speeches of radical politicians than in systematic political theory and serious academic works or in the works of the 'classics'.

In my view, however, these ideals are implicit not only in popular discussion about democracy, as Plamenatz maintains, but in democratic theory and mainstream political science as well.[8] The classical doctrine is not just a 'straw man'. Many political scientists and democratic theorists accept the elements of this popular idea, often as a *shadow theory*, as Robert

---

4 Danilo Zolo, *Complexity and Democracy* (Cambridge: Polity Press, 1992), p. 76.
5 Joseph A. Schumpeter, *Capitalism, Socialism and Democracy* (London: Unwin, 1987), p. 250.
6 Plamenatz, *Democracy and Illusion*, pp. 96–7; Carole Pateman, *Participation and Democratic Theory* (Cambridge: Cambridge University Press, 1970), p 17; David Held, *Models of Democracy* (Cambridge: Polity Press, 1987), pp. 178–9.
7 Plamenatz, *Democracy and Illusion*, p. 39.
8 Cf. Joseph Femia, *Against the Masses* (Oxford: Oxford University Press, 2001), pp. 2–3.

Dahl called the implicit, unreflected assumptions behind democratic theories.[9]

A contrasting view of the role of leadership in modern democracy was provided first by Max Weber and Joseph Schumpeter. Both of them put *leadership* at the centre of the political process and into the centre of their democratic theory. They were sceptical of the view of democracy as rule by the people. Neither of them regarded democracy in this form as feasible or even a desirable form of government. They were also sceptical of the view that public policy might be based on issue-preferences of rational and autonomous citizens and of the view that leaders or governments could be held accountable for their policy on specific issues. They saw the role of the citizen as limited to participation in the selection of rulers or leaders.

Using the terminology of Max Weber, I will call this model of the relation between leaders and citizens, which contradicts the classical doctrine, *leader democracy*.[10] Below I will try to reveal some further elements of the model of leader democracy and compare them to the classical doctrine. My essay will have four parts. In the first part I will try to show that the model of leader democracy, since it acknowledges the role of leadership, gives a more adequate account of the political process and the working of the democratic political institutions (elections, representation) than the classical view. In the second part I would like to explore how the contrasting views of the political process given by the two theories can be attributed to their different underlying set of assumptions. While the classical view is based on more optimistic assumptions, the theory of leader democracy is more realistic and sceptical. The classical doctrine is built on assumptions that are empirically unrealistic and logically questionable. Furthermore, the empirical reality and normative preferences are sometimes mixed up.[11] In the third part I will compare leadership both to guardianship and to self-government. My thesis is that leadership means a more serious challenge for classical democracy theory than guardianship. Finally I would like to refer shortly to the normative implications of the two models of democracy. My proposition is that although leader democracy is an analytical and realist model, it has important normative qualities. Some of the alleged normative qualities of the classical view, in contrast, are dubious.

---

9   Robert Dahl, *Democracy and its Critics* (New Haven and London: Yale University Press, 1989), p. 36.
10 András Körösényi, 'Political Representation in Leader Democracy', *Government and Opposition*, Vol. 40, no 3 (Summer 2005), pp. 358–78.
11 The notion of 'enlightened understanding' in Dahl's *Democracy and its Critics* is an example for that (p. 111).

1. The Contrasting Interpretations of Democratic Political Process and Institutions

Bottom-up vs. Top-down Depiction of the Political Process

The two approaches of democracy provide contrasting pictures of the political process. In the classical doctrine, the starting point is the will of the people, which is usually interpreted as an explicit view of the people on major issues of public policy. This will is expressed through the issue-votes of citizens in elections, and the government must be responsive. The *'responsive rule'* must prevail, as John May calls it, even if citizens formally give their votes to candidates and, unlike in referendums, do not vote on individual issues.[12] That is, democratic procedures must ensure a way — either through the mechanism grasped by the mandate-theory (see below), or through delegation or through proportional representation — whereby the government will implement public policy decisions according to the expressed preferences of the people. The common good can be achieved through responsive public policy based on the will of the people.

According to this theory of democracy, decision-making is a 'bottom-up' process, in which no room is left for leaders. Office-holders, elected representatives are *delegates*, i.e. 'executives' of the popular will, and not representatives in the traditional sense.[13] Using the market metaphor of politics, it is a demand- or citizens-driven political-market. The classical view depicts the political process for example in the aggregative model of democracy, which ensures the continuing responsiveness of the government to the preferences of the citizens.[14] Democracy is equated with self-government of the people, which can be achieved through representation as an adaptation of assembly democracy to large-scale society. Representation is considered as a necessary means to the end in this view of democracy.[15]

Unlike in the 'bottom-up' description of the political process presented by the classical view of democracy or the adaptation theory of representation, political process in a leader democracy is generated by political leaders. The popular will is an 'empty space', policy-programs are presented

---

12   John. D. May, 'Defining Democracy: A Bid for Coherence and Consensus', *Political Studies*, Vol. 26, no 1 (1978), pp. 1–14.
13   Hanna Pitkin, *The Concept of Representation* (Berkeley, LA/London: University of California Press, 1967), p. 146.
14   Robert Dahl, *Polyarchy. Participation and Opposition* (New Haven and London: Yale University Press, 1971), pp. 1–2 and his *Democracy and its Critics*, pp. 109–13.
15   Dahl, *Democracy and its Critics*, pp. 13–33.

by leaders and not by citizens or by the people.[16] In democratic elections, citizens vote for candidates, i.e. for persons rather than for issues. Leaders, who emerge from the ranks of ordinary citizens, compete for power. In this struggle they mobilize followers with various means they have at their disposal, e.g. with their image, charisma, ideological appeal or issue-position. Leaders in governmental positions, as long as they can mobilize support, provide public policy rather autonomous from the citizens. Leader democracy is a representative system, where leaders rule, while citizens may participate at most in the selection of rulers. Although leaders may be responsive to certain wishes of the citizens, leader democracy does not provide a responsive government *per se*. It may produce at most a *responsible government* in an optimistic account,[17] or just a *minimalist conception* of democracy in a more sceptical account.[18] Citizens have some role in the competitive leadership selection and democracy is perceived as consent to be lead.

Mandate vs. Accountability Theory of Representation

We have seen above that the two theories have very different views about the role of elections in democratic political process. The difference can be well illustrated by the contrast between the mandate and the accountability theory of representation.[19]

The mandate theory shares the wider assumption that the crucial criterion of democratic and representative government is the responsiveness of public policy to the preferences of the citizens.[20] Specifically, the mandate theory states a government is deemed representative if it is responsive to the citizens will expressed in elections through the given mandate. The mandate of the politicians and/or parties who form the government is to carry out that specific policy promised in their electoral manifesto.

---

16 Frank Cunningham, *Theories of Democracy. A Critical Introduction* (London: Routledge, 2002), pp. 64–5 and 186.
17 Plamenatz, *Democracy and Illusion*, pp. 109–14 and 184–5.
18 Norberto Bobbio, *The Future of Democracy: A Defence of the Rules of the Game* (Cambridge: Polity Press, 1987), pp. 24–25 and Adam Przeworski, 'Minimalist conception of democracy: a defence', in Ian Shapiro and Casiano Hacker-Cordón (eds.), *Democracy's Value* (Cambridge: Cambridge University Press, 1999), pp. 23–55.
19 Bernard Manin, Adam Przeworski and Susan Stokes, 'Elections and Representation', in Adam Przeworski, Susan Stokes and Bernard Manin (eds.), *Democracy, Accountability and Representation* (Cambridge: Cambridge University Press, 1999), pp. 29–54.
20 This wider assumption is broadly shared in empirical political science, see e.g. Benjamin I. Page and Robert Y. Shapiro, 'Effects of public opinion on policy', *The American Political Science Review*, Vol. 77, no 1 (March 1983), pp. 175–90; Lawrence R. Jacobs and Robert Y. Shapiro, 'Studying Substantive Democracy', *Political Science and Politics*, Vol. 27, no 1 (March 1994), pp. 9–17; Sarah Binzelt Hobolt and Robert Klemmemsen, 'Responsive Government? Public Opinion and Government Policy Preferences in Britain and Denmark', *Political Studies*, Vol. 53 (2005), pp. 379–402.

The function of elections in this view is the selection of policies to be accomplished by the future government and the selection of the politicians who carry out *these* policies. If the public policy is in accordance with the electoral mandate of the government, then the will of the people is realized. The mandate view fits well into the wider frame of the classical doctrine, since elections are seen as a linkage between people's will and public policy.

In the accountability theory the role of elections is to provide an ex post evaluation of the government's record; not the expression of the will of the citizens on policy-issues to be carried out in the future, but making the rulers accountable for their policy record in the past and for the impact of the public policy. Accountability of government is ensured by consecutive elections, since in accordance with Friedrich's rule of anticipated reactions, elections motivate the incumbents seeking reelection to anticipate citizens' future reactions to their public policy.[21]

The two theories grew out from two distinct traditions of political thinking. While the intellectual source of the mandate theory is the classical view of democracy, the source of the accountability theory is the principle of representation. While the mandate theory assumes a more responsive public policy, which is sensitive to citizens' preferences, the accountability theory assumes a more autonomous role of the government.[22] The former is the theory of a responsive; the latter is that of a responsible government. Therefore the accountability view is, in a normative sense, closer to a more optimistic version of the theory of leader democracy, where citizens can hold leaders accountable. In a more sceptical account of elections, as in the above mentioned minimalist concept of democracy, the possibility of ousting the incumbents does not necessarily result in their accountability as Friedrich's rule assumed.

The classical doctrine in general and the mandate theory in particular assume that citizens are equally well-informed and competent in public policy matters. Only competent and autonomous citizens are able to set up a preference order for each policy issue. According to a more sceptical view shared by the accountability theory and the theory of leader democracy, these conditions are not met, and for epistemological and anthropological reasons cannot be met either.

I conclude that the institution of democratic elections provides poor means to achieve the normative aims of the classical doctrine, such as the self-rule of the people, or to realize the will of the people in specific public

---

21 Carl Joachim Friedrich, *Man and His Government: An Empirical Theory of Politics* (New York: McGraw-Hill Book, 1963), pp. 195–215.
22 Bernard Manin, *The principles of representative government* (Cambridge: Cambridge University Press, 1997), pp. 203–4. See also Pitkin, *The Concept of Representation*, pp. 55–9 and 144–56.

policy issues. Citizens, in a political sense, cannot be regarded as autonomous and competent actors; they fall far behind the political leaders in this respect. Leaders are those actors, who usually take the risk of and the political responsibility for initiating public policy decisions and for making public choice.

Taking a more optimistic reading of Weber and Schumpeter, citizens at most are able to give an ex post judgement on the record of government. This consequently enables them to hold their rulers accountable, as we have seen above. In the theory of leader democracy therefore the function of elections is first of all to select the rulers, i.e. the establishment of government that is consistent with empirical and institutional reality. An asymmetry between leaders and followers, between politicians and citizens is maintained, which follows from the more sceptical assumptions of leader democracy. Voters decide through consenting to be lead by particular persons rather than through autonomous initiative or choice.

Principles Behind Government: Identity vs. Representation

In this section I would like to highlight the contrast between the classical doctrine and the theory of leader democracy through the question of representation. The theory of leader democracy can be understood as a specific version of the traditional concept of representative government. The representatives are political leaders in public office, who are authorized to govern and who are responsible to the citizens; they themselves shape the political alternatives in contingent political situations. They do not act *instead of* the represented, but do act on their own. Representation has neither a 'standing for' nor an 'acting for' meaning; political representation is leadership.[23] Through democratic elections, accountability is attached to representation, as we have seen above in the case of accountability theory.

Unlike leader democracy, the classical doctrine is rooted in the concept of democracy, as self-rule by the people. In contrast to representation, it is the principle of *identity* of the rulers and the ruled (of the representatives and the represented) that provides its founding principle.[24] Representation gains a role only as a useful institutional technique, an inescapable means to institutionalize and accomplish the idea of self-government of the people in modern large-scale societies.[25] Representative bodies and institutions (e.g. an elected assembly) provide linkage between the will of the people and government policy, but they are not institutions with the autonomous political role of leadership. This 'channelling' role is

---

23 Körösényi, 'Political Representation in Leader Democracy', p. 377.
24 Carl Schmitt, *Verfassungslehre* (Berlin: Duncker & Humblot, 1928), pp. 150–2, p. 235.
25 This is the underlying thesis of Dahl's *Democracy and its Critics* (see e.g. pp. 215–16 and 225–31).

expressed by the mandate theory of democratic election and government. Government is required to carry out public policy according to the given mandate, in an analytical as well as in a normative sense. Representation, as an autonomous and substantive activity 'for' others, is out of the scope of this approach. [26] It has, instead, a descriptive meaning; i.e. the *re*-presentation or mirroring of the will of the people, which is expressed through the issue-votes of the citizens.

However, in my view, the reality is the opposite. Theoretically, the principle of equality could be preserved and institutionalized not by representation, but through lottery. It could also be substituted with institutions like the bounded mandate and the recall of the representatives, or with the regular application of referenda. Historically, the principle of equality has been applied through the extension of the franchise to a representative system, which already existed before. Representative democracy is therefore not an adjustment of democracy as a self-rule of the people to the circumstances of large-scale societies, as Dahl states,[27] but an egalitarian reform of the system of representative government.[28]

2. Contrasting Assumptions of Classical and Leader Democracy

The sharp contrast in the depiction of the democratic political process in the classical view and in leader democracy is due to the different and incompatible assumptions about the major actors of democracy. Therefore in the second part of my essay I would like to explore the differences between the underlying assumptions of the two theories of democracy, considering first the equality of citizens, secondly the political competence (of the common man), thirdly the nature of the political preferences and volition, fourthly the question of responsibility, and finally the nature of the common good. We will see that the classical doctrine and leader democracy have very different assumptions regarding these aspects, and these differences shape the inner logic and the normative implications of the theories in question.

Equality vs. Leadership. The Epistemological Argument for Equality

Democracy as a self-rule of the people assumes equality of citizens in various respects. The major weakness of the classical view both in a descriptive and a normative sense is that it assumes a *symmetric* relationship among citizens therefore it excludes the very notion of leadership. Lead-

---

26 See Pitkin, *The Concept of Representation* pp. 112–43.
27 Dahl, *Democracy and its Critics*, pp. 83, 97 and 106.
28 András Körösényi, *Vezér és demokrácia. Politikaelméleti tanulmányok* (Budapest: L'Harmattan, 2005), p. 163.

ership, as a leader-followers relation, which is a structural element of the political process, is necessarily a dynamic and asymmetric relationship.[29] Asymmetry unavoidably implies a kind of political inequality. It does not mean exclusion by birth, race, etc., but it means the acknowledgement of the reality that democratic political processes, for structural reasons, distribute political influence unequally among individuals. It may be feasible and desirable to aim at equality in a *formal* or legal sense, nevertheless an asymmetric relationship emerges inevitably between leaders and citizens. Therefore, in contrast to the classical doctrine, in a leader democracy the *political* equality presumption is given up in both descriptive and normative sense.

One of the justifications of the equality assumption is epistemological. Let me recall the argument provided by Robert Dahl as well as by Michael Saward. Their aim is to justify the equality assumption of democracy through the rejection of guardianship, or to put it more precisely, through the rejection of the thesis that guardianship could be justified by superior knowledge. A classical case for guardianship and against democracy is the notion of the superior knowledge of a minority. Guardians are 'qualified to govern by reason of their superior knowledge and virtue'.[30] But if the claim to superior knowledge in politics cannot be made clear the case for equality and democracy is justified, conclude both Dahl and Saward. But we will see, that even if guardianship cannot be justified, their conclusion concerning equality and democracy is premature.

Saward emphasizes that '(t)he need to adopt the equality assumption arises from the fact that there is no secure ground upon which it can be said that one person or group has better insight in this field than any other'.[31] He applies an epistemologically sceptical argument, *the principle of fallibilism*, to challenge the view of superior knowledge in politics. In Pierce's words, 'fallibilism is the doctrine, that our knowledge is never absolute but always swims, as it were, in a continuum of uncertainty and of indeterminacy'.[32] The fallibilist argument provides a refutation of superior knowledge, or of the absolute certainty of knowledge.

Saward draws a difference between 'contingent knowledge' (a specialized, technical, partial knowledge), which is relevant in a certain sphere of activity and 'non-contingent knowledge', which is 'general', not confined

---

29 See Blondel, *Political Leadership*, p 13; James MacGregor Burns, *Leadership* (New York: Harper and Row, 1978), p. 18; and Robert C. Tucker, *Politics as Leadership* (University of Missouri Press, 1995), p. 7.
30 Dahl, *Democracy and its Critics*, p. 52.
31 Michael Saward, 'Democratic Theory and Indices of Democratization', in David Beetham (ed.), *Defining and Measuring Democracy* (London: Sage, 1994), p. 13.
32 Cited by Saward, *Ibid.*, p. 9.

to any subsystem of the political community. He concludes, that while contingent knowledge claims can overcome the fallibilist objection (therefore an expert knowledge, in fact, can be superior in a specific sphere), non-contingent superior knowledge does not exist. Unlike the argument of Plato, which does not differentiate between specialized technical and general, political knowledge, Saward accepts Aristotle's argument and claims that political knowledge is qualitatively different. He argues, that '…politics is not a realm where contingent claims to specialized, superior knowledge are legitimate; rather, it is a realm in which only non-contingent claims are admissible in principle'.[33] Therefore the superior knowledge claim in the realm of politics cannot escape the fallibilist critique. Having agreed that there is no superior knowledge in politics, it follows that the equality assumption is legitimate, and 'individuals must be adjudged the best judges of their own interests'.[34]

Saward's reasoning is a renewal of the argument that Robert Dahl has applied in his *Democracy and Its Critics* earlier. Dahl also tried to justify the equality assumption of democracy in an indirect, negative way, rejecting the arguments for guardianship. However, the weakness of their argument is that a disproval of guardianship does not necessarily justify the equality assumption of democracy. There may be other (e.g. anthropological) sources of inequality than *epistemé* (i.e. absolute knowledge or knowledge with certainty).[35]

In my view, the equality assumption of democratic theory has to face a more serious challenge than guardianship, namely the challenge of leadership. Leadership does not require absolute knowledge while it is clearly based on some kind of superior faculty or ability. Leaders do have practical knowledge (*praxis*), a type of knowledge needed in politics, which distinguishes them from ordinary citizens of democracy.[36] The nature of this faculty will be depicted below.

Political Autonomy vs. Citizens' Incompetence

'Democracy—rule by the people—can be justified only on the assumption that ordinary people are, in general, *qualified* to govern themselves', Dahl defines another crucial assumption of democracy as self-rule of the people.[37] What does this mean? It requires the rational and moral capacity, the political autonomy (independence) and the competence of the citi-

---

33 *Ibid.*, p. 12.
34 *Ibid.*, p. 13.
35 These anthropological sources of equality are not related to the socio-economic structure, but they have their roots in the human nature.
36 Körösényi, 'Political Representation in Leader Democracy', p. 372.
37 Dahl, *Democracy and its Critics*, p. 97.

zens. It follows from the thesis of Dahl, that, if ordinary people are, in general, not *qualified* to govern themselves, then democracy, as a self-rule of the people cannot be justified. We will see below, that we may have to settle for a more sceptical assumption on the political competence of ordinary citizens and therefore we cannot justify democracy as rule by the people, but merely in a weaker or minimalist sense.[38]

The equal moral capacity of human beings is a traditional moral assumption, upon which liberal democracy is based. Arguing from Aristotle's thesis, Dahl claims, that an 'adequate level of moral competence is widely distributed'.[39] Therefore every citizen is ultimately the best judge of his or her own interest. The question is, what follows from this principle for the field of politics. Can we conclude from this, that political competence is also widely distributed? Can we arrive to the conclusion that individuals possess political autonomy? In my view, this is not the case. From the general anthropological assumption of the autonomy and rationality of man does not *necessarily* follow his or her *political* autonomy and competence.

Usually the *political* autonomy of individuals is taken for granted without any serious argument. Schumpeter challenged this conventional view with his famous *infantilism argument*, which aimed at demonstrating the degradation of political competence of average citizens. He differentiates between spheres of human action: the narrower, little field and the wider political field.[40] The first one is the field of the everyday life, where the individual citizen's household, profession, family, neighbourhood and hobby lie. It is the area, which the individual knows well, where things are under his or her personal control. This little field consists of '…the things which are familiar to him independently of what the newspaper tells him, which he can directly influence or manage and for which he develops the kind of responsibility that is induced by a direct relation to the favourable or unfavourable effects of a course of action'.[41]

As opposed to this, in the political field an ordinary citizen does not have direct, personal experience, does not know its rules and conventions well; he gains all his knowledge indirectly, through transmitters, and is not able to consider the long-term consequences of political actions. His reduced sense of reality 'accounts for a reduced sense of responsibility but also for the absence of effective volition', for ignorance and lack of

---

38   Przeworski, 'Minimalist conception of democracy: a defence', pp. 43–50.
39   Dahl, *Democracy and its Critics*, p. 59.
40   Schumpeter, *Capitalism, Socialism and Democracy*, pp. 258–61.
41   *Ibid.*, p. 259.

judgement in matters of domestic and foreign policy.[42] While in this smaller field, the ordinary citizen is capable of more or less rational and purposeful actions, in the political field this is much less the case. That is the reason, why an ordinary man does not have an effective volition in politics and therefore becomes sensitive to persuasion and external influences.[43]

For our purposes it is even more important what is implicit in Schumpeter's argument. While entering the field of politics the ordinary citizen behaves like a child, a professional politician is at home in this field. What is the wider, political field for ordinary people is the narrower, little field for a political leader. Politics is the sphere of his or her everyday activity, where he or she is familiar with the rules, conventions and other realities of life. Therefore there is a wide gap between the competence of political leaders and ordinary citizens in this field. Although ordinary citizens can be autonomous and rational actors in their own narrower field, they become politically heteronomous and non-rational in the political field.

Schumpeter's infantilism argument challenges the epistemological justification of equality provided by Dahl and Saward. It follows from Schumpeter's argument, that political leaders may have a 'contingent', specialized knowledge claim in their own narrower field, i.e. in the political field. Thus they have a superior ('non-contingent') knowledge claim vis-à-vis ordinary citizens, using Saward's term. Saward, however, made a difference between political and other types of knowledge, claiming, that the absolute or superior knowledge claim was irrelevant in the field of politics.

Even if we share the view that absolute knowledge is irrelevant in the field of politics, therefore guardianship cannot be justified, Schumpeter's infantilism argument reveals that there is a kind of 'superior' knowledge, or competence, which is available only for professional politicians and not for ordinary men. Besides democracy as a self-rule of the people and guardianship there is a third type of rule. This is leader democracy, which acknowledges and institutionalizes the role of leadership. Although political leaders do not have absolute knowledge (episteme), they do have practical knowledge (praxis), which includes certain traits of 'contingent' knowledge as well. Modern politics, including democratic politics, is a sphere that possesses its own 'laws' or traits.

---

42   *Ibid.*, p. 261.
43   Therefore, concludes Schumpeter, '…the typical citizen drops down to a lower level of mental performance as soon as he enters the political field. He argues and analyzes in a way which he would readily recognize as infantile within the sphere of his real interests' (*Ibid..*, p. 262).

Volition of Leaders vs. Preferences of Citizens

The adaptation theory of the classical view assumes the existence of the people's will, which can be defined and expressed, through some method of aggregation, from the preferences of rational and autonomous individual citizens. The theory of leader democracy is sceptical to this view in two respects. Firstly, it challenges whether any definite collective choice could be aggregated from individual preferences at all. It shares the scepticism of classical elitism in this respect.[44] Instead of people's will, the volition of political leaders prevails in the political process. The populistic democracy or the classical doctrine often explores the democratic and the governmental decision-making process as if it were a social choice problem. According to this approach, people's will is to be derived from citizens' issue-preferences in a way, in which the preference of each citizen is assigned an equal value.[45]

The well-known results of Kenneth Arrow and other authors of the social choice literature, however, challenge the view that an unambiguous social or collective choice could be aggregated from ex ante given individual preferences at all (e.g. Arrow-paradox, voting-cycles, path-dependency).[46] It is revealed that individual rationality may produce irrational social choice.[47] And William Riker shows that certain individuals in strategic positions, manipulating the agenda-setting process or through '*heresthetics*', can mould the social choice according to their own interests.[48]

While the will of the people cannot be unambiguously defined within the rational choice paradigm, the role of leadership can be very much grasped. Political leaders can be defined as the individuals who, through

---

[44] Femia, *Against the Masses*, p. 90.
[45] Robert Dahl, *A Preface to Democratic Theory* (Chicago & London: The University of Chicago Press, 1956), pp. 34–62.
[46] Kenneth Arrow, *Social Choice and Individual Values* (New York: John Wiley and Sons, 1951), and see also William H. Riker, *Liberalism Against Populism* (San Francisco: W. H. Freeman and Company, 1982).
[47] *Ibid.*
[48] *Heresthetics* is a term coined by William Riker to denote the art and science of manipulation of the structure of tastes and alternatives within which decisions are made. It is an alternative means to rhetoric for political leaders to gain support before decisions are made. The concept is explored within the context of social choice theory, and involves the manipulation of the agenda and of the salience of dimensions of judgement. From the works of William H. Riker see especially 'Political Theory and the Art of Heresthetics', in Ada W. Finifter (ed.), *Political Science: The State of the Discipline* (Washington, D.C.: The American Political Science Association, 1983), pp. 47–67. Riker grounded the concept in his *Liberalism Against Populism*.

the manipulation of voters' preferences, are able to shape the collective choices.[49]

Secondly, leader democracy challenges whether individual preferences can be regarded as a starting point of the political process or as a basis of any sort of political will (see above the first part of this essay). According to this approach, instead of people's will, it is the volition of political leaders that prevails in the political process. Due to the equality assumption, it is assumed in the framework of the classical view that each citizen has preferences on policy-issues. Anthony Downs and Robert Dahl assume that citizens individually and therefore collectively do have political will and precisely that will evokes the reaction of politicians. But this assumption seems to be unrealistic. The faculties for various arts are not evenly distributed, and neither is the ambition to carry out these faculties. The model of leader democracy therefore assumes that political leaders are different from ordinary citizens in this respect. While citizens often do not have any definite preferences on policy-issues, leaders not only have such a clear vision of what they want, but they also have *stronger* political preferences than ordinary men. One of the motivational sources of becoming a politician may be to have strong, definite political views. Therefore they are the persons who instigate other people to follow them in certain political or policy endeavours. As Bertrand de Jouvenel writes, precisely this instigation sets into and keeps the political process in motion.[50]

Leaders are people of political action, but clearly formulated preferences themselves are not enough for action. Strength of preferences does matter, but will is also a necessary component of action. It is precisely the effective volition, what ordinary citizens do not have in the field of politics in Schumpeter's view. 'The reduced sense of reality account not only for a reduced sense of responsibility but also for the absence of *effective volition*. One has one's phrases of course, and one's wishes and daydreams and grumbles: especially, one has one's likes and dislikes. But ordinarily they do not amount to what we call a *will* — the psychic counterpart of purposeful responsible action'.[51]

Certain human characteristics, like determined will, risk taking, etc. are more conducive to political action than others (e.g. thoughtfulness). Among the various motivational sources of becoming a political leader will of power also must be taken into consideration, beside other elements like having a passionate commitment to a cause or having some vision of

---

49 Cf. Kenneth A. Shepsle and Mark S. Bonchek, *Analyzing Politics. Rationality, Behavior, and Institutions* (New York and London: W. W. Norton & Company, 1997)., pp.380-404.
50 Bertrand de Jouvenel, *The Pure Theory of Politics* (Indianapolis: Liberty Fund, 1963)., 91-125.
51 Schumpeter, *Capitalism, Socialism and Democracy*, p. 261.

the national interest, as emphasized by Max Weber.[52] The desire for greatness, honour and glory also can be added to this list.[53] These sources of the volition of political action are also unevenly distributed among the citizens of a polity. This ambition for and capacity of leadership characterizes only a small minority of the citizens. Political leaders are selected from those few, who take the risks, the responsibility, and who take part in the competition or struggle for power. Citizens themselves, in democratic polities, usually get some role in the last phase of this selection process only. The selection of leaders is in this way first of all means *self-selection* of leaders, where the voters' role is confined to the recognition of leaders in public office or the rejection of them.[54] According to the leader democracy approach, citizens' democratic role is limited to giving *consent* to the leaders in public office or cancelling it.

In summary, leaders are autonomous actors in politics, not just followers of citizens' wishes, or representatives of ex ante given individual preferences or group interests as the aggregative-model of classical democracy assumes. They do have their own will concerning what to do, have their own policy-position with which they try to mobilize followers, and precisely that is what makes them leaders. It is the political will of leaders that moves political actions therefore the whole political process.

Individual vs. Political Responsibility

Liberal political theory regards individuals as autonomous and hence responsible agents. *Individually*, everybody is responsible for his or her own choices and actions. The meaning of this is clear in ethics, in private life and in the world of private goods. A collective choice in a democracy, which is derived from the citizens' preferences or wishes through an aggregative procedure, however, does not establish public or *political* responsibility in any respect. The classical theory of democracy abolishes political responsibility, or more precisely, dissolves it into the self-government of the people. Due to the identity-principle of democracy[55], the people is identical with itself therefore cannot make itself accountable, since accountability presumes a principal-agent relationship.

A further trait of collective choice and action is, especially in large communities, that it eliminates the *sense* of responsibility of the individuals.

---

52 Max Weber, *Political Writings*, eds. Peter Lassman and Ronald Speirs (Cambridge: Cambridge University Press, 1994), p. 353.
53 Zoltán Balázs, 'Greatness as the Integrative Value of Politics', *Telos*, no 137 (Winter 2006), pp. 143–70.
54 As Mosca writes, 'the representative has himself elected by the voters' (cited by Femia, *Against the Masses*, p. 89).
55 Schmitt, *Verfassungslehre*, pp. 151–2.

The relation between citizens' vote and the impact of their choice is so ambiguous, uncertain and remote, that a voter's decision does not imply *the feeling* of responsibility in any meaningful sense. Additionally, a secret ballot does not make it visible who is in fact responsible for specific decisions. If democracy means complete responsiveness to citizens, the responsibility of political leaders for public policy vanishes. Leaders turn into delegates rather than into representatives. Responsiveness to the popular will abolishes both leadership and political responsibility. This way the classical doctrine of democracy excludes the problem of responsibility, as seen in Dahl's *Democracy and its Critics*, which completely neglects the question.[56]

In contrast to the above mentioned approach, in a representative government the representative is an agent, who is responsible (for his or her actions) to the principal. Accordingly, in a leader democracy the problem of responsibility is closely connected to the concept of representation and leadership. Similar to the liberal view of representative government, Weber and Schumpeter also emphasize the relative autonomy as well as the responsibility of leaders.[57] They regard political leaders and not citizens to be the subject of responsible political action. Unlike citizens, leaders do have the sense of responsibility, since they can give a more thorough judgement on the potential impact of policy propositions, as Weber emphasizes in his account of political ethos.[58] Their institutional accountability and Friedrich's law also endorse the development of the sense of responsibility. As for Schumpeter, he underlines in his infantilism argument that ordinary men, in contrast to leaders, have only a reduced sense of responsibility in national policy issues.

John Stuart Mill emphasizes in his *Considerations on Representative Government* that even the members of an assembly do not feel personal responsibility to the same degree as the members of the executive, like ministers, who have one man responsibility in their jurisdiction.[59] The problem is multiplied in the case of large-scale societies. The nature of collective, democratic decision-making fosters irresponsible collective choices (e.g. the increase of state expenditures based on public

---

56 See also Michael Saward, *The Terms of Democracy* (Cambridge: Polity Press, 1998).
57 John Stuart Mill, *Considerations on Representative Government* (Charleston: BiblioBazaar, 2007); A.H. Birch, *Representative and Responsible Government* (London: Unwin, 1964); Plamenatz, *Democracy and Illusion*. The difference lies in the question that to which extent can be leaders held accountable. While the liberals are more optimistic, Weber and Schumpeter are more sceptical in this respect.
58 Weber, *Political Writings*, p. 353.
59 Mill, *Considerations on Representative Government*, p. 74..

indebtment), as Bobbio notes referring to the problem of *ungovernability*.[60] It is only responsible leadership, which can challenge the policy of ever increasing demands for government expenditures from various interest groups.

My conclusion is that taking responsibility is an essential virtue, and this virtue is an attribute of political leaders rather than that of their followers.

Objective, Aggregative or Innovative Nature of the Common Good

The classical doctrine of democracy shares the view that for every proper polity a single common good exists, but it challenges through an epistemological argument guardianship, i.e. the notion that anybody or any group of persons could have an exclusive knowledge of it. Its conclusion arrives at the equal political competence of citizens, who are rational and autonomous agents. Therefore democracy as a self-government of the people is the only form of government which corresponds to the public good.

Modern political theory has produced different variations of the classical doctrine. Each describes differently the way, how collective decisions are formed from citizens' views or preferences. According to the utilitarian approach appropriate public policy is formed through the aggregation of citizens' preferences, according to participative democrats it is rooted in the participation of citizens in the political process and finally, according to deliberative democrats it is revealed through the process of rational argumentation in an 'ideal speech situation'.

Robert Dahl provides a synthesis of these currents of the classical view. According to him, common good is both substance and process. Dahl defines the common good in terms of the democratic process; but the depiction of the process is different from that of Schumpeter's pure procedural criteria. The procedural claim includes *normative* conditions in Dahl's account. He states that 'an essential element in the meaning of the common good among the members of a group is what the members would choose if they possessed the fullest attainable understanding of the experience that would result from their choice and its most relevant alternatives'.[61] To put it another way, the common good is composed of democratic procedures of collective choice and of outcomes arrived at through

---

60 Bobbio, *The Future of Democracy: A Defence of the Rules of the Game*, p. 39. See also Samuel Brittan, 'The Economic Contradictions of Democracy', *British Journal of Political Science*, Vol. 5, no 2 (April 1975), pp. 129–59 and Michael Crozier, Samuel P. Huntington and Joji Watanuki, *The Crises of Democracy* (New York: New York University Press, 1975).
61 Dahl, *Democracy and its Critics*, p. 308.

such procedures under conditions of *enlightened understanding*.[62] Dahl takes enlightened understanding as a normative criterion of the democratic political process, as a necessary element of the common good.[63] This criterion ensures, firstly, that citizens must be well informed, since it is a precondition of responsible decision-making; secondly, that the impact of collective decisions is taken into consideration; and thirdly, that the harmony between individual interests and the common good is kept. Enlightened understanding therefore provides that a person's good is more than self-regarding interest.[64] It involves the understanding of and the responsibility for others to provide a human centred ground for collective decisions.[65] 'Insofar as a citizens' good or interests requires attention to a public good or general interest, then citizens ought to have the opportunity to acquire an understanding of these matters'.[66]

The procedures for making decisions should furnish citizens with opportunities to understand means and ends. It shows that Dahl's approach shares the criteria and the optimism of the *developmental* concept of democracy, in which democratic institutions and citizens' participation are not just means of decision-making but do have normative functions. Firstly, the notion of 'enlightened understanding' seems to transcend the conflict between individual and common interest. Secondly, it also seems to transcend the condition of contingency, which characterizes every political situation. Thirdly, it seems to neglect the lesson from the epistemological argument. In their critique of guardianship, Dahl and Saward object to the possibility of absolute knowledge in politics and the justification of anybody's rule based on this knowledge. However, assuming that the public good or public interest exists in any political community, the argumentation of Dahl implicitly concludes that if citizens are well-informed and competent, the common good can be potentially known and accomplished. His reasoning suggests that the common good has an objective and knowable nature. This potential is provided in Dahl's theory through normative assumptions regarding citizens' capabilities and democratic procedures.

The 'enlightened understanding', as a normative criterion of the democratic political process, is a clear signal that Dahl adheres to the classical doctrine of democracy. It also shows that a simple aggregation of ex ante preferences or the equal consideration of them, according to Dahl, does

---

62 Joshua Cohen, 'Review: Institutional Argument ... Is Diminished by the Limited Examination of the Issues of Principle', *The Journal of Politics*, Vol. 53, no 1 (February 1991), p. 224.
63 Dahl, *Democracy and its Critics*, pp. 111–12.
64 Ibid., pp. 72–3.
65 Ibid., p. 229.
66 Ibid., p. 112.

not necessarily lead to the common good. It is 'enlightened understanding' itself which ensures that rule by the people in an aggregative democracy may achieve the common good. The substantive outcome depends on the degree of 'enlightenment' of citizens' preferences. It suggests, if an appropriate level of enlightenment is achieved, the common good is attainable.

The theory of leader democracy, however, challenges this proposition, claiming, first, that empirically it is not a realistic account of the capacity of ordinary man in the field of politics and secondly, that it also disregards the nature of the political process. 'Enlightened understanding', as a normative criterion of the democratic political process and that of the common good, has an implicit empirical assumption. It attributes to citizens a capacity that seems to be unrealistic, regarding the uncertainties and contingencies in the political process and the complexity of the modern world. It also neglects Schumpeter's infantilism argument and the paradox of individual and collective rationality. According to the more realistic theory of leader democracy, the common good (i) is rooted always in concrete situations; (ii) has a particularistic nature; (iii) it is always political, i.e. a result of decisions taken in contingent situations; (iv) it cannot overcome conflicts; and (v) an ex post consensus can be reached on at most regarding the common good. The common good has an intuitive and voluntarist nature and it might be discovered or defined by innovative leaders. I will explain the role of leaders in the discovery of the common good in the rest of this essay.

3. Guardianship, Self-Government, Leadership. The Consequences of the Assumptions

As we have seen above, Dahl and Saward try to justify the equality assumption through objecting to the possibility of the absolute or superior knowledge-claim shared by guardianship. An additional argument of Dahl is, in this respect, that guardianship requires a procedure for the selection of rulers that can select individuals with superior knowledge with high certainty in order to authorize them to govern the people.[67] Since we do not have such a procedure in the field of politics, guardianship is not simply a type of rule, which cannot be justified, but it is unfeasible at the same time. Although Dahl's argument objects to guardianship, it cannot justify, in my view, the assumption of equality and the political autonomy of individuals.

One of the traditional arguments for guardianship is the application of the parent-child relation to politics as an analogy. A child relies on paren-

---

[67] *Ibid.*, pp. 52–9.

tal care and protection, since she is not capable of independent, autonomous and responsible action and life-conduct. Her parents or guardians know better what is in her interest. The classical doctrine assumes that each adult citizen has equal capacity to conduct his or her life, each of them is responsible for his or her actions, therefore they are equals or they should be regarded as equals. The legal order and Western civilization itself relies on these presumptions. In my view, however, it does not follow from this, that this capacity of adult citizens including their sense of judgement would be equal. It assumes only that each has a sense of judgement, therefore individuals can be held responsible and/or accountable for their deeds.

Guardianship takes for granted that there are similar differences in moral and cognitive competence among the members of a political community, which resemble to the parent-child relationship. We often need advice in our private life, but even more in public matters; we accept and follow the guidance of others. It is in the public interest, if individuals with superior, 'parental' knowledge rule. However, since we are not able to say how to select the excellent guardianship, it cannot be better than arbitrary rule, at least that is how its critics argue.

My thesis is that both guardianship and the classical doctrine are mistaken. The former presupposes that politically relevant inequalities of competence and knowledge are absolute, while the latter does not acknowledge that inequalities exist at all. Conversely, the theory of leader democracy is based on assumptions, which are in an 'in between' position and which rely on a more realistic view of man.[68] It shares such politically relevant anthropological and epistemological assumptions, which acknowledge that besides the elements of equality, there are inequalities among men regarding politically relevant information, political competence, intensity of preferences, volition, willingness of taking political responsibility, will of power and desire for glory. In addition to this, these inequalities are not distributed equally among the members of the political community, but they are cumulated in a smaller or larger extent, and serve as sources of an asymmetrical relationship between leaders and citizens. The theory of leader democracy assumes that there is a mixture of equality and inequality in human relationships and that the relation between leaders and followers is neither hierarchical, nor symmetrical. Mutuality as well as asymmetry characterizes this relationship.

---

68 See Emilio Santoro, 'Democratic theory and individual autonomy. An interpretation of Schumpeter's doctrine of democracy', *European Journal of Political Research*, Vol. 23 (1993), pp. 121–43.

4. Summary and Conclusions: Analytical and Normative Implications

The classical doctrine, associating democracy with self-government of the people, cannot give an adequate account of the political process, since (i) it excludes leadership from the political process; (ii) it perceives elections as issue-votes; and (iii) it considers representation as a technical means of mirroring the popular will. It relies on assumptions like equality and autonomy of citizens, which proved to be empirically questionable. These assumptions also include overestimated competence of citizens, like Dahl's 'enlightened understanding' or the aggregative approach of the common good, which is not tenable in the world of incomplete information.

As we have seen above, Arrow's voting-paradoxes, Downs' thesis of rational ignorance, Schumpeter's infantilism-argument and Olson's free-rider argument all demonstrate that social choice and collective action cannot be based solely on citizens' preferences. The aggregative and deliberative theories of democracy are not only too idealistic, but untenable, if the unavoidably emerging world of incomplete information, or agenda and strategic manipulation are taken into consideration. Political situations belong necessarily to the world of incomplete information and do have a contingent nature. The output and impact of political processes therefore are highly uncertain; and the ever-growing complexity of the world increases the unpredictable nature of political actions.[69] We do not (and cannot) have absolute knowledge about the common good, which has neither an objective nor an aggregative nature. Therefore we cannot have absolute knowledge about the proper political action conforming to the public interest. Due to these factors, arbitrary elements and volition do have a role in every political action seeking to accomplish any concept of the common good. Political leaders play a crucial role in creating rival alternatives of the public good.

The more realistic assumptions of the theory of leader democracy make possible a more adequate account of the political process (elections, representation) and that of the role of leaders in democratic politics. The political process itself is generated by the rivalry of political leaders. Leaders are initiators and persuaders, who manipulate the political process. They strive to shape rather than follow public opinion and the 'will of the people'. In this way, issue-vote cannot be separated from their role, since instigation, agenda-setting and the manipulation of preferences are amongst the primary roles of leaders. Political leadership is an asymmet-

---

[69] Femia, *Against the Masses*, pp. 102–9, and see also Zolo, *Complexity and Democracy*, pp. 4–14 and 54–64.

ric, but mutual relationship. In democratic elections citizens vote first of all for candidates or parties; therefore democracy is feasible either as a selection of rulers or as a means of giving consent to the rule of the office-holders, or retrieving it if that is the case. Democracy works, instead of self-rule, as an egalitarian version of representative government. It does not satisfy the criteria of the *mandate-theory* of elections; but if asymmetry between leaders and citizens does not turn to be of extreme proportions, the criteria of accountability-theory might be met.

All of this has important normative consequences. While some of the allegedly normative values of the classical doctrine, which usually are taken for granted, have been challenged, leader democracy has unexpected normative potential. Firstly, the theory of leader democracy gives up the assumption of political equality, since it has been proven to be unrealistic in a descriptive sense, and challenges the desirability of this very political equality at the same time. Secondly, due to incomplete information and the differences in citizens' competence, the common good cannot be revealed through an aggregative procedure. Therefore it is not in the public interest if the preferences of ignorant and indifferent citizens (would) have the same weight in collective decisions as that of the committed, competent and responsible ones. Thirdly, the selection of political leaders relies partly on self-selection or self-appointment. The emergence of leaders from among the citizens (even in a democracy) is not necessarily an evil. The role of leaders is fundamental for any collective action. Leaders themselves create alternatives of the common good. Any vision about the common good and collective action includes components of intuition, will, vision and is accompanied by a certain sense of arbitrariness. Fourthly, leadership also has a role in reducing the complexities of politics (through agenda-setting and other means of manipulation), which makes politics more comprehensible for ordinary citizens. The penultimate point views leadership as an autonomous action and includes responsibility-taking. Responsibility-taking is an important, often neglected political virtue, which is a trait of leadership, but it does not characterize followers. The final point is that a political leader is a representative of the people. Representation in the theory of leader democracy, unlike in the classical doctrine of democracy, makes it possible to grasp institutionally the responsibility and accountability of governmental leaders.[70]

---

[70] The method of elections turns to be a method of selection, i.e. it has a meritocratic impact. See Manin, *The principles of representative government*, pp. 134–49, and Giovanni Sartori, *The Theory of Democracy Revisited*, Vol. 1–2 (Chatham, NJ: Chatham House Publishers, 1987), pp. 169–71.

Jules Townshend[1]

Getting from Here to There
Marxism and the Paradoxes of Leadership

Leadership' has different styles as exemplified in such phrases as 'taking a lead', implying leadership by consent, in contrast to 'leading by the nose', involving domination. Yet, whatever the contrasting nuances, in essence political leadership is an instrumental activity, about how 'we' or 'they' get from 'here' to 'there'. It is conceived within Marxism as political practice of a strategic kind, enabling the proletariat to get from the capitalist present to the communist future. Marxists as much as anarchists, in striving for societal transformation, have been deeply preoccupied with the nature of political leadership. The difference between them was that anarchists, profoundly committed to 'horizontal' forms of self-governance saw any kind of *institutionalised* leadership, entailing either force or consent, as an unnecessary evil, whilst Marxists held that it had a vital function: in order to bring about the 'there' of an egalitarian, 'stateless', self-governing society, a political party was needed, as well as some type of coercive state — some leading by the 'nose'. Thus, a potential paradox arose, between authoritarian means and emancipatory ends. However, for Marx and his followers this paradox was more apparent than real. They held that with appropriate forms of political engagement and under suitable social, economic and political conditions, leadership, at least in the form of a 'vanguard' party and state, would eventually 'wither' away. This would occur for the simple reason that since political power was the product of class division, of class domination, it would become redundant once a socially harmonious and transparent society had been created. True, even in such a society power of a sort would exist, but it would be in the form of a democratic polity in which 'all' would participate,

---

[1] Thanks to Joe Femia for his helpful and thought-provoking comments.

without the need for a specialised political caste.² This sort of political arrangement that Marx modelled on Ancient Athenian democracy has been felicitously described by Hunt as 'democracy without professionals'.³ In other words under communism leadership in an institutional-strategic sense would disappear. Hence, for Marx any discrepancy between ends and means could be ultimately overcome.

Significantly, a second, unintended paradox arose: the history of twentieth century Marxism has amply demonstrated that Marxists when in power have been anything but 'self-dissolving' in their actions, with the party and state assuming totalitarian dimensions. Many critics of Marxism, as well as post-Marxists, have held that there is indeed a 'genetic' relation between these two paradoxes, that Marxist discourse although at the declaratory level might want democracy, freedom and equality for all, does not have the theoretical resources to produce a form of political practice that avoids authoritarianism.⁴ This chapter will explore the theoretical and practical strategies of Marx and some of his principal followers, namely Kautsky, Lenin and Gramsci, aimed at avoiding left-wing authoritarianism. It will also briefly look at the post-Marxist response to this issue. And *en passant* it will consider the question of whether there is something inherently anti-democratic in Marxist theory that inevitably leads to an anti-democratic practice that has led post-Marxists, at least, to search for other explanatory paradigms to ensure that the 'progressive' cause does not lead to the Gulag.

Marx's Synthesis — Avoiding the Jacobin Temptation

Marx's work could be interpreted a rather long tutorial in training the radical imagination, or as a meditation on the question of political leadership and its role in achieving human emancipation, particularly on how to avoid the failed radicalism of the French Revolution of 1789. He sought to circumvent the egalitarian authoritarianism that led to the Jacobin Reign of Terror (1793-4), and combat Robespierre's conspiratorial imitators, such as August Blanqui and Wilhelm Weitling, as well as anarchists, especially Bakunin, all of whose thinking was fatally flawed by a commitment to what he termed the 'will principle' of politics. He stated: 'Far from identifying the principle of the state as the source of social ills, the heroes of the

---

2   Karl Marx, 'Critique of Hegel's Doctrine of the State', in *Early Writings* (hereafter *EW*), introduction Lucio Colletti, trans. R. Livingstone and G. Benton (Harmondsworth: Penguin, 1975), p.185. See also Joseph V. Femia, *Marxism and Democracy* (Oxford: Clarendon Press, 1993), pp. 69–76.
3   Richard N. Hunt, *The Political Ideas of Marx and Engels*, Vol. 1 (London and Basingstoke: Macmillan) 1975, p. 82.
4   Joseph V. Femia, *Marxism and Democracy*, ch. 4 *passim*.

French Revolution held social ills to be the source of political problems'. Hence, Robespierre regarded 'great wealth and great poverty as an obstacle to *pure democracy* and therefore wished to establish a universal system of *Spartan* frugality. The principle of politics is the *will* ... the more perfect *political* understanding is the more completely it puts its faith in the *omnipotence* of the will; the blinder it is towards the *natural* and *spiritual* limitations of the will, the more incapable it becomes of discovering the real source of the evils of society.'[5] Similarly, he noted that for Bakunin: 'The *will*, and not economic conditions, is the foundation of his social revolution.'[6] Elsewhere, he famously condemned the 'alchemists of the revolution', who forestalled 'the process of revolutionary development, pushing it artificially to a revolutionary crisis', and made a 'revolution impromptu, without the preconditions for a revolution'.[7] Thus, political action had to take full cognisance of different types of conditions, whether they were political, social, economic or indeed cultural. He pitted against the 'will principle' a number of interrelated principles, the most important of which we may term a 'condition-dependency' principle, when he asserted that, 'It is not enough that thought should strive to realize itself; reality must itself strive towards thought'.[8] In other words, effective political action—its possibilities and limits—required contextual understanding and evaluation

Intimations of his attempt to distance himself from egalitarian-authoritarian radicalism can be seen at the outset of his political and intellectual career in a letter to his friend Arnold Ruge (1843). In musing about the role of a radical political intellectual, he did not want to confront the world with 'new doctrinaire principles' and or provide 'true-campaign slogans'. He aimed to develop 'new principles' from the 'existing principles of the world' and show 'why it is struggling, and consciousness of this is a thing it *must* acquire whether it wishes it or not.'[9] He sought to make the world 'aware of its own consciousness, in arousing it from a dream of itself, in *explaining* its own actions to it.' He did not wish to draw a 'sharp

---

5   Karl Marx, 'Critical Notes on "The King of Prussia and Social Reform"', in *EW*, p. 413. Marx's emphasis.
6   Karl Marx, 'Conspectus of Bakunin's *Statism and Anarchy*', in Karl Marx, *The First International and After*, ed. & trans. D. Fernbach (Harmondsworth: Penguin, 1974), p. 335. Marx's emphasis. For another example, see Marx's unfavourable juxtaposition of 'will' and 'actual conditions' in opposition to the Blanqui inspired Willich-Schapper faction of the Communist League. 'Minutes of the Central Committee Meeting of 15 September 1850' in Karl Marx, *The Revolutions of 1848*, edited and introduced by David Fernbach (Harmondsworth: Penguin, 1973), p. 341.
7   Quoted Hal Draper, *Karl Marx's Theory of Revolution* (New York: Monthly Review Press, 1986), Vol. 3, p. 162.
8   'Critique of Hegel's Philosophy of Right. Introduction', in *EW*, p. 252.
9   *EW*, pp. 208–9. Marx's emphasis.

mental line between past and future but to *complete* the thought of the past.' Mankind should not begin any *'new* work', but should 'consciously bring about the completion of its old work.' His 'credo' was 'the self-clarification ... of the struggles and wishes of the age.' From this we can deduce an opposition to a radical elitism of doctrinaire sloganising based on *a priori* ethical principles, and the importance he attached to getting involved in *existing* struggles, and of the need to help those in struggle to become self-aware by connecting their empirical wills to greater contextual understanding ('explaining' their own actions to them). And finally, we see an emphasis on relating theory to *existing* practices of struggle (*'praxis'*), and on the notion that the underpinnings of political intervention should based upon *immanent critique* (completing 'old' work).

Marx, then, aimed to give radical intellectuals a more modest historical role, by not allowing them to impose external values or 'scientific' nostrums on those struggling to overcome their suffering. Moreover, the theory/practice (*praxis*) relation could be interpreted in a non-elitist way, especially if we heed his later remark in his 1845 third *Theses on Feuerbach*, which refers to the need of the 'educator' to be educated through a *'revolutionising practice'*.[10] And optimistically he claimed that those involved in struggle would become less theory-dependent. In the *Poverty of Philosophy* (1847) he held that: 'In the measure that history moves forward, and with it the struggle of the proletariat assumes clearer outlines, [socialists and communists] no longer need to seek science in their minds; they have only to take note of what is happening before their eyes and become its mouthpiece'.[11] And the corollary of this, as he stated in *The Communist Manifesto*, was that communists 'do not set up any sectarian principles of their own by which to shape and mould the proletarian movement', because their 'theoretical conclusions' were not based upon 'ideas or principles' invented by 'this or that would-be reformer'. Rather, they expressed 'in general terms, actual relations springing from an existing class struggle, from an historical movement going on under our very eyes'.[12] Hence communism could not be an ideal to which reality would have to 'adjust'. Rather, it was a *'real* movement which abolishes the present state of things.'[13]

10 Karl Marx, 'Theses on Feuerbach', in Karl Marx and Frederick Engels, *Selected Works*, vol. 2 (hereafter, *MESW2*) (Moscow: Foreign Languages Printing House, 1962), p. 404. Marx's emphasis.
11 Karl Marx, *Poverty of Philosophy* (Moscow: Progress Publishers, 1955), p. 109.
12 Karl Marx, 'The Communist Manifesto' (hereafter *CM*), in Karl Marx and Frederick Engels, Selected Works, vol.1 (hereafter *MESW1*) (Moscow: Foreign Languages Printing House, 1962, p. 46.
13 Karl Marx and Frederick Engels, *The German Ideology* (hereafter *GI*) (Moscow: Progress Publishers, 1968), p. 48. Marx's and Engels' emphasis.

Despite this attempt to render the radical intellectual less significant in the historical process, Marx in effect made their role pivotal in giving *meaning* to these struggles ('in *explaining* [the world's] own actions to it'). Here we come to the vital issue of how Marx and his followers *chose to interpret* how 'reality' might 'strive towards thought'. Marx, intellectually never far from Hegel, in order to comprehend how the past, present and future developed, employed what we can call a 'dialectical ontology' ensuring that the drawing of 'sharp mental lines' could be avoided. Crucially, this meant that political intervention could be based upon immanent critique, completing the 'old work', rather than imposing abstract ethical principles upon a benighted multitude, potentially involving compulsion. In a sense, this meant that intervention was educational in nature, entailing acts of persuasion by an appeal to the 'facts' thrown up by an emerging reality, thereby making explicit what was deemed implicit in the historical process.

In broad terms his dialectical account of this process enabled him to highlight the progressive, freedom and equality-giving potential of the two great revolutions of his time, namely, the French and Industrial Revolutions. This perspective when analysing the development of politico-economic formations entailed the terms 'sublation' or 'aufhebung', meaning simultaneously preservation and transcendence. The 'completion' of these Revolutions in the intertwined political and economic spheres meant overcoming the contradiction between their content and form, preserving the universalistic content or promise of freedom and equality for all, whilst transcending their particular and particularistic form, grounded upon private property.

His early work focused on the political sphere in response to Hegel's statism (and by implication Robespierre's). For Marx, the state rather than being the *solution* to the conflicts within the private realm of civil society, was in fact their *expression*. The public, political sphere of the state whilst in effect projecting an imagined community of free and equal citizens, in reality served the interests of the private property owners, who dominated 'civil society', along with the bureaucracy that supposedly constituted a 'universal class'. The separation of the public and private spheres was indeed symptomatic of the domination of the property-owning minority over the propertyless majority. In the *German Ideology* he explained this separation and putative independence of the state from society in terms of the division of labour between rulers and ruled, which allowed narrow class interests to prevail.[14] The resolution of the separation between state and society Marx argued lay in workers getting the

---

14 Marx and Engels, *GI*, p. 45.

vote, or more precisely ' *unrestricted* active and passive *suffrage*'. Electoral reform, or as he later said, winning the 'battle of democracy' in the '*abstract political state* ... implies the *dissolution of civil society.*'[15] Thus, once the propertyless had the right to vote, the private sphere of civil society would become politicised and private property abolished, thereby dissolving the public/private distinction. Representatives would truly represent the interests of the majority in society, that is the working class. Marx's notion of representation involved full-scale democratic participation—'active suffrage', or as he later stated, government 'of the people by the people',[16] which as we have already noted Hunt has characterized as 'democracy without professionals'.[17] Not only was the specialised division of labour between leaders and led overcome, but also the institutional division between the legislative and executive arms of government. The abolition of specialisation also involved the abolition of a standing army, as later depicted in the Paris Commune. [18] As already remarked, Marx clearly believed that leadership in any institutional sense would be redundant[19].

Marx's dialectical view of the state's functions meant that its 'social functions',[20] or 'legitimate functions'[21] would remain, but it would lose its 'political' character[22] when classes had disappeared. Whilst this phase of 'sublation' was described by Marx as a 'dictatorship of the proletariat', it had little in common with the Jacobin dictatorship. As more recent commentators have indicated, it merely meant class rule by the proletarian majority, over a bourgeois minority,[23] which as we have seen assumed a democratic form. Thus we can see that Marx's condition-dependency principle gave rise to the *democratic principle*, that the propertyless struggling to improve their living conditions would also struggle to democratise the state and civil society, which entailed the 'sublation' of both.

15 Karl Marx, 'Critique of Hegel's Doctrine of the State' in *EW*, p. 191. Marx's emphasis.
16 'The Civil War in France', in *MESW1*, p. 527.
17 Hunt, *The Political Ideas of Marx and Engels*, vol 1, p. 82.
18 'The Civil War in France', in *MESW1*, pp. 519–20.
19 Marxists and those strongly influenced by Marx have however proposed that under communism there could a need for leadership with parties having to compete democratically with other 'vanguard' parties for the right to lead. See Chris Harman, 'Party and Class' in *Party and Class*, essays by Tony Cliff, Duncan Hallas, Chris Harman and Leon Trotsky London: Pluto Press, n.d.), p. 63; Lucio Magri, 'Problems of the Marxist Theory of the Revolutionary Party', *New Left Review*, no.60 (1970), p. 128; C.B. Macpherson, *The Life and Times of Liberal Democracy* (Oxford: Oxford University Press, 1977), p. 111.
20 'Critique of the Gotha Programme', in *MESW2*, p. 32.
21 'The Civil War in France', in *MESW1*, p. 520.
22 *CM*, p. 54.
23 Hal Draper, *The 'Dictatorship of the Proletariat' from Marx to Lenin* (New York: Monthly Review Press, 1987), pp. 24–6. See also Hunt, *The Political Ideas of Marx and Engels*, Vol. 1, p. 298.

His later work, starting with *The German Ideology*, concentrated more closely on the contradictions *within* civil society, especially within the capitalist mode of production, a system that provided the underlying dynamic of reality striving 'towards thought'. Capitalism's material productivity held out the promise of an equality that was not an equality of 'want' as in the Babouvian egalitarian schema of 'crude communism'.[24] Yet, its growth was fettered by the tendency of the rate of profit to fall. The other major contradiction of capitalism was between its 'content' involving the increasingly sophisticated social production of use values, and its 'form' as exchangeable commodities, that enabled capitalists privately to appropriate this socially produced wealth.[25] Completing the 'old work' (or 'negating') here merely involved rendering privately owned productive assets into common property, and in ending property relations that were inherently exploitative, and creating a classless epoch in which the promise of prosperity for all and the universality of (non-private) ownership was no longer an abstraction.

So far Marx's condition-dependency principle has been interpreted as relying heavily on a dialectical view of social, economic and political reality. We should note however that Marx in his historical writings, or in his commentaries on current socio-economic and political contexts had a far less schematic approach to condition-dependency, as indicated by one of his oft-quoted phrases: 'Men make their own history, but they do not make it just as they please in circumstances chosen by themselves, but under circumstances directly encountered, given and transmitted from the past.'[26] Condition-dependency here could be interpreted as suggesting a contingent, more open-ended approach to political calculation. Even in *The Communist Manifesto*[27] he noted that different demands were appropriate for different countries. In his speech on the Hague Congress of the First International in 1872, he maintained that that 'road' to workers' power was not the 'same everywhere', and that heed must be paid to the 'institutions, customs and traditions of the various countries'. From this he speculated that peaceful revolutions were possible in the United States, England and possibly Holland, whereas force would be needed in most continental countries.[28] And where capitalism was relatively unde-

---

24 'Economic and Philosophic Manuscripts', *EW*, p. 346; *GI*, p. 47.
25 Karl Marx, *Capital*, Vol. 1, Intro. Ernest Mandel, trans. Ben Fowkes (Harmondsworth: Penguin, 1976), p. 929.
26 'The Brumaire of Louis Bonaparte', in *MESW1*, p. 247.
27 *CM*, p. 53.
28 'Speech on the Hague Congress ', Karl Marx, *The First International and After*, editrd and introduced by David Fernbach (Harmondsworth: Penguin, 1974), p. 324. Context sensitivity also led him to speculate that the Russian peasant villages, or *obshchinas* might serve as a

veloped, class alliances with the bourgeoisie, or even petit bourgeoisie as in Germany where the bourgeoisie was politically weak would be necessary.[29] Nevertheless, consistent with his dialectical perspective, such alliances were aimed at speeding up capitalist development, or creating a political framework that enabled the proletariat to mobilise and develop its sense of political efficacy, for example, struggles to bring about national unification during the 1848 revolutions, or agrarian revolutions, or the democratisation of the state, especially the creation of a democratic republic.

In reality 'striving' towards thought Marx evidently held that a subjective, voluntaristic element was necessary to counter the Jacobin mind-set. This element involved the consciousness and organisational capacities of the working class, the key agent in bringing to completion the 'old work'. This we may term the 'self-emancipatory' principle. Indeed, for Marx communism was the product of working class *self*-emancipation. 'The emancipation of the working classes must be conquered by the working classes themselves ... ' as he wrote in the General Rules of the International Working Men's Association.[30] The significance of this self-emancipatory principle was not merely that this ruled out the idea of radical intellectuals drawing up utopian schemes for the 'good' society — 'recipes for the cook-shops of the future',[31] but also that they should be coming to the aid of workers in their struggle for self-emancipation.

Another implication was that the workers in their struggles would set up their own political party, rather than one being created by well intentioned intellectuals *for* the workers. This position helps us understand Marx's attitude towards the idea of a political party. As has been noted he attached different notions to the meaning of 'party', ranging from a group of his followers to an historical movement of workers.[32] The self-emancipatory principle led him to oppose conspiratorially organised parties, such as the League of the Just, which became the Communist League. He joined it on condition that it became open and democratic.

'starting-point for communist development' following a successful workers' revolution in the West. 'Preface to the Russian Edition of 1882' of the Communist Manifesto', in *MESW1*, p. 24. Nevertheless, apart from his observation, towards the end of his life that the middle class was a growing proportion of the working population Karl Marx, *Theories of Surplus Value*, part three (London: Lawrence and Wishart, 1972), p. 63, this form of condition-dependency did not seem have serious implications for his dialectical ontological version, since such villages would not provide the global dynamic for a global socialist revolution.

29   'Address to the Central Committee of the Communist League', in *MESW1*, p. 110.
30   'General Rules of the International Working Men's Association', in *MESW1*, p. 386.
31   Karl Marx, 'Postface to the Second Edition' in *Capital*, Vol. 1, p. 99.
32   Monty Johnstone, 'Marx and Engels and the Concept of the Party', in Ralph Miliband and John Saville (eds.), *Socialist Register*, (London: Merlin Press, 1967), p. 122. See also, Hunt, *The Political Ideas of Marx and Engels*, Vol. 1, p. 283.

Marx was also not particularly fetishistic about any particular ('the') party, which he thought would come and go, according to the vicissitudes of the class struggle.

For Marx proletarian self-emancipation also implied self-transformation, an awareness of its historical, anti-capitalist destiny and capacity to become a ruling class that could act in the interests of the whole of humanity. This self-belief would grow, according to Marx, as it developed its sense of political efficacy, or sense of 'political competence'.[33] Class combat clearly had a key role, in which a revolution would rid the working class of all 'the muck of ages' and enable it to 'become fitted to found society anew'.[34] Just as dramatically Marx asserted that: 'We will tell the workers: if you want to change conditions and make yourselves capable of government, you will have to undergo fifteen, twenty or fifty years of civil war'.[35] Yet less dramatically, he thought that universal suffrage could enhance political efficacy. With reference to mid-nineteenth century France, it enabled the 'majority of the people' in a revolutionary period to pass 'through the school of development'.[36] Equally, the workers' capacity for self-organisation was a crucial prefigurative element in a successful revolution. Thus, in a letter Hyndman he indicated that the German working class to sustain a revolution would need 'previous organisation, acquirement of knowledge, propaganda and ... (word illegible).[37] Generally, in prefigurative terms, trade unions were vital as 'organised agencies for superseding the very system of wage labour and capital rule.'[38] Various workplace reforms within capitalism itself were also useful in promoting efficacy, especially the reduction of the working day: 'A preliminary condition, without which all further attempts at improvement and emancipation must prove abortive, is the limitation of the working day. It is needed to restore the health and physical energies of the working class ... as well as secure them the possibility of intellectual development, social intercourse, social and political action.'[39]

---

33   Carole Pateman, *Participation and Democratic Theory*, (Cambridge: Cambridge University Press, 1970), p. 46.
34   GI, p. 87.
35   'Minutes of the Central Committee Meeting of 15 September 1850', Karl Marx, *The Revolutions of 1848*, p. 341.
36   Karl Marx, 'Class Struggles in France', in *Surveys from Exile*, ed. and intro. David Fernbach (Harmondsworth: Penguin, 1973), p. 134.
37   'Marx to Hyndman' 8/12/1880, in Karl Marx and Frederick Engels, *Selected Correspondence* (Moscow: Progress Publishers, 1955), p. 334.
38   Karl Marx, 'Instructions for Delegates to the Geneva Congress', in *The First International and After*, p. 91. Marx's emphasis.
39   *Ibid.*, p. 87.

Whilst we can see that there was clearly an intentional, voluntaristic element in this dialectical process, the significance of these actions is in terms of their 'objective', unintended consequences, with for example struggles of workers against the capitalists creating organisations such as trade unions that would form the basis of new class rule. This 'unintended consequence' standpoint enabled Marx to provide an optimistic gloss as to the meaning of their struggles, of how capitalism, or the bourgeoisie in its political struggles, unwittingly created its own gravediggers or (in 'Hegelese') 'begets ... its own negation'.[40] The proletariat, which had no stake in capitalist society, could only improve its living conditions by overthrowing capitalism. The improved means of communication under modern capitalism also helped unify the proletriat.[41] The bourgeoisie in its struggles with the *ancien regime* dragged the proletariat into the political arena supplying it with its 'own elements of political and general education', which could be utilised as 'weapons for fighting the bourgeoisie'.[42] Not surprisingly Marx optimistically concluded from all this that: 'mankind always sets itself only such tasks as it can solve ... it will always be found that the task itself arises only when the material conditions for its solution already exist or are in the process of formation.[43]

The upshot of his dialectical ontology was an historical teleology of 'inevitability', of the consciousness that the world (unintentionally) *'must* acquire whether it wishes it or not.'[44] And whilst communists should not impose 'sectarian principles' on the workers' movement, they understood 'the line of march'.[45] The role of the intellectual was to 'shorten and lessen the birth pangs' of the new society.[46] Therefore, radical intellectuals rather than attempting to impose their own abstract, ethical principles upon the ignorant masses, should acknowledge how 'good' practices (for example the socialisation of labour, the growth of democracy, working class political efficacy, the Paris Commune of 1871, and the like) were emerging from an unfolding reality, a process going on 'under our very eyes'.[47] Thus the task of communists was to 'fight for the attainment of the immediate aims, for the enforcement of the momentary interests of the working class; but

---

40   Karl Marx, *Capital*, Vol. 1, p. 929.
41   CM, p. 42.
42   Ibid., p. 43.
43   'Preface to a Contribution to a Critique of Political Economy', in *MESW1*, p. 363.
44   *EW*, pp. 208–9. Marx's emphasis).
45   CM, p. 46. See also 'Marx to J. Weydemeyer', 3/5/1852 What he did that was 'new' was to 'prove' among other things that the 'class struggle necessarily leads to the *dictatorship of the proletariat*'. Marx and Engels, *Selected Correspondence*, p. 69.
46   Marx, 'Preface to the First Edition', *Capital*, Vol.1, p. 92.
47   CM, p. 46.

in the movement of the present, they also represent and take care of the future of the movement'.[48]

From all this we can see that Marx sought to avoid leftwing authoritarianism by synthesising a number of principles that would negate the Jacobin 'will' principle of politics. His pivotal condition-dependency principle suggested that the 'good' society relied far more on the existence of material and institutional conditions than the exercise of will and imagination, of reality striving 'towards thought'. Marx's account of this reality as we have shown was framed by a dialectical ontology, which involved drawing out the logics of the two major revolutions of his time. However, the voluntaristic, subjective element was also an essential precondition for revolutionary success: the working class needed the knowledge, confidence and organisational capacity to become a ruling class. In the course of its struggles against the capitalists it would develop its own political organisation with the help of intellectuals such as Marx. As we have noted, apart from aiding workers in their practical day-to-day struggles, such an organisation would invest them with an historical significance by showing how these struggles contained anticipations of the future in which the proletariat would become the hegemonic force in society. To limit the historical role of the intellectual we have also seen that the self-emancipatory principle attempted to ensure that other groups within society could not act on behalf of workers, and that moreover this self-emancipation would assume a democratic form. Although Marx thought that a synthesis of these principles would avoid the Jacobin temptation, they were clearly quite optimistic and simultaneously demanding ones, with which his followers had to deal, as capitalism and the workers' movement developed around the world. Marx's primary expectation was that as capitalism matured so would the workers' revolutionary capabilities and desires. What if capitalism developed in unforeseen ways, and relatedly workers preferred a larger portion of the capitalist cake, rather than controlling the bakery? What if workers' empirical wills failed to coincide with Marx's revolutionary dialectical assumptions? What if 'reality' was not striving 'towards thought'? Overall we can see that Marx was supremely confident about his dialectical framework and empirical reality ultimately coinciding, about the potential hegemonic capacities of the working class and capitalism's capacity to self-destruct. He was equally optimistic about the state losing its coercive, 'political' and 'independent' character, as democratic participation increased and the post-capitalist society moved towards classlessness.

---

48   *Ibid.*, p. 64.

Breaking the Synthesis: From Kautsky and Lenin to Gramsci

Just as people do not make history in 'conditions of their own choosing', neither do Marxists. 'Reality' after Marx's death was not striving towards 'thought' in any simple way, although until Gramsci the key strategic thinkers, particularly Kautsky and Lenin, did their utmost to convince themselves and others that 'history' was on the proletariat's side. Unfortunately, for both Kautsky, the chief ideologist of European Marxism and Lenin, the creator of Soviet Marxism, 'reality' began to disrupt Marx's synthesis of leadership principles.

Until the First World War at least Kautsky could maintain a great fidelity to the spirit of Marx's anti-Jacobinism with a clear correlation between capitalism's development, especially in Germany, and the growth of workers' power going on 'under our very eyes', evidenced in the rise of trade unions and the electoral support of the Social Democratic Party (SPD). Indeed, Kautsky could share the optimism of Engels who asserted in the 1895 preface to *The Class Struggles in France, 1848–1850*: German Social Democracy's two million voters were the 'decisive "shock force" of the international proletarian army ... its growth proceeds as spontaneously, as steadily, as irresistibly, and at the same time as tranquilly as a natural process. All government intervention has proved powerless against it ... if it continues in this fashion [it will] grow into the decisive power in the land, before which all other powers will have to bow, whether they like it or not.'[49] Like Marx, Kautsky held that capitalist conditions created the link between democracy and socialism: the logic of democracy was socialism, once capitalism had made the proletariat the majority of the working population, and went into deeper crisis.[50] Again, following Engels he recognised that the German army could not be confronted head-on, but had to be subverted through the democratic process itself, by rendering it 'faithless to its rulers'[51], especially by demonstrating the size of working class support, and how the capitalists were in a minority. Furthermore, democratic institutions, whether trade unions, local government or parliament were vital in promoting the organisational cohesiveness and the ruling skills of the proletariat.[52]

Perhaps influenced by Max Weber, he saw parliament as part and parcel of modernity, as the product of an ever growing division of labour:

---

49 Frederick Engels, 'Introduction' to 'The Class Struggles in France, 1848–1850', in *MESW1*, p. 135.
50 Karl Kautsky, *The Road to Power*, Bloch, Chicago, 1909, p. 7; Karl Kautsky, *The Social Revolution* (Chicago: Kerr, 1913[1902]), pp. 189–91.
51 Karl Kautsky, *The Social Revolution*, p. 88.
52 *Ibid*, p. 81; Karl Kautsky, *The Class Struggle* (New York: W.W. Norton, 1971[1892]), 187–88.

'The problems of the modern state have grown so enormously that it is impossible to solve them without an extensive division of labour and a high grade of professional knowledge'. Capitalists were too involved in competition to govern. 'They must leave that to wage workers and bureaucratic employees. The capitalist class reigns, but does not govern.'[53] A parliamentary legislature was necessary to prevent the 'arbitrary and corrupt procedures' of the bureaucracy, so that the forces of production could grow unhindered.[54] In other words there had to be a division between the legislative and executive functions.[55] A crucial implication for the leadership question was that for Kautsky unlike other Marxist thinkers, including Marx himself, leadership in an institutional sense would not wither away in a post capitalist society, since a sophisticated division of labour would have to be expertly coordinated.

Moving to the strategic implications, given the obvious benefits of the division of labour Kautsky wanted to minimise the effects of a revolutionary rupture. A violent revolution would destroy the economic base required for a socialist economy, producing a 'crippled capitalism'.[56] He did however recognise that in order for parliament to be fully amenable to proletarian wishes it might in itself need revolutionising: 'Parliamentarism far from making a revolution useless and superfluous, is itself in need of a revolution in order to vivify it.'[57] During the German revolution of 1918 his favoured form of governance was a combination of parliament and workers' councils.[58] The socialist transition had to take account of modernity with its sophisticated division of labour, the growth of large scale political organisations and the emergence of economic organisations such as trade unions and employers' associations. Modern economic and political conditions therefore suggested that even if the ultimate end-state was a revolution in class and production, it would be the result of a gradual process and a working class majority in parliament, represented by the SPD. The implication of this was that the proletarian party should represent the *whole* of the working class, not just a 'vanguard', with its elitist and coercive potentialities. This notion of representation formed the basis of Kautsky's famous 'centrism', his attempt to balance the radical and pragmatic wings of the SPD. The Party might be

---

53 *Ibid*, pp. 29–30.
54 Pat Goode (ed.), *Karl Kautsky, Selected Political Writings* (London: Macmillan, 1983), p. 107.
55 Karl Kautsky, *The Labour Revolution* (New York Dial Press, 1925), p.77; Massimo Salvadori, *Karl Kautsky and the Socialist Revolution, 1880–1938*, trans. Jon Rothschild (London: New Left Books, 1979), p. 14.
56 *Ibid*, p. 89.
57 Karl Kautsky, *The Social Revolution*, p. 80.
58 Massimo Salvadori, *ibid*, p. 237.

an educational 'vanguard' instilling in the proletariat its historical mission and a sense of an 'inevitable' revolution (however involving acts of will[59]). Yet his insistence on the existence of objective socio-economic and subjective preconditions, and a virtually rupture-free revolution led him to describe the party as 'revolutionary, but not revolution-making'.[60]

In broad terms Kautsky attempted, at least in a formal sense, to remain true to Marx's anti-Jacobin leadership principles, retaining the connection between socialism and democracy, showing how 'reality' was striving towards 'thought', uniting theory and practice, and emphasising the importance of the objective and subjective preconditions of revolutionary action. However, he was patently risk-averse, unwilling to allow the SPD to have an actual leadership role in 'making' a revolution, which implied that if one was to occur it would be outside the direction of the Party. Thus, although the Party was meant to represent the working class it would seem to have a restricted role in proletarian self-emancipation insofar as it required some form of revolution. He had in effect a 'light touch' view of leadership, with the Party more alongside the working class than ahead of it. Further, given his model of socialist transition there would seem to be little allowance for the role of contingency, of events for which this model could not provide the basis for effective political intervention. Indeed, the tumultuous events of the First World War that gave rise to intense political struggles, especially in Russian and to a lesser extent in Germany revealed Kautsky's Marxism as a distinctly fair-weather kind, waiting in port until the seas had calmed. Indeed, they did, but just as the European proletariat at the outset of the World War put loyalty to country above class, so afterwards it prioritised reform over revolution. The 'reality' that was striving towards 'thought', which Kautsky seemed to acknowledge, was more Weberian than Marxist, insofar as it was a managed capitalism. The logic of these large scale state and non-governmental organisations was the promotion of workers' living standards within capitalism. Eduard Bernstein, the first Marxist revisionist, at the beginning of the twentieth century had already drawn out many of the implications of a stabilised capitalism for a reformist political practice. Small wonder that Kautsky towards the end of his life acknowledged that he and Bernstein were 'Siamese twins'.[61] The SPD with distinctly Marxist origins by the 1920s had changed into a form of parliamentary

---

59   Karl Kautsky, *The Class Struggle*, p. 90.
60   Quoted Gary P. Steenson, *Karl Kautsky, 1854–1938* (Pittsburgh, PA.: University of Pittsburgh Press, 1978), p. 141.
61   Douglas Kellner (ed.), *Karl Korsch: Revolutionary Theory* (Austin, TX: University of Texas Press, 1977), p. 179.

social democracy, as did post-Stalinist European Communist parties *de facto* in the post-war years, and then formally in the 1970s.

Lenin too sought to apply Marx's leadership principles, and as with Kautsky not under conditions of his own choosing. Yet, unlike Kautsky he was, with the Bolsheviks, directly involved in 'revolution-making', whilst the Kautsky-influenced Mensheviks stood on the side-lines after the February revolution. If for Kautsky leadership was 'light touch', for Lenin it was 'heavy duty'. Although Lenin was strongly influenced by Kautsky before the First World War, it became clear that the latter's model of socialist transition did not address the immediate problems confronting the international working class thrown up by War in general, and confronting Russian society in particular. Another key difference was that Kautsky was essentially a party theoretician, interpreting the world, whilst Lenin was also a practitioner, involved in revolutionary *actualitié*, of taking power with its unpredictable outcomes of action and reaction. Nevertheless, there is little doubt that Lenin attempted in his own mind to remain loyal to Marx's synthesis of leadership principles both before and after the October revolution of 1917.

Lenin's thought was strongly underpinned by an historical teleology, of a 'reality' striving towards 'thought' in a particular way that was reinforced by his reading of Hegel during the First World War. Strategically, before 1917 he held to a stages theory of revolution in the light of Russia's political and economic backwardness. He called for the most democratic political superstructure possible, to promote capitalist development, especially an agrarian revolution, and in order to situate the proletariat most favourably within the 'bourgeois' body politic in preparation for the next revolution. As for his theory of the party, this too was teleologically informed as Neil Harding indicates: 'The teleology of capitalist development through ascending phases to its apogee or essential expression was matched by Lenin's account of the development of consciousness and of the party.'[62] His call for a party of professional revolutionaries and denigration of 'amateurism', stemmed not only from the need to avoid detection by the Tsarist police, but also from the notion that the development of the party should parallel the development of industrial organisation from domestic, handicraft to factory production. Although his professional and centralised conception of the party led to charges of 'Jacobinism', which Lenin conceded, on closer inspection it is clear that he rejected historical parallels dragged up from the past. His aim through tightening membership rules was to prevent the party degenerating as a result of an influx of 'professors and high-school students', who were 'afraid of the

---

62 Neil Harding, *Lenin's Political Thought*, Vol. 1 (London: Macmillan, 1977), p. 247; p. 137.

dictatorship of the proletariat'.[63] He wanted to create a genuine proletarian vanguard, combining the 'thinking' and 'doing' elements.[64]

Lenin's strategic reorientation during the First World War, which led him essentially to reject stages theory and see a proletarian revolution in Russia as the beginning of a world-wide revolution, was again marked by a teleological approach. His *Imperialism, the Highest Stage of Capitalism* (1916) suggested that the First World War was indeed *the* crisis of global capitalism in its final, imperialistic phase. The notion that the Russian proletariat could be a global vanguard, albeit temporarily, was for Lenin reinforced by the creation of Soviets that formed the basis of the February revolution in 1917. *The State and Revolution* (1917), based upon copious quotations from Marx and Engels, championed the idea of workers' self-emancipation, stressed the link between socialism and democracy and called for a stateless society. He viewed the Soviets as embryonic forms of proletarian democracy. Yet, despite advocating democracy from the bottom up the Marxist party had a distinctly vanguardist, educational role : 'By educating the workers' party, Marxism educates the vanguard of the proletariat which is capable of assuming power and of *leading the whole people* to Socialism, of directing and organising the new order, of being the teacher, the guide, the leader of all the workers and exploited in the task of building up their social life without the bourgeoisie and against the bourgeoisie'.[65] The central educational task of the party was to make the proletariat aware of its 'revolutionary role in history. The culmination of this role is the proletarian dictatorship.'[66] Although at the same time he rejected charges of of 'Blanquist adventurism' on the grounds that the majority had to be won over in the Soviets, that it was a question of '*struggle for influence within*'[67]them, there was clearly a potential disjunction between the empirical desires of workers and their capacity to become a new ruling class on the one hand, and the demands of the party whose *raison d'etre* was the facilitation of their historic destiny, on the other. For Lenin this difficulty was clear by 1919 when he noted in a report to Party Congress in March 1919 as a result of the 'low cultural level' of the working class, 'the Soviets, which by virtue of their program are organs of government *by the working people*, are in fact organs of government *for the*

---

63 V.I. Lenin, 'One Step Forward, Two Steps Back', in *Collected Works*, Vol. 7 (Moscow: Progress Publishers, 1961), p. 381.
64 Marcel Leibman, *Leninism under Lenin* (London: Merlin Press, 1980), pp. 45–9.
65 V.I. Lenin, 'The State and Revolution', in *Selected Works* (London: Lawrence and Wishart, 1969), p. 281.
66 *Ibid.*
67 V.I. Lenin, 'Letters on Tactics' in *The April Theses* (Moscow: Progress Publishers, 1970), p. 17. Lenin's emphasis.

working people by the advanced section of the proletariat, but not the working people as a whole.'[68] By 1921 he identified the dictatorship of the proletariat no longer with Soviet power but with the Marxist party: 'the dictatorship of the proletariat is impossible except through the Communist Party'.[69] This 'substitutionism' was even clearer when he said in the same year: 'Even when the proletariat has to live through a period of being declassed, it can still carry out its task of conquering and retaining power.'[70] Thus, proletarian dictatorship became increasingly associated with the leading organs of the state, rather than workers' self-government, to such an extent that even in 1918 he saw the Cheka (secret police) as 'directly exercising the dictatorship of the proletariat'.[71]

What is clear in all these formulations is that 'reality' was no longer striving towards 'thought', as it seemed to be doing in the heady days of 1917, and that Lenin in reality was making a virtue out of a necessity. In many ways he became an easy target for Kautsky, whom Lenin had dubbed a Marxist 'renegade'. 'Our Bolshevist comrades have staked all on the card of the general European Revolution. As this card has not turned up ... they had to defend Russia without an army against powerful and implacable enemies [and] establish a regime of well-being for all in a state of general dislocation and impoverishment'. And the less the material and intellectual conditions existed 'the more they felt obliged to replace what was lacking by the exercise of naked power, by dictatorship ... So it became inevitable that they should put dictatorship in the place of democracy.'[72]

As the revolution failed to go global, it became more obvious to right and as well as left-wing Marxist critics of the Bolshevik strategy before and after the October revolution that material and political conditions were indeed premature, that the global proletarian element of civil society was not ready to take power. What became clear was the re-emergence of the 'will' principle of leadership that did indeed embody a statism that reflected an undeveloped civil society in Russia.[73] Thus, rather than its

---

68 Quoted Hal Draper, *The Dictatorship of the Proletariat From Marx to Lenin*, p. 136. Lenin's emphasis.
69 Quoted Ralph Miliband 'Lenin's *The State and Revolution*', in Ralph Miliband and John Saville (eds) *Socialist Register* (London: Merlin Press, 1970), p. 312.
70 Quoted, Tony Cliff, 'Trotsky on Substitutionism' in *Party and Class*, p. 32.
71 Quoted, Hal Draper, *The Dictatorship of the Proletariat from Marx to Lenin*, p. 104.
72 Karl Kautsky, *The Dictatorship of the Proletariat* (Ann Arbour: University of Michigan Press, 1964 [1919]), p. 64.
73 What is interesting about Gramsci's famous distinction between 'East' and 'West' is that he did not go on to conclude that although a 'war' of manoeuvre was successful in the East in terms of seizing power, this signified conditions that were not ripe for a proletarian revolution with an undeveloped 'civil society'. Antonio Gramsci, *Selections from the Prison Notebooks*

struggles being interpreted as an expression of history's directionality, the Soviet working class was compelled to conform to the 'grand narrative' of the Party. This was based upon Marx's 'Preface to a Contribution to a Critique of Political Economy', which suggested that the meaning of history centred on the growth of human productivity. Accordingly, Lenin in the early days of the revolution recommended the use of Taylorist piece-work techniques, and the German model of 'state capitalism' with its efficient organisation of labour.

Although the later Gramsci in a number of respects was a Leninist, especially in his emphasis on the role of the Marxist Party in the transition to communism, one of his significant revisions of Marxism was to break with any sense of fatalism grounded on a teleological account of an unfolding reality. He strongly criticised 'immanentist conceptions'[74] that he saw even in Marxism: 'It should be noted how the deterministic, fatalistic and mechanical element has been a direct ideological "aroma" emanating from the philosophy of praxis, rather like religion or drugs (in their stupefying effect)' whose purpose was to provide solace in time of proletarian defeat.[75] Such conceptions therefore discouraged 'initiative' or leadership. For Gramsci the 'intelligence' could not encourage the 'optimism of the will' as Marx had assumed in the *Communist Manifesto* when referring to an 'historical movement going on under our very eyes'.[76] For Gramsci an 'objective' situation could not be automatically, or 'mechanically' reflected in proletarian consciousness. He stated that economic crises would not force the bourgeoisie 'to abandon their positions, even among the ruins'.[77] He concluded that leadership and organisation were pivotal in enabling the working class to become the dominant force in society.

As is well known after the defeat of the Turin Factory Councils between 1919–20, he focused on the construction of a Communist Party, a 'Modern Prince' that would achieve such hegemony. He now saw that an 'elite' (that is a Party) was needed: 'innovation cannot come from the mass … except through the mediation of an *elite* for whom the conception implicit in human activity has already become to a certain degree a coherent and systematic ever-present awareness and a precise and decisive will.'[78] He constructed a number of concepts, such as 'hegemony', 'passive revolu-

---

(hereafter *SPN*), ed. & trans. Quintin Hoare and Geoffrey Nowell Smith (London: Lawrence and Wishart, 1971), p. 238.
74 Gramsci, *SPN*, p. 371.
75 *Ibid.*, p. 336.
76 *CM*, p. 46.
77 Gramsci, *SPN*, p. 253.
78 *Ibid.*, p. 335. Gramsci's emphasis

tion', 'war of position', war of movement' and 'organic intellectual' to analyse the ideological and political terrain. Unsurprisingly, his emphasis on leadership led him to share with Lenin some identity with Jacobinism—a return to the 'will principle of politics'? Although the *Prison Notebooks* contain many positive references to Jacobinism, he acknowledged that it could become rightfully a 'derogatory' term when applied to a 'politician who was energetic, resolute and fanatical, because fanatically convinced of the thaumaturgical virtues of his ideas, whatever they might be. This definition stressed the destructive elements derived from hatred of rivals and enemies, more than the constructive one derived from having made the popular demands of the masses one's own; the sectarian element of the clique, of the small group, of unrestrained individualism, more than the national political element.'[79] Gramsci seemed to be advocating what we might term a 'democratic Jacobinism' characterised by a democratic militant political party deeply embedded in the working class making 'the popular demands of the masses one's own'.[80] Thus, certainly within the Italian context, his relative pessimism about the working class's capacity to become a ruling class led him to put a much greater emphasis on leadership than Marx, and perhaps even than Lenin, who only had to engage in a 'war of manoeuvre', involving a relatively quick physical contestation of power. This pessimism induced him to claim that 'the proletariat as, a class, is poor in organizing elements. It does not have its own stratum of intellectuals, and can only create one very slowly, very painfully, after the winning of State power.[81] Thus, his faith in the capacity of workers to develop their political efficacy in struggling against capitalism, evident in the period of the Turin factory occupations,[82] was somewhat dented.

Overall, we can see that Gramsci during the Factory Council period embraced many aspects of Marx's anti-Jacobin leadership principles, involving self-emancipation, political efficacy, praxis and democracy. Yet later, he endorsed a certain kind of Jacobinism whilst strongly disassociating himself from an optimistic, immanentist, historical teleology characteristic of Marx, Kautsky and Lenin. Nevertheless, although he no longer assumed that 'reality' was striving towards 'thought', he upheld Marx's far more contingent, open-ended version of the condition-dependency principle that did indeed acknowledge the importance of

79 Ibid., p. 66.
80 Ibid., pp. 155; 429.
81 Ibid., p. 462.
82 Antonio Gramsci, 'The Instruments of Labour', in *Selections from Political Writings, 1910–1920*, selected and ed. Quintin Hoare and trans. John Mathews (London:, Lawrence and Wishart, 1977), p. 162.

'institutions, customs and traditions', especially in the 'West'. Whilst understandably he sought to reconcile political effectiveness that required leadership, organisation and 'discipline' within the context of Fascism, with a democracy that would eventually overcome the division between 'rulers and ruled',[83] we are still left with Marx's question posed in the third thesis on Feuerbach: who is to educate the educators?

The Post-Marxist Moment–Synthesis Abandoned

Post-Marxists were no longer faithful to Marx's or Marxism's synthesis of leadership principles. They could not be described as 'neo-Marxists; yet neither could they be portrayed as 'ex' Marxists, as in most case cases they subscribed to at least one of Marx's or Marxism's 'spirits', to use Derrida's formulation.[84] And whilst many theorists might not call themselves 'post Marxist', such as Habermas, they are here being labelled as such, *post hoc*,[85] because they came out of the Marxist tradition and often combined Marxism in some way with other explanatory paradigms, or were still asking Marxist questions without necessarily coming up with Marxist answers. From the 1960s onwards, they were responding to the failure of the western working class to become a hegemonic, revolutionary subject, and looked for other kinds of radical subjectivity, leading many of them to support what became known as 'identity politics', centring on the politics of 'experience'. Generally, they rejected the notion that class location was the primary determinant of consciousness. Rather, it stemmed from the human psyche or language.

What most of them had in common—Deleuze and Guattari, Lyotard, Derrida, post-Marxist feminists, such as Haraway and Barrett, Laclau and Mouffe, Habermas and Heller, to name but a few, was a rejection of any attempt to marry democracy with proletarian emancipation, entailing an historical teleology and the transcendence of capitalism. They fought shy of any explicit 'grand narrative'. They had little sympathy with Marxism's account of the working class as *the* revolutionary subject, the privileging of 'science' over other forms of human knowledge, along with the 'knowing' vanguard Party, and finally the implicit assumptions about democracy, which owing to an over-simple class analysis, could not accommodate differences of value and identity.[86] Indeed, the post-Marx-

---

83 Gramsci, *SPN*, p. 144.
84 Jacques Derrida, *Specters of Marx, the State of the Debt, the Work of Mourning, and the New International*, trans. P. Kamuf, and intro. Bernd Magnus and Stephen Cullenburg (London: Routledge), p. 75.
85 Goran Therborn, *From Marxism to Post-Marxism?* Verso, London, 2008, pp. 165-6.
86 Simon Tormey and Jules Townshend, *Key Thinkers from Critical Theory to Post-Marxism* (London: Sage, 2006), pp. 5-6.

ist prioritisation of lived experience and its plurality led them to argue that in political terms democracy was the supreme value, whether of a 'radical' (Laclau and Mouffe) or liberal (Heller and Habermas) stripe. In the light of the Soviet experience, rather than opt for some form of substantive equality on an authoritarian basis, they chose democracy as the preferable ideal. They devoted little attention to thinking about how possible substantive economic, social and political arrangements would promote human freedom. Moving away from the classic Marxist interest in political economy, they derived their inspiration from the paradigms of language and psychoanalysis. Nevertheless, in all probability they had substantive egalitarian commitments at least by default. From this we might deduce that for them a radical egalitarian had to wear two distinct 'hats', one democratic, the other egalitarian, and that Marx' and Marxism's problem was the assumption that a proletarian victory in the 'battle of democracy' would automatically lead to a substantive egalitarianism.

Of all the Post-Marxist thinkers, perhaps Laclau and Mouffe were perhaps the most troubled by the leadership issue, as the title of their influential book *Hegemony and Socialist Strategy*[87] suggests. In a sense like Marx, they forthrightly distanced themselves from the 'Jacobin imaginary' of the French Revolution,[88] but held that unfortunately Marx's own deterministic and teleological discourse that privileged workers' struggles over any other, and thereby 'its' Party, helped create a regime as equally brutal as Robespierre's in the Soviet Union and elsewhere. For them the sites of conflict, of 'antagonism' in the modern world had proliferated, and were no longer confined to the class struggle, or could be explained within its terms. The champions of radicalism, of 'radical democracy', were the New Social Movements, of race, ethnicity and gender, of identity politics, as well as the single issue campaigners for peace and the environment. The struggle for socialism was only part of an ongoing for the democratization of all spheres of society that began with the French Revolution of 1789, one of its 'moments', which involved challenging subordination in social life in whatever form.[89] Rather than a progressive hegemony being a semi-automatic reflex of class struggle, as implied at least in pre-Gramscian Marxism, it had to be politically constructed. Building on Gramsci's notion of hegemony, the Left had to 'articulate' freedom and equality with democracy, as opposed to the Right's

---

87 Ernesto Laclau and Chantal Mouffe, *Hegemony and Socialist Strategy* (hereafter *HSS*), Verso, London, 1985.
88 Laclau and Mouffe, *HSS*, pp. 2; 152; 172; 177.
89 *Ibid.*, p. 155.

anti-egalitarian conception of freedom.[90] Given the 'radically open character of the social', the experience of democracy 'should consist of the recognition of the multiplicity of social logics along with the necessity of their articulation', which should be 'constantly re-created and re-negotiated.'[91] Laclau and Mouffe proposed a 'democratic revolution', consisting of the 'multiplication of spaces and ... institutional diversification.' This would allow for a genuinely anti-authoritarian hegemony to arise through some form of discourse developed by the New Social Movements. Thus, just as Eurocommunists in the 1970s 'de-Leninized' Gramsci's notion of hegemony to justify their final reconciliation with capitalism, so Laclau and Mouffe embraced a 'de-Leninized' version in which the 'Party' is ruled out as a vehicle for radical political mobilisation *tout court*.

Interestingly, Laclau and Mouffe were closer to some of Marx's 'spirits' than some of their detractors would seem to allow. Just as Marx sought to do, they wanted to 'decentre' the role intellectuals in the dynamic of social transformation, even if that entailed encouraging a 'polyphony of voices', rather than an 'irreducible discursive identity'.[92] There is a sense of a 'utopia-in-the-making' through constructing 'new' principles from the 'old', as suggested in the notion of an unfolding 'democratic revolution', realizing Marx's ideal of a society in which the 'freedom of each is a condition for the freedom of all'.[93] This process for Laclau and Mouffe was also fostered by 'extra-discursive' conditions, which implied a notion of condition-dependency. This meant that the political terrain was shaped by 'objective' factors created by modern capitalism, for example, the commodification of social life outside the sphere of production, creating the ethos of a consumer society and an ecological backlash.[94] Nevertheless, whatever these circumstances were like, Laclau and Mouffe highlighted the irreducible psychological dimensions of human antagonism. Employing Lacan's psychoanalytic theory, all human beings experienced a primordial 'lack' of a 'full' identity arising from the trauma of separation from the mother in early childhood. The blocked identity could very easily be blamed on the 'Other'.[95] The only way to ensure non-authoritarian outcomes from this form of conflict was through a democratization of social relations.

90 *Ibid.*, p. 166.
91 *Ibid.*, p. 188.
92 *Ibid.*, p. 191.
93 *Ibid.*, p. 183.
94 *Ibid.*, pp. 161–2.
95 Laclau and Mouffe, *HSS*, p. 125.

Laclau and Mouffe in a sense were representative of the post-Marxist 'turn', in wanting to expunge from radical theory any hint of potential authoritarianism by strongly reaffirming its democratic commitments. Yet in terms of 'leadership' this came at a price. Just as Derrida was vague about the content of his proposed 'new international',[96] so they advocated a 'radical democracy' without any precise institutional prescriptions. We are left with little sense of what a 'post-Marxist' political intervention might look like except in the most general terms. Perhaps we could not expect anything more, given the historical collapse of Communism and post-Marxism's 'social being' firmly located in the academy.

Conclusion

What we have traced is how Marx's anti-Jacobin leadership principles came under increasing stress as the kind of reality as depicted in *The Communist Manifesto* refused to unfold, that in fact the attempt to articulate democracy with a substantive freedom and equality for all, in itself proved to be paradoxical: where Marxists took democracy seriously, especially in Western Europe the majority of the working class were not prepared to make significant inroads into private property, and where Marxists took social equality and social ownership seriously, they dispensed with democracy. In other words, in the East Marxists surrendered to the Jacobin temptation, and in the West any Jacobin temptation gave way to a *de facto* Bernsteinian revisionism. Put another way Marx's attempted synthesis of principles aiming to resolve the leadership paradox grounded upon a dialectical ontology, proved to be too fragile as the empirical wills of the working class diverged from the demanding ideal of self-emancipation. Of course, this divergence could be interpreted as something preordained, as an accompaniment to the growth of instrumental rationality, as Weberians or Critical Theorists would have it, or as the outcome of class struggle as Marxists of whatever variety would continue to claim. Nevertheless, if 'reality' is not striving towards 'thought', the most well-constructed leadership principles based upon mutual consent, enabling us to realize a radical egalitarian future, are bound to have little traction even in Marxist terms. Thus, whatever theoretical consistency there may be, the requirements of political intervention in a world not fully congenial to these principles meant that they could not all be applied equally at the same time. Indeed, in Kautsky's case it would seem that the cost of maintaining these principles was a form of political quietism, whereas for Lenin the price of intervention was the corruption of their meaning. As for Gramsci, whatever his earlier syndicalist inclina-

---

96 Derrida, *Specters of Marx*, p. 8.

tions and later working class self-emancipatory aspirations, the defeat of the Turin Factory Councils and his Leninist turn meant that a question mark hung over how the Marxist Party would represent the empirical wills of its putative constituents, of how *they* would 'educate' the Party. The post-Marxist response to the paradox of leadership was, as we have seen, to jettison the whole idea of a political party, and put their trust in democratic principles to effect social change.

Whether there is a 'genetic link' between Marxism's attempt to resolve theoretically the leadership paradox and the historical paradox between Marxist theory ('taking a lead') and practice ('leading by the nose'), the answer as the forgoing discussion suggests has to be prefaced by a question: which Marxism? The 'Marxism' of Marx? Of Kautsky? Of Lenin? Of Gramsci? In the language of post-Marxists, Marxism itself in having to adapt to inclement conditions became something of a 'floating signifier'. Nevertheless, such a response ignores the possibility of another paradox: if 'reality' is not 'striving' towards thought, there is the danger of an anti-utopian utopianism that does not give sufficient consideration to non-capitalist and non-class sources of power (especially bureaucracy and patriarchy), conflict and oppression even more evident in an epoch of what we may term 'mature modernity'. If this is so, even with socialised production relations as advocated by Marx and his followers, leadership in an institutional sense may be around for some time. Indeed, Kautsky perhaps alone among the classical Marxists recognised that developed socialised production relations were built on a complex division of labour, that required coordination and expertise, that is leadership if by another name. And we have already noted that some twentieth century Marxists proposed a multi-party democracy in a post-capitalist society. Such thoughts may render a less optimistic Marxism, indeed a post-Marxism of some sort, but they may have slightly more historical purchase.[97]

---

97 See footnote 19.

Donald D. Searing & Marco R. Steenbergen

Virtues and Vices of Liberal Democratic Leadership

Introduction

The aim of every political constitution is, or ought to be, first to obtain for rulers men who possess most wisdom to discern, and most virtue to pursue, the common good of the society, and in the next place, to take the most effectual precautions for keeping them virtuous whilst they continue to hold their public trust (James Madison).[1]

The quality of leadership in modern liberal democracies is a subject that for fifty years has been neglected by political theorists and empirical researchers alike.[2] During the same period, public confidence in democracy's political leaders has collapsed, leaving in its wake widespread discontent and confusion about appropriate standards. What is an excellent liberal democratic leader? What are the criteria by which leaders should be judged? As political scientists, we ought to be able to offer publics and politicians convincing standards justified by normative theory and grounded in empirical research.

We will argue that leadership is an essential component of any comprehensive theory of liberal democracy that addresses feasible as opposed to ideal models of such regimes.[3] And we will argue that good liberal democratic leaders are those who excel at the motivations and skills needed to protect and promote liberal democratic institutions and cultures. We will identify key motivations and skills, which we will call 'civic virtues'; and we will link them to liberal democratic leadership's principal functions: regime building, governing, accountability, and representation.

---

1   James Madison, Alexander Hamilton and John Jay, *The Federalist Papers*, intro. Clinton Rossiter (London: Penguin Group, 1961), Federalist No. 57.
2   Suzanne Dovi, *The Good Representative* (Oxford: Blackwell, 2006).
3   András Körösényi, 'Political Representation in Leader Democracy', *Government and Opposition*, vol 40, no. 3 (2005), pp. 358–78.

From this perspective, we offer a complementary essay to William Galston's celebrated article on the virtues of liberal democratic citizenship.[4] Although Galston considered leadership too, he concentrated on desirable capabilities for liberal democracy's citizens. We will expand on and deepen his suggestions about leadership virtues and add to them an account of plausible leadership vices. Our goal is to develop normatively informed concepts suitable for a dialogue between democratic theory and empirical research programs and, in particular, for an empirical research program that we are developing on this topic. Leadership's virtues and vices are practiced in institutional settings, but they are fundamentally psychological phenomena. Therefore research programs must focus on their psychological dynamics, as well as on their political contexts and consequences. And our discussions in this paper will link the political theory of virtues and vices to relevant work in political psychology.

What do Citizens want?

To formulate prescriptions for democracy, we need first of all to listen to the views of democracy's citizens. So, what kind of government do citizens want? There is much confusion here, but there is also some consensus. Survey research persistently finds one very striking cross-national pattern: strong support for the idea of liberal democratic government, and strong dissatisfaction with most liberal democratic leaders.[5] Thus, citizens endorse liberalism's ideals of liberty and rights, even if they disagree about the specifics. And they endorse democracy's electoral and civic participation, even when they do not practice what they preach.[6] In short, they like liberal democracy. But they don't like liberal democracy's leaders.

Public dissatisfaction with politicians and government officials has plummeted steadily since the 1960s. In fourteen out of sixteen countries for which data are available, confidence in public officials has reached lower levels than most observers believed possible.[7] Citizens question both the competence and character of their leaders. This mistrust, a disappointment over absent virtues and a cynicism about present vices, feeds

---

[4] William Galston, 'Liberal Virtues', *American Political Science Review*, 82, 4 (1988), pp. 1277–90.
[5] Russell J. Dalton, *Citizen Politics: Public Opinion and Political Parties in Advanced Industrial Democracies*, 4th edn. (Washington, D.C.: CQ Press, 2006).
[6] Donald D. Searing, Pamela Johnston Conover and Ivor Crewe, 'The Elusive Ideal of Equal Citizenship: Political Theory and Political Psychology in the United States and Great Britain', *Journal of Politics*, 66 (2004), pp. 1036–68.
[7] Russell J. Dalton, *Citizen Politics*, pp. 252–6.

political corruption and is in turn fed by it.[8] Candidate evaluations have become increasingly important in campaigns and elections, even in parliamentary systems where citizens vote more for parties than for people. Views about leading party figures interact with partisanship and issue preferences in determining votes.[9] Criteria for such evaluations typically emphasize competence: 'They all talk a good game', complained Marie-Claude Verrier about the candidates for the French presidential election, 'But none of them has any idea how to fix the problems of France.' And they emphasized integrity: 'All the politicians smile and make promises', charges Sébastien Gomard, 'and then they disappoint'.[10]

Competence and Integrity

Citizens want governments that are effective in running the shop and solving problems. They want governments that are reasonably free of large scale corruption. And to guide such governments they want political leaders who are suited for the job by intellect and by temperament, by skills and by character. Some of the most desirable skills and character traits seem obvious, but many turn out on closer inspection to be little more than empty pieties that politicians parade for public consumption. Other skills and character traits, however, are not at all obvious, because recognizing them and appreciating how they work requires more knowledge than most citizens possess about regime building, governing, accountability, and representation, about the specific functions that political leaders perform in contemporary liberal democratic states.

Discovering the virtues and vices that are, in the abstract, needed for good government is not a chimerical quest but instead a practical challenge for democratic theory and political psychology. We need to know what the key virtues and vices are, and how they work, in order to better select and evaluate political leaders and improve the institutional learning mechanisms that shape and reinforce these traits. First, however, we must wade through the conceptual underbrush that has accumulated during fifty years of neglect and that blocks our pathway to understanding what leadership in liberal democracy is and why it matters. Some democratic theorists (not ordinary citizens, however) regard 'liberal democratic *leadership*' as an oxymoron. And some social scientists (again, not ordinary citizens) think that it does not matter much at all.

---

8   Donatella della Porta, 'Social Capital, Beliefs in Government and Political Corruption', in Susan J. Pharr and Robert D. Putnam (eds.), *Disaffected Democracies* (Princeton: Princeton University Press, 2000), pp. 202–30.
9   Russell J. Dalton, *Citizen Politics*, pp. 215–20.
10 *New York Times* (28 March 2007).

What is Leadership in a Liberal Democracy?

For liberal democracy, leadership poses two problems. One arises from its difficulties in serving, at the same time, individual liberty and majority rule. The other arises from its inconsistencies with each core project. To bring to light leadership's place in liberal democracy's world, we need to define leadership, define liberal democracy, and then consider the relationship between them.

Leadership and Democracy

'Leadership', writes the political historian, James MacGregor Burns, 'is one of the most observed and least understood phenomena on earth.'[11] There are at least as many definitions of leadership as there are of 'democracy', the classic example of an over-stretched concept. At least sixty-five different classification schemes have been published during the past fifty years.[12]

Nearly all of the earliest and most persistent definitions emphasize 'agency' in shaping policies, institutions and perspectives.[13] Thus, in political science, leadership is typically seen as an activity that produces social, economic and political changes by shaping the needs and preferences of others.[14] Political leadership is valued for its instrumental utility. It achieves goals that leaders share with citizens, sometimes with all of them, more often with only some. Most importantly, leaders modify followers' minds as well as adapting to them. This is the essence of their authority, the engine of their success.[15] 'Follower-leaders', are leaders in name only. For the essence of leadership is agency, where the agent's lead is followed,

> ...because he is loved, admired, respected or feared, because he can coerce, persuade or manipulate group members, because he can offer psychic as well as material rewards and punishments, or because compliance with his wishes is sanctioned by habit, traditional or legal-rational behavior norms.[16]

The amount of agency that leaders exercise is remarkably variable. Very few leaders have very much agency. But because 'leadership' is a goal-oriented concept, we imagine it less in terms of 'prototypes' than in

---

11 James MacGregor Burns, *Leadership* (New York: Harper and Row, 1978), p. 2.
12 Peter G. Northouse, *Leadership: Theory and Practice* (London: Sage Publications, 2004).
13 Ralph M. Stogdill, *Handbook of Leadership* (New York: Free Press., 1974), p. 7ff.
14 James MacGregor Burns, *Leadership* (New York: Harper and Row, 1978), p. 3.
15 Donald D. Searing, 'The Psychology of Political Authority: A Causal Mechanism of Political Learning Through Persuasion and Manipulation', *Political Psychology* 16 (1995), pp. 667–96.
16 Lewis J. Edinger, 'Editor's Introduction', in Lewis J. Edinger (ed.), *Political Leadership in Industrialized Societies* (New York: Wiley, 1967), p. 5.

terms of ideal or extreme examples like Churchill, Roosevelt or DeGaulle.[17] The prototypes are less exciting: they listen a lot and offer a little inspiration during election campaigns; they mind the shop and tend the machinery of national parliaments and local politics; they manage wearisome committees and patient discussions with constituents. They may influence their colleagues, their constituents and their political cultures. But, typically, 'it's little grains of sand and little drops of water all the time'.[18] Apart from great upheavals and crises, contemporary leaders in most liberal democracies work from institutional positions that constrain their thinking and behavior as much as they enable it.

The concept of 'Liberal Democracy' is not only ambiguous but also contested. Let us try to span its spectrum with help from Albert Weale, Benjamin Barber and Barry Holden.

Thus, 'democracy' is a regime where (a) 'important public decisions on questions of law and policy depend, directly or indirectly, upon public opinion, expressed both formally and informally',[19] and where (b) there exists a democratic community that honors the equality inherent in the concept 'citizen' and practices civic engagement.[20] The adjective 'liberal' modifies the noun 'democracy' by protecting individual freedom from collective power, particularly from majority rule and majority prejudices.[21] Hence, all citizens need the liberal protections of (c) equal political, civil, economic and social rights, and (d) restrictions on concentrated power in governments, corporations and communities. Today's liberal democracies exhibit these characteristics in quite different degrees and mixtures. But it would be a concept-stretch too far to count as liberal democratic any regime that does not possess at least a reasonable modicum of (a), (b), (c) and (d).[22]

Inconsistencies and Contributions

Now, since democracy is committed to majority rule and popular sovereignty, while liberalism is committed to individual liberty and limited government, tensions between liberal democracy's democratic and liberal principles are inevitable. They arise when the laws and public opinion of majorities interfere with the efforts of individual citizens to

---

17 Susan T. Fiske and Shelley E. Taylor, *Social Cognition*, 2nd edn. (New York: McGraw Hill, 1991), p. 110.
18 Donald D. Searing, *Westminster's World: Understanding Political Roles* (Cambridge: Harvard University Press, 1994), p. 35.
19 Albert Weale, *Democracy* (New York: Palgrave, 1999), p. 14.
20 Benjamin Barber, *Strong Democracy* (Berkeley: University of California Press, 1984), p. 230ff.
21 Barry Holden, *Understanding Liberal Democracy* (London: Philip Allen, 1988), pp. 12–13.
22 Giovanni Sartori, *The Theory of Democracy Revisited* (Chatham, New Jersey: Chatham House Publishers, 1987), ch. 13.

construct their own lives for themselves.²³ Liberalism has always worried about democracy's comfort with conformity, while democracy has always had difficulties with liberalism's atomistic tendencies. This has been a marriage of paramount importance, but never an easy relationship. And leadership is caught in the middle. The effectiveness of its virtues in serving one side can undercut the other.

Both partners further suspect leadership because its essential agency feels incompatible with their essential missions. Leadership leads in particular directions and thereby privileges particular goals and ways of life, which potentially constricts citizens' choices and constrains majority rule.²⁴

Liberalism does not accept the idea that particular ways of life are preferable for most circumstances. Instead, it is dedicated to maximizing individual liberty by enabling citizens to explore different goals and construct for themselves ways of life that they prefer and choose.²⁵ The liberal state should merely establish a system of rights to protect individuals and their choices from interference.²⁶ To the extent that leadership tries to shape citizens' aims, values and ways of life by manipulative or coercive processes, its activities are inconsistent with liberalism's core project.

For democracy, the problem with leadership is likewise its agency. From the theories of Pareto, Mosca, Michels, Weber, and Schumpeter to recent empirical studies like those of John Higley, it is clear that elites have always been central actors in liberal democratic regimes.²⁷ And even fenced in by constitutions and institutions, their agency inherently reaches beyond existing public preferences.²⁸ Leadership threatens majority rule and popular sovereignty. It can, of course, facilitate them by working within frameworks of widely shared goals and assumptions. But it also gets in the way.

Liberals are pleased that leadership gets in democracy's way. In fact they design constitutions to ensure that it does. James Madison and John Stuart Mill worried about destructive popular passions and hoped to use

---

23 Andrew Heywood, *Political Ideologies: An Introduction* (New York: Palgrave Macmillan, 2003), pp. 43–4.
24 William A. Galston, *Liberal Purposes: Goods, Virtues and Diversity in the Liberal State* (Cambridge: Cambridge University Press, 1991), pp. 213–17.
25 John Galston, *Liberalism* (Minneapolis: University of Minnesota Press, 1986); Amy Gutmann, *Identity in Democracy* (Princeton: Princeton University Press, 2003), p. 5; John Rawls, *A Theory of Justice* (Cambridge: Harvard University Press, 1971), p. 511; Raymond Plant, *Modern Political Thought* (Oxford: Basil Blackwell, 1991), pp. 110–15.
26 Michael J. Sandel, *Democracy's Discontent* (Cambridge: Harvard University Press, 1996).
27 John Higley, 'Democracy and Elites', in Fredrik Engelstad and Trygve Gulbrandsen (eds.), *Comparative Studies of Social and Political Elites* (Amsterdam: Elsevier, 2007), pp. 250–1.
28 András Körösényi, 'Political Representation in Leader Democracy'.

democracy's leaders to head them off.[29] Hamilton concurred.[30] The public makes mistakes for lack of information or because it is misled by 'ambitious, avaricious or desperate' men who, to serve themselves, whip up support for divisive and undesirable policies. In such cases, it is the duty of the people's representatives to discourage, divert, and delay such programs till the public has had 'time and opportunity for more cool and sedate reflection.' Ironically, liberalism turns to a leadership it distrusts to defend itself against a democracy that it distrust even more.

In sum, the theory of liberal democracy, which focuses on ideals, has difficulties with leadership because it limits both liberalism and democracy. But, at the same time, in the everyday world of contemporary liberal democratic states, leadership protects and promotes liberalism and democracy, mediates their tensions and even defends the one against the other. This is the critical contribution that enables us to integrate robustly normative theory with empirical research.

Does Leadership Matter?

Political leadership is about agency, and there have always been powerful traditions in the social sciences eager to depreciate agency's importance, either by excluding it from their explanations or by treating it as a constant.[31] Does political leadership actually matter then?

Greats to Traits

Would Germany have been united without Bismark? Would the October Revolution have occurred without Lenin's arrival at the Finland Station? Such questions recall the 'Great Men in History' debates of the nineteenth and early twentieth centuries. Thomas Carlyle famously argued that social phenomena could be fully explained by the great acts of great men, and legions of historians provided supportive examples and accounts.[32]

When this heroic perspective on leadership fell out of favor, historians passed the baton to sociologists, psychologists and researchers in management studies who constructed its more democratic successor, the 'Trait Approach'.[33] The effectiveness of leadership's agency would now be explained by distinctive qualities of leaders that were much more common and uniform across all fields and contexts. Hundreds of studies cata-

---

29 James Madison, Alexander Hamilton and John Jay, *The Federalist Papers*, Federalist #53; John Stuart Mill, *Considerations on Representative Government* (New York: Bobbs- Merrill, 1958).
30 James Mill, Alexander Hamilton and John Jay, *The Federalist Papers*, Federalist #71.
31 Alexander Rosenberg, *Philosophy of Social Science* (Oxford: Oxford University Press, 1988).
32 Sidney Hook, *The Hero in History* (Boston: Beacon Press, 1955), p. 195.
33 Alvin Gouldner, *Studies in Leadership: Leadership and Democratic Action* (New York: Harper and Brothers, 1950), p. 21ff.

logued personality characteristics like self-control, courage and flexibility, and skills like good judgment and quick decisions taking, which marked particular people as well-suited to shape events and institutions.

Social Forces to Situations

The great men in history approach was undermined by social theorists like Hegel, Marx, Spencer, Spengler, Weber and Durkheim, who maintained that major events were best explained not by great men but instead by 'Social Forces', by evolving, context-shaping processes, systemic and institutional. Political leadership was simply a transmission belt for these powerful factors, they claimed, and not itself an important part of the explanation. This type of long-term deterministic thinking about social causation persists in many areas of contemporary social science, where it generates theoretically and methodologically sophisticated research that systematically ignores political leadership's explanatory significance.[34] Thus, historical institutionalists in comparative politics, neo-realists and world system theorists in international relations, and rational choice theorists in economics and political science all suggest that the driving forces behind political outcomes are systemic and institutional conditions that determine the behavior of the actors involved.[35]

Just as the great men in history approach to leadership was discredited at the macro level by social forces, so its immediate successor, the 'Trait Approach', lost out at the micro level to a 'situationist' attack which, like its social forces cousin, was quite deterministic and 'democratic'. Leaders, according to the 'Situationist Approach', are not born with unusual leadership traits that enable them to shape events and institutions. Instead they are simply cogs in the wheels of their immediate contexts. Either they are selected for very specific characteristics that fit pre-existing institutional roles or, once selected for their positions, they learn the appropriate skills there. Furthermore, they adapt to the goals of their colleagues and 'followers'. They succeed by consulting and assisting group members, sometimes even by helping them 'feel comfortable' about themselves.[36] According to the Situationist Approach, it makes no sense to talk about leadership traits in general, because institutional contexts are so control-

---

34 Cf Paul Pierson, *Politics in Time* (Princeton: Princeton University Press, 2004).
35 Michael Taylor, 'Structure, Culture and Action in the Explanation of Social Change', *Politics and Society*, 17 (1989), pp. 115–62; Alexander Wendt, 'The Agent-Structure Problem in International Relations Theory', *International Organization*, 4 (1987), pp. 335–70.
36 Peter G. Northouse, *Leadership: Theory and Practice* (London: Sage Publications, 2004), pp. 87–9.

ling that leaders who seem self-confident and dominant in one can readily become insecure and disoriented in another).[37]

Social forces and situations won the day but not the argument, for in seeing off their competitors they went to extremes in the opposite direction. The balance lies in seeing how structure and agency are interdependent and understanding that the relationship between them is often the most important part of the explanation. Identical structures do not cause identical desires and beliefs in political actors because institutional rules and incentives are integrated by such actors with the desires and beliefs that they bring to their roles.[38] Indeed, one of the most influential applications of agency by political leaders is the construction and reconstruction of political institutions themselves. 'Let us remember, then', John Stuart Mill wrote,

> that political institutions ... are the work of men, owe their origin and their whole existence to human will. Men did not wake on a summer morning and find them sprung up. Neither do they resemble trees which, once planted, 'are aye growing' while men 'are sleeping'. In every stage of their existence they are made what they are by human voluntary agency.[39]

Character versus Institutions

How, in light of these debates, are we to think about the foundations for good government? There is an institution-based answer to this question which concentrates on constitutional rules and shares assumptions with the social forces theorists and situationists. And there is a character-based answer to this question which focuses on leadership virtues and echoes the great man and trait traditions.

Many liberal theorists do not believe in leadership virtues and certainly do not wish to rely upon them, for they sympathize with the doctrine of psychological egoism and tend to assume that leaders are inevitably motivated by selfish desires. Hence, the governments that liberal theorists prescribe are governments of good rules, not good people.[40] These rules are carefully constructed institutional arrangements that control self-interested politicians by manipulating their incentives so that they will behave in ways that promote the general interest.

---

37 Peter G. Northouse,, *Leadership*; Ralph M. Stogdill, *Handbook of Leadership* (New York: Free Press, 1974); Alvin Gouldner, *Studies in Leadership: Leadership and Democratic Action* (New York: Harper and Brothers, 1950).
38 Martin Hollis, *The Philosophy of Social Science* (Cambridge: Cambridge University Press, 1994); Michael Taylor, 'Structure, Culture and Action in the Explanation of Social Change'; Fred Greenstein, *Personality and Politics* (Chicago: Markham, 1969), pp. 40–57.
39 John Stuart Mill, *Considerations on Representative Government*, p. 5.
40 William A. Galston, 'Pluralism and Civic Virtue', paper presented at the University of North Carolina (Chapel Hill, 2007); Suzanne Dovi, *The Good Representative*.

This mechanistic Mandevillean model was, in the eighteenth century, an Enlightenment dogma shared by Immanuel Kant, David Hume, Adam Smith and James Madison among many others: 'the powers of each selfish inclination' could be, by constitutional design, 'so arranged that one moderates or destroys the ruinous effects of the other. The effect is the same as if none of them existed'.[41] The trick was to bring into alignment the self interests of leaders with the general interests of society. This could be accomplished through checks and balances. But it could be accomplished most securely through regular elections where, to achieve office or to avoid losing it, ambitious politicians would be compelled to satisfy the peoples' preferences.[42]

Political psychologists reject such one-directional models where the behavior of leaders is determined by institutional settings. In their view, institutions circumscribe behavior but do not dictate it. Structure and agency are interdependent, not institution-determined. And their interdependence is negotiated (and can be manipulated) by the political actors involved. Fear of losing office, for instance, has been blunted by political leaders who have introduced mechanisms like safe seats and positions on party lists. Good rules are important, but character counts as well. Madisonian faith in the magical powers of institutional constraints has worn thin over the last two hundred years, despite the continuing support of macro determinists, micro situationists, and rational choice institutionalists who sometimes sound more fundamentalist than Madison himself.

Against Madison's confident arguments that artfully designed democratic institutions would produce good government, Michels found mechanisms that aligned leaders' self interests with the 'iron law of oligarchy.'[43] No doubt he exaggerated as well. Still, too many liberal democratic politicians over the past two hundred years have come to care less, not more, about the common interest than about their own self interests or the reckless pursuit of their obsessions. Too many have rewarded 'us' and ignored 'them.' Too many political spins have spun into official deceits in evading the rule of law, manipulating voting arrangements, undermining rules of the game and straining the system's limits. Surely the burden today is on our institutional fundamentalists to support their sanguine deterministic claims with convincing empirical evidence. Until then, we

---

41 Roy Porter, *Enlightenment* (London: Penguin Books, 2000), pp. 262–3.
42 Robert S. Erikson, Michael B. MacKuen and James A. Stimson, 'Public Opinion and Policy: Causal Flow in a Macro System', in Jeff Manza et al (eds.), *Navigating Public Opinion* (Oxford: Oxford University Press, 2002).
43 James Madison, Alexander Hamilton and John Jay, *The Federalist Papers*; Robert Michels, *Political Parties* (New York: Collier Books, 1962).

deserve more plausible models that take both character and institutions seriously.[44]

What are Virtues and Vices?

Virtues

The Greek word 'areté' translates into modern English as 'virtue', but it is closer in meaning to our ideas about 'excellence of character', to traits, like intelligence and integrity, that citizens would like to see in their political leaders.[45]

Virtues are embedded in social structures and cultures. Their contextual nature is revealed by the incompatibilities among lists drawn up in golden age Greece for leading a successful life in city states (justice, wisdom, courage, self-control), by Christian theologians who focused on pathways to heaven (faith, hope, charity and humility), or by Benjamin Franklin thinking about respectability and prosperity in colonial America (cleanliness, silence, industry, thrift).[46]

Virtues are 'practices' defined in relation to particular activities in which they are a form of excellence and toward which they are directed. MacIntyre offers politics and teaching as examples.[47] We will define liberal democratic leadership's virtuous practices in relation to the principal functions that leaders perform in contemporary liberal democracies: regime building, governing, accountability and representation. The psychological core of the virtues of liberal democratic leadership, then, will be the key motivations and skills that prepare leaders to perform these activities well.[48]

Vices

Vices, by contrast, ('kakia') are faults, defects or flaws.[49] These must be considered too, for they are often the excesses or defects of particular virtues, in other words, extremes on the same continua. They are exactly

---

44 Suzanne Dovi, *The Good Representative*; William A. Galston, 'Pluralism and Civic Virtue'.
45 Some contemporary commentators refer to virtues as 'excellences', which is an awkward noun when alternatives like talents, abilities, capabilities, qualifications or capacities might do. Because these concepts are less heavily value laden than 'virtue' or 'excellence', empirical social scientists are more comfortable with them. By contrast, citizens want the strong evaluative connotations, which we might put back in with adjectives like desirable, admirable and valuable. (Alasdair MacIntyre, *After Virtue* (Notre Dame: University of Notre Dame Press, 1984), pp. 122-3; William A. Galston, *Liberal Purposes*; Aristotle, *The Nicomachean Ethics* (Oxford: Oxford University Press, 1925), p. xxvi).
46 Alasdair MacIntyre, *After Virtue*, pp. 181-7.
47 Ibid., p. 187 ff.
48 Suzanne Dovi, *The Good Representative*.
49 Aristotle, *The Nicomachean Ethics*, p. xxvi.

what, following Aristotle, good government needs to avoid or, following Madison, to recognize and harness.

In Aristotle's ethics, extreme manifestations of desirable dispositions are undesirable. With each virtue, there is usually a more, the excess, and a less, the defect, and then the 'desirable mean'.[50] This desirable intermediate approach, Aristotle's moderation, must be identified with reference to particular institutions and circumstances.[51] For empirical work in political psychology, this curvilinear model creates methodological challenges. Tolerance, ambition, compromise and many other character traits are currently measured on linear scales that treat unqualified endorsements, not 'desirable means', as the optimal dispositions.

Madison, of course, regarded some of these moral vices, the excesses, as invaluable incentives that could be harnessed and compelled to work as political virtues. He wrote that virtues like a sense of duty did have some motivational force. But he thought these sorts of motivations too weak to ensure good government, to overcome the temptations to which politicians are always drawn.[52] Virtues might face politicians in the right direction; but *moving* them in the right direction required the spur of vices like anger, pride, vanity, ambition or fear, in his view much more powerful and dependable dispositions.[53]

Moral versus Civic

Madison's idea that moral vices might do as political virtues recalls Plato's 'noble lies', Machiavelli's 'virtù', and contemporary discussions of the 'problem of dirty hands.' These puzzles are rooted in the important distinction between moral and civic virtues.

Moral virtues like courage, charity or cleanliness are ends in themselves. They are intrinsic goods, valued for their own sake in the sense that they bring goodness of character to the people who practice them.[54] This is Aristotle's archetypal view of moral virtues, and it is quite self-centered, focused less on serving society than on helping oneself become a better person.[55] Moral virtues prescribe being well by doing well in a 'practice' of reciprocal causation. We become virtuous by doing virtuous

---

50 David Ross, *Aristotle*, 6th edn. (London: Routledge, 1995), pp. 202–3.
51 Alasdair MacIntyre, *After Virtue*, p. 154.
52 James Madison, Alexander Hamilton and John Jay, *The Federalist Papers*, Federalist #51–63.
53 Leonard R. Sorenson, 'Madison on Sympathy, Virtue and Ambition in the Federalist Papers', *Polity*, 27 (1995), pp. 431–46.
54 Alasdair MacIntyre, *After Virtue*, p. 148.
55 David Ross, *Aristotle*, p. 235.

acts which, in turn, reinforce our dispositions to behave virtuously, to do the right thing, and to do it from the right motive.[56]

By contrast, civic virtues like toleration, independence and law-abidingness are instrumental. They serve ends beyond themselves and are judged first and foremost by their contributions to sustaining a political community.[57] Thus, liberal democratic civic virtues serve the liberal democratic institutions in which they are embedded: governmental, social, economic, and cultural. They conserve and are therefore conservative. Their commitment to help sustain a regime implies that this regime is basically desirable and should be improved, not dismantled. They are defined in terms of their hypothesized institutional consequences, definitions which require empirical investigation. We need to know how they work psychologically and how they are constrained, enabled, selected for and modified by the political institutions where they are practiced.

What is the relationship between civic and moral virtues? Many citizens say they want good leaders who are also good people. But it is not even clear that the virtues of the good citizen and the good person are the same. They may overlap, but they also differ because citizenship virtues are instrumental and focused on sustaining political institutions.[58] Nor is it clear that the civic virtues and moral virtues of political leaders are the same. To perform their instrumental civic duties well, politicians may sometimes need to take actions that would, outside the world of politics, be regarded as signs of questionable moral character.[59]

In sum, the civic virtues of liberal democratic leaders are dispositions 'to act rightly' in certain kinds of institutional contexts. These valuable leadership motivations and skills help to preserve and promote liberal democratic regimes in both their liberal and their democratic aspects. The first order of the business of good government, according to John Stuart Mill, is the proper operation of these institutions and thereby their protection.[60] The second is the ability of leaders to invent and adapt new solutions for new problems that their polities face.

---

56 *Ibid.*
57 William A. Galston, 'Pluralism and Civic Virtue'.
58 William A. Galston, *Liberal Purposes*.
59 Michael Walzer, 'Political Action: the Problem of Dirty Hands', *Philosophy and Public Affairs*, 2 (1973), pp. 160–80; Martin Hollis, 'Dirty Hands', *British Journal of Political Science*. 12 (1982), pp. 385–98; Dennis F. Thompson, *Political Ethics and Public Office* (Cambridge: Harvard University Press, 1987); Stephen Garrett, *Conscience and Power: An Examination of Dirty Hands and Political Leadership* (New York: St Martins, 1996); Laurie Calhoun, 'The Problem of "Dirty Hands" and Corrupt Leadership', *The Independent Review*, 8 (2004), pp. 363–85.
60 John Stuart Mill, *Considerations on Representative Government*, pp. 18–20.

The Virtues and Vices of Liberal Democratic Leadership

To understand what liberal democratic leaders are expected to protect and superintend, we need to work with models of existing political systems. But to understand what they might be expected to promote and reform, we need to pay attention to feasible aspects of normative models as well. In other words, we need to focus on how contemporary liberal democracies actually work, but also on what we can expect of them.[61]

Eventually it will be necessary to construct a regime typology and assess key leadership virtues against it, sorting out virtues of leadership in liberal democracies in general, and of types of liberal democracies in particular. First, however, we need to get a general sense of the motivations and skills that political theorists have thought important. We begin with Aristotle, the essential virtues theorist, and with James Madison and John Stuart Mill who, more than most, considered the interactions of leaders' character traits with liberal democratic institutions.

Virtues and Vices Serving Multiple Functions

AMBITION, when held in moderation, is one of Aristotle's moral virtues.[62] As a civic virtue of leadership, its admirable form is the desire to achieve high office primarily to benefit citizens through policies and institutional reforms. Its undesirable form is seeking high office primarily to benefit oneself. Ambition's pervasiveness, constancy and intensity are exaggerated, while its potential for corruption is much commented on. Madison, for example, believed that representatives come out of elections with positive sentiments toward the electorate, but that these are quickly eroded by the exercise of power.[63] Surrounded by worshipful sycophants and applauded by the public, tempted by special interests pushing selfish inclinations and short-sighted perspectives, political leaders can lose their way. Mill had similar concerns.[64] In fact, Harold Lasswell launched the field of political psychology with psychodynamic studies of political leaders whose desire for power drove them, in his famous epigram, 'to displace their private motives on public objects and rationalize their behavior in terms of the public good.'[65] Many are disciplined by Madi-

---

61 Ian Shapiro, *The State of Democratic Theory* (Princeton: Princeton University Press, 2003), p. 2.
62 Aristotle, *The Nicomachean Ethics*.
63 James Madison, Alexander Hamilton and John Jay, *The Federalist Papers*, Federalist #57.
64 John Stuart Mill, *Considerations on Representative Government*, p. 100ff.
65 Harold Lasswell, *Psychopathology and Politics* (New York: Viking Press ,1960 [1930]); Harold Lasswell, *Power and Personality* (New York: Viking Press, 1962 [1948]).

son's institutional constraints. But many are not, and some engage in rigid, self-destructive and dangerous behavior.[66]

HONOR is another strong motive that politicians have for seeking and holding office. It is related to ambition but may be more prevalent and influential. The admirable and moderate form of honor is the disposition to seek respect. Its excess is hubris; and its defect low self-esteem. Aristotle identified the seeking of honor or proper pride as a desirable motivator for political leaders, one less dangerous than wealth.[67] This sense of honor develops from respect shown by others and from a sense of achievement. Madison and Hamilton agreed that the pursuit of honor could lead politicians to the public good, but they had more faith in the spurs of honor's excesses: hubris, fame, pride and vanity, which they proposed to yoke alongside it.[68] Aristotle believed that these excesses were released by intemperance and by luxurious lifestyles, sexual escapades and trappings of office. The danger for liberal democracy is that they encourage political leaders 'to become worshipers of themselves and think themselves entitled to be counted at a hundred times the value of other people...'[69] Equally dangerous is honor's defect, low self-esteem. Leaders with pathologically low self-esteem and high narcissism may be unusual, but in positions of genuine power they cause a great deal of distress.[70]

PRACTICAL WISDOM is one of Aristotle's intellectual virtues, which he explicitly associated with leadership positions.[71] This is a capability for comprehending and constructing one's own well-being (when focused on oneself) and the well being of the political community (when focused on the citizenry). Firmly aimed at taking action, practical wisdom is based on expertise acquired through experience. It is also supported by good judgment, which Aristotle described as a mode of thinking that 'knows the right thing to do without arriving at it by a process of deliberative analysis—a wisdom about details which is found in those who have had a cer-

---

66 Alexander George 'Power as a compensatory Value for Political Leaders', *Journal of Social Issues*, 24 (1968), pp. 29–50; David G. Winter, 'Leader Appeal, Leader Performance, and the Motive Profiles of Leaders and Followers: A Study of American Presidents and Elections', *Journal of Personality and Social Psychology*, 52 (1987), pp. 196–202.
67 David Ross, *Aristotle*.
68 James Madison, Alexander Hamilton and John Jay, *The Federalist Papers*, Federalist #57, Federalist #72.
69 John Stuart Mill, *Considerations on Representative Government*, p. 57.
70 Paul M. Sniderman, *Personality and Democratic Politics* (Berkeley: University of California Press, 1975); Vamik D. Volkan, Norman Itkowitz, and Andrew W. Dod, *Richard Nixon: A Psychobiography* (New York: Columbia University Press, 1997).
71 Aristotle, *The Nicomachean Ethics*.

tain experience in life even if they cannot formulate general principles'[72] This skill has been investigated by Philip Tetlock in a field study examining the efficacy of key attributes of reasoning and decision making, including understanding one's limits, appreciating new evidence, and entertaining counterfactuals.[73] Finally, Aristotle identifies 'understanding' as another virtue that supports practical wisdom. This form of expertise entails being knowledgeable about topics in which one specializes and about major policy questions of the day.[74]

The Function of Regime Building

The instrumental purpose that civic virtues serve in liberal democracies is protecting and promoting the regime. This mandate applies to building key liberal democratic institutions (governmental, economic and social) and core values and practices of civic engagement. Institutions and culture come together in the rules of the game.

RULES OF THE GAME. Because he frames the virtues concept in practices, MacIntyre understands virtues as dispositions to obey certain rules.[75] And obedience to liberal democratic rules of the game may be the quintessential leadership virtue. Mill emphasized its centrality: ' The very existence of some governments, and all that renders others endurable, rests on the practical observance of doctrines of constitutional morality ...'[76] When the attitudes and actions of political leaders undermine the legitimacy of their regime's rules of the game, then they have done the greatest damage that they can do.[77] The appropriate dispositions are driven by a sense of duty to protect these rules and a dutiful approach to governing in general. Madison allowed that such a sense of duty, which is a form of civility, had some motivational force of its own, but he preferred to rely upon sanctions and rewards.[78] This debate continues today in both theoretical and empirical literatures. The issue is whether dutiful action is based more on a desire to engage in appropriate conduct, or on instrumental calculations of costs and benefits.[79]

LIBERAL DEMOCRATIC VALUES. Beyond support for the rules of the game, regime building requires commitments to core liberal democratic

---

72 David Ross, *Aristotle*, p. 225.
73 Philip E. Tetlock, *Expert Political Judgment* (Princeton: Princeton University Press, 2005).
74 Aristotle, *The Nicomachean Ethics*.
75 Alasdair MacIntyre, *After Virtue*, p. 244.
76 John Stuart Mill, *Considerations on Representative Government*, pp. 176–7.
77 Suzanne Dovi, *The Good Representative*.
78 James Madison, Alexander Hamilton and John Jay, *The Federalist Papers*, Federalist #57.
79 James G. March and Johan P. Olsen, *Rediscovering Institutions: The Organizational Basis of Politics* (New York: Free Press, 1989), p. 21ff; Tom March, *Why People Obey the Law* (Princeton: Princeton University Press, 2006).

values. Although core values and their understandings vary across polities, some are shared by all liberal democratic regimes. First, democracy itself, including its appreciation for equality, for a great deal of political equality, some economic equality and, increasingly, social equality as well.[80] Dispositions to support such values accompany support, on the liberal side, for liberty, human rights, tolerance and limited government.[81] Values of the liberal economy are more controversial, because capitalism and liberal democracy are interdependent and at the same time in tension with each other. Capitalism's market economy produces the economic growth and strong middle class that liberal democracies need (Dahl 2000, Ch. 14). But it also produces an economic inequality that undermines the democratic community.[82] There is surprisingly little empirical research on fundamental values that leaders embrace. Most of it appears in political biographies as characterizations of world views. Instruments similar to Rokeach's value scales have, however, been used with some national politicians, including values such as capitalism, community, freedom, participatory democracy, and social progress.[83]

POLITICAL EDUCATION. Good liberal democratic leaders must not only support rules of the game and core values. They must also educate the public in these liberal principles and democratic values and explain their connections with particular policies and practices. Political education builds legitimacy and trust in government and anchors it in attentive publics who scrutinize the conduct of political leaders and hold them to the mark.[84] Good liberal democratic politicians work to enhance the self-governing capacities of citizens, because liberty will only be secure when citizens are self-reliant and able to construct their own lives for themselves.[85] Mill regarded this personal autonomy as the essence of psychological freedom. Liberal democratic governments should be judged, he argued, by how well they perform in giving citizens the tools and guidance that enable them to develop as free human beings.[86] Such govern-

---

80 William A. Galston, *Liberal Purposes*.
81 Ibid., pp. 213–16
82 Frank Cunningham, *Theories of Democracy* (London: Routledge, 2002), pp. 41–51.
83 Milton Rokeach, *The Nature of Human Values* (New York: Free Press, 1973); Ivor Crewe and Donald D. Searing, 'Ideological Change in the British Conservative Party', *American Political Science Review*, 82 (1988), pp. 361–84; Donald D. Searing, 'Measuring Politicans' Values: Administration and Assessment of a Ranking Technique in the British House of Commons', *American Political Science Review*, 72 (1978), pp. 65–79.
84 John Stuart Mill, *Considerations on Representative Government*, pp. 24–5; William A. Galston, *Liberal Purposes*; Suzanne Dovi, *The Good Representative*.
85 William A. Galston, *Liberal Purposes*, p. 222.
86 John Stuart Mill, *Considerations on Representative Government*, p. 28.

ments also have a primary duty to encourage political participation.[87] The best form of liberal democratic government is one where, at least occasionally, all citizens are called upon to take part.

The Function of Governing

Political leaders are usually visualized as larger than life characters forging common purposes and national projects. But most of the time they protect and promote their liberal democratic regimes by performing the more mundane tasks of minding the shop and tending the machinery of government.

THE GENERAL INTEREST. Political justice consists of working to benefit the citizenry, of pursuing the common interest.[88] Good liberal democratic leaders will be concerned with the impact that public policies have on their constituents. But they will be even more concerned with the impact on all the nation's citizens – the general interest.[89] The general interest differs in different times and places depending on the wants and needs of the citizenry and considerations of fairness and legitimacy.[90] It is best discovered in context by leaders with Aristotle's practical wisdom, a wisdom prized by Madison as well.[91] Nonetheless, Mill offered three general guideposts.[92] The first follows from the fact that the interests of the weak and excluded are always in danger of being overlooked. To pursue the general interest, therefore, it is important to hear their wants and include their interests in the mix. Second, contra psychological egoism's claims, it is indeed feasible to pursue the general interest. Everyone has both selfish and unselfish motivations, and the ones most likely to prevail in any given circumstance depend on habituated character. Lastly, it is desirable that leaders look to the long run, to what Mill called 'comprehensive and distant views' which can be undermined by short sighted perspectives.[93] Unless they consider the long term, it matters little how competently leaders manage the present.

OPEN MINDEDNESS refers to the disposition to seek out and consider conflicting perspectives on political issues and to avoid dogmatic mind sets and 'group-think'.[94] Tetlock's distinction between hedgehogs and foxes is relevant here, but much other well known work in political psy-

---

87 Suzanne Dovi, *The Good Representative*.
88 Aristotle, *The Nicomachean Ethics*, 1131a.
89 Suzanne Dovi, *The Good Representative*.
90 John Stuart Mill, *Considerations on Representative Government*.
91 James Madison, Alexander Hamilton and John Jay, *The Federalist Papers*, Federalist #57.
92 John Stuart Mill, *Considerations on Representative Government*, pp. 96-7.
93 *Ibid.*
94 William A. Galston, *Liberal Purposes*.

chology is important as well. Mill believed it essential that liberal democratic leaders seek out, listen to, and consider seriously different opinions about policy issues.[95] They need to encourage rather than discourage unorthodox recommendations whether they adopt them or not. His *On Liberty* is an extended argument about the value of deliberation across a wide variety of views about facts, values, and ways of life. Only by colliding such views together, he suggested, would one be likely to discover truth and develop reasonable understandings and strategies. The social psychologist Milton Rokeach was one of the first to measure open-mindedness.[96] He constructed scales for its vice, dogmatic and rigid thinking. More recently, Kruglanski has shown that people who score high on the need for closure systematically ignore important relevant evidence.[97]

DELIBERATION. Goodness in deliberation is one of Aristotle's intellectual virtues.[98] Those who have the disposition to engage in structured deliberation listen carefully to the views of others, explain their own views to them, and take time together to think over a matter thoroughly. They are willing to defend their views in public and to listen with an open mind to the views of others.[99] They are wary of manipulation (changing minds without giving the real reasons), dislike coercion (forcing behavior without changing minds), and disparage sound bites. Good representation requires calm deliberation and representatives ready to engage in it. It is, in Mill's opinion, one of the most important functions that parliaments perform.[100] Much the same might be said of executive and judicial institutions. But it is parliaments that bring to light the important wants in the country and evaluate the reasons behind them. Moreover, policy programs and goals acquire legitimacy by having their rationales aired, explained, and tested against alternatives.[101] Political psychologists are increasingly investigating the psychological foundations of this character trait.[102]

---

95 John Stuart Mill, *Considerations on Representative Government*, pp. 197–8.
96 Milton Rokeach, 'Political and Religious Dogmatism: An Alternative to the Authoritarian Personality', *Psychological Monographs*, 70 (1956).
97 Arie W. Kruglanski, *The Psychology of Closed Mindedness* (New York: Psychology Press, 2004).
98 Aristotle, *The Nicomachean Ethics*.
99 William A. Galston, *Liberal Purposes*.
100 John Stuart Mill, *Considerations on Representative Government*, pp. 82–3.
101 Jürgen Habermas, *Moralbewusstsein und kommunikatives Handeln* (Frankfurt: Suhrkamp, 1983).
102 Arthur Lupia, 'Deliberation Disconnected: What Does it Take to Improve Civic Competence?', *Law and Contemporary Problems*, 65 (2002), pp. 133–50; Marco R. Steenbergen, André Bächtiger, Markus Spörndli and Jürg Steiner. 'Toward a Psychology of Deliberation', paper delivered at the Swiss Chair Conference on Empirical Approaches to Deliberative Politics, European University Institute, Florence (May 21–22, 2004).

COMPROMISE, which Mill characterized as a disposition toward '*conciliation*', is indispensable because liberal democratic politics is expected to reconcile diverse and conflicting interests. The conciliation in compromise smoothes its way with a willingness to overcome distrust and animosity by pleasant behavior and civility: 'One of the most indispensable requisites in ... the management of free institutions, is conciliation – a readiness to compromise, a willingness to concede something to opponents, and to shape good measures so as to be as little offensive as possible to persons of opposite views....'[103] Such dispositions are further facilitated by recognition that politics is 'the art of the possible' and that 'half a loaf is better than none.' Studies in political psychology identify several motivations that impede compromise and others that support it. Narcissistic and aggressive leaders, for example, are notoriously bad at compromise and unnecessarily escalate conflicts.[104] The prospects of compromise arouse their fears of powerlessness and resentments toward others perceived as more powerful than them.

The Function of Accountability

The function of accountability refers to processes by which ministers, governments, civil servants and individual representatives are scrutinized, evaluated and critiqued. Mill believed that accountability should be the most important responsibility of parliamentary institutions.[105] Parliaments can be institutionally engineered for watching and controlling governments, for investigating their policies and procedures, for compelling them to justify what they do, and for exposing and driving from office political leaders who have betrayed the people's trust.

INTEGRITY is the ethical goal of accountability. Government cannot successfully pursue the common interest if its representatives are systematically corrupted.[106] Truthfulness is one of Aristotle's moral virtues.[107] But to what extent is complete truthfulness a civic virtue as well as a moral one? Are the ethics of good government different from the ethics of everyday life? As a civic virtue, integrity or rectitude is bounded by its vices, over-scrupulousness the excess, corruption the defect. Compared to other virtues, the range of appropriate conduct for integrity is especially contextual and difficult to see. Its image is murky because nearly all the time, and at different levels of awareness, political leaders work with 'dirty

---

103 John Stuart Mill, *Considerations on Representative Government*, p. 187.
104 Jerrold M. Post, 'Current Conceptions of the Narcissistic Personality: Implications for Political Psychology', *Political Psychology*, 14 (1993), pp. 99–121.
105 John Stuart Mill, *Considerations on Representative Government*, p. 81.
106 *Ibid.*, p. 24.
107 Aristotle, *The Nicomachean Ethics*.

hands'.[108] It is a fact of political life that developing consensus among disparate groups requires emphasizing some things to one audience and other things to another.[109] It is a fact of political life that liberal democratic politicians must sometimes give evasive answers, especially when they are in government, and especially on TV.[110] It is a fact of political life that they must sometimes construct instrumental relationships with colleagues and constituents and treat them more as means than ends. It is a fact of political life that they must sometimes do lesser bads in order to achieve greater goods: lying to protect the nation's currency, to facilitate an important negotiation, or to discourage terrorists from destructive plots. When they have effectively protected and promoted our institutions we may judge them good political leaders. But, at the same time, we may feel they are morally compromised human beings.[111]

Some themes from Machiavellianism in political philosophy have been directly investigated in psychological studies. Unfortunately the measurement has been too linear to distinguish convincingly the virtue of integrity/rectitude from its excesses. That said, it has been quite revealing. For instance, it has been found that those who score high on Machiavellianism believe that most people are not only psychological egoists but deceitful and manipulative as well. And they themselves are very likely to accept deceit and manipulation as legitimate tools of the political trade.[112]

TRANSPARENCY AND PUBLICITY. There is little philosophical or psychological commentary on leaders' commitments to transparency and publicity, but this modern liberal democratic civic virtue has become

---

108 Michael Walzer, 'Political Action: the Problem of Dirty Hands', *Philosophy and Public Affairs*, 2 (1973), pp. 160–80; Martin Hollis, 'Dirty Hands', *British Journal of Political Science*, 12 (1982), pp. 385–98; Dennis F. Thompson, *Political Ethics and Public Office* (Cambridge: Harvard University Press, 1987); Stephen Garrett, *Conscience and Power: An Examination of Dirty Hands and Political Leadership* (New York: St Martins 1996); Laurie Calhoun, 'The Problem of "Dirty Hands" and Corrupt Leadership', *The Independent Review*, 8 (2004), pp. 363–85.
109 '[Gordon] Brown is anti-Europe when he talks to [Rupert] Murdock and pro-Europe when he talks to Chatham House.' He is 'New Labour when he talks to the City and Old Labour when he is at a trade union dinner', Kettle, Martin, 'Martin Kettle v. Jackie Ashley', *The Guardian* (30 March 2007).
110 They are more guarded when they are in government because they are being scrutinized and criticized, which is to say because they are being held accountable for what they are doing by colleagues and publics. They are more guarded when they are on TV because their comments are being recorded as well as broadcast and can get them into a great deal of trouble; White, Michael, 'The Slippery Slope', *The Guardian* (5 April, 2007).
111 Suzanne Dovi, 'Guilt and the Problem of Dirty Hands', *Constellations: An International Journal of Critical and Democratic Theory*, 12 (2005), pp. 128–46
112 Richard Christie and Florence L. Geis, *Studies in Machiavellianism* (New York: Academic Press, 1970).

increasingly important for accountability.¹¹³ It is a disposition to conduct the public's business in public and to expect others to do so as well. The virtue encourages suspicion of measures like official secrets acts and favorable attitudes toward freedom of information programs.

AVOIDING COGNITIVE DISTORTIONS. The function of accountability is threatened by cognitive biases that impede decision-making.[114] Here we consider them as leadership vices, as defects in skills needed for good government. Among such biases are heuristics that result in flawed retrospective assessments of the probabilities of certain outcomes, lack of empathy that impedes putting oneself in another leader's shoes, overconfidence in initial assessments, and ego-centric bias. The defensive avoidance of uncomfortable information and wishful thinking simply distorts leaders' images of the world.[115] All these errors spoil evaluations of past performances and proposed policies. Beyond this research on psychological heuristics, common cognitive distortions that weaken accountability include causal (mis)attribution, improper use of analogical reasoning, and unrealistic 'operational codes.'

The Function of Representation

Representation is effected by: advocacy, whereby representatives serve as agents to advance their constituents' interests and the interests of the nation as a whole;[116] by descriptive representation, for it is believed that what representatives do flows from who they are;[117] and by opinion representation, when representatives keep abreast of their constituents' opinions, speak on behalf of those opinions, and press to see them enacted into public policy.[118]

---

113 William A. Christie, *Liberal Purposes*.
114 Ibid.
115 Janice Gross Stein, 'Building Politics into Psychology: The Misperception of Threat', *Political Psychology*, 9 (1988), pp. 245–71.
116 Anthony H. Birch, *Concepts and Theories of Modern Democracy*, 4th edn. (London: Routledge, 2001); Anthony H. Birch, *Representative and Responsible Government* (London: Unwin, 1964).
117 Thus, the representative body should mirror the socio-economic-cultural profile of the nation, and particular attention ought to be paid to seeing that historically disadvantaged groups are represented by members of those groups who have strong mutual relationships with them. Dovi, Suzanne, 'Preferable Descriptive Representatives: Will Just any Woman, Black or Latino Do?', *American Political Science Review*, 96 (2002), pp. 729–43; Suzanne Dovi, *The Good Representative*.
118 Populistic interpretations of opinion representation encourage participatory democracy and cross the borders of direct democracy with devices like referenda and initiatives Benjamin Barber, *Strong Democracy* (Berkeley: University of California Press, 1984). Thinner more liberal versions echo John Stuart Mill's prescriptions (in *Considerations on Representative Government*, pp. 82–3) for a 'congress of opinion' where representatives articulate the general opinion of the nation and the concerns of its important sections. The duty of representatives is to find out

ATTENTIVENESS TO PUBLIC OPINION. This is a disposition to be attentive to public opinion both during elections and between them. It is a disposition to be sensitive and responsive, while protecting the polity's liberal democratic institutions and culture.[119] Pandering is the excess, conceit the defect. Liberals fear that demagogues will generate immoderate public demands and that political opportunists will satisfy them.[120] These fears have not changed much since Madison and Hamilton wrote that one of the most important duties of political leaders is to discourage, divert, and delay popular but immoderate proposals till the public has had 'time and opportunity for more cool and sedate reflection.'[121] Conceit is as common as pandering but far less discussed or investigated. It grows in representatives who grow detached from the public and come to believe that their own views and intuitions invariably represent the public interest and the public mind.

EMPATHY, SYMPATHY AND CONNECTIONS. Some politicians have a great deal of empathy for their constituents' concerns and situations and for the difficulties of vulnerable groups in their society. The excess here is the charitable affection that turns representatives into nurturing social workers who lose their taste for public policy. The defect is contempt, which, like conceit, is a more widespread vice than generally realized.

Sympathy for ordinary citizens suggests a relationship of concord with them, including respect and gratitude, liking and shared outlooks.[122] Madison hypothesized that the experience of campaigning and of being elected would encourage a respect and liking for the public that had regarded them so well that it returned them to office.[123] Successful liberal democratic leaders must also be able to connect in ways that make citizens feel they are being listened to, and that the listeners care about what they have to say. Media savvy is part of it. But successful presentation is highly context-dependent within liberal democracies and among them. The concept of 'charisma' has become a label for very different presentations. Machiavelli's famous advice about these matters was that if leaders cannot be both loved and feared, better to be feared, for fear is something they can control. Liberal democratic leaders do not have this choice, however, because they lead mainly by authority, not power, and authority works best when it rests on being liked as well as respected.

CAPACITY TO FORGE A SENSE OF COMMON PURPOSE, the last virtue of liberal democratic leadership on our list, builds upon empathy and sympathy with citizens and adeptness in connecting with them. This is the skill most commonly visualized as 'political leadership' in liberal democracies, despite the fact that liberals are supposed to be wary of common purposes, and democrats of being forged. The process of forging a sense of common purpose is typically associated with grand projects, but it may simply be what leaders qua leaders are expected to do every day, with staff, colleagues and interest groups as well as the public.

With regard to the grand undertakings, Galston argues that it begins with an ability to recognize the polity's core goals, what MacIntyre characterizes as the nation's central projects: the structures and traditions that are rooted in its history and guide its development.[119] The key is having (a) the good judgment to sense intuitively those core goals and assumptions that are widely shared among the public at a particular time, (b) the skill to analyze convincingly the polity's pressing needs and problems in terms of them and, finally, (c) the dispositions to communicate these visions to the public and win its support. Symbolic uses of politics loom large here, yet another topic on which there has been little systematic research.[120]

Conclusion

Research programs can be driven by universalistic theories, specific methodologies or the availability of data. They can also be problem-driven.[121] The problem that concerns us here is the evaluation of political leaders in contemporary liberal democracies. We propose to develop criteria for judging the character of these leaders, criteria that can be readily understood by the general public and convincingly justified by normative theory and empirical research.

The first step is to identify key virtues and vices of liberal democratic leadership, particularly ones with strong psychological roots, for we plan to investigate not only their institutional consequences but also their dynamics and how they are learned and modified in the course of political careers. In this paper we have begun to construct the groundwork for our research program by exploring the suggestions of political theorists who have reflected on this subject and matching some of their ideas with relevant empirical work from political psychology. We expect to encounter disagreement with our choice of key virtues and vices and with the ways we have defined them. But if this leads to controversy and discussion, then, all the better, for the topic has lain dormant far too long while the character of liberal democratic leaders has become a critical problem,

---

119 William A. Galston, *Liberal Purposes*; Alasdair MacIntyre, 'Is Patriotism a Virtue?', in Igor Primoratz (ed.), *Patriotism* (New York: Humanity Books, 2002).
120 Murray Edelman, *The Symbolic Uses of Politics*, (2nd edn.) (Champagne-Urbana: University of Illinois Press, 1985).
121 Ian Shapiro, 'Problems, Methods, and Theories in the Study of Politics, or: What's Wrong with Political Science and What to Do About It', in Ian Shapiro, Rogers Smith, and Tarek E. Masoud, *Problems and Methods in the Study of Politics* (Cambridge: Cambridge University Press, 2004).

partially because of their conduct, but mainly because citizens are deeply disillusioned. Leadership in contemporary liberal democracies exhibits too many vices and too few of the virtues that publics want to see.

The virtues of liberal democratic leadership are civic, key motivations and skills required for good government, for the effective performance of regime building, governing, accountability, and representation, for preserving and promoting liberal democratic regimes. Among those that serve multiple functions, ambition, honor, and practical wisdom stand out. In its admirable form, ambition seeks office primarily to benefit citizens through public policy and institutional change. It is supported by honor, the desire for respect, and guided by practical wisdom, a capacity for comprehending and constructing the community's well-being. The function of regime building turns our attention to support for liberal democratic rules of the game and values like freedom and equality, and to promoting these ideals through political education. At the same time, these regimes must be governed with sufficient open-mindedness, deliberation and compromise to ensure that citizens' wants and needs are met with consideration for security, fairness and prosperity. The history of liberal theory and liberal democracy testify to both the feasibility and the failures of accountability in focusing governments on the general interest and seeing that they conduct themselves with integrity. Liberalism and democracy came together to ensure liberty and compel attentiveness to public opinion, to give all citizens a stake in the conduct of public policy. This goal is captured in the function of representation, which requires empathy and sympathy for members of the public and skill in connecting with them.

It is difficult to write about this subject without feeling both fatuous and frustrated; fatuous in the role of a social scientist reflecting on ideal virtues for liberal democratic leaders, frustrated in the role of the citizen reflecting on their more egregious recent vices. Thoughtful observers who have written about the subject have usually managed, however, to analyze it productively as a puzzle, a puzzle about the intersection of character and structure, motivations and constraints. They disagree so much about the relative importance of the one versus the other because we know so little about the relationships between individuals and institutions, about conformity and habits, calculations and sanctions and institutional learning. The beginning of the story is captured in the insight that institutions do not dominate the conduct of political leaders, for they enable as well as restrain them. But that is just the beginning of a story yet to be investigated and spelled out.

In sum, structure and agency are interdependent and negotiated; exactly how that works is what we need to discover in order to understand what institutions do to leaders and what leaders can do to them. The Madisonian project of liberal constitution making to guarantee good government by using institutions to manipulate leaders' incentives gets a mixed report. The key mechanism of regular competitive elections has indeed secured liberal democratic governments and cut short some of the worst abuses. But constitutional constraints have not in general been nearly as effective as expected by our Enlightenment ideology, and therefore character very much needs to be returned to the equation. Like Madison, Mill worked hard at thinking through the capacity of countervailing political institutions to fence in potentially corrupt political leaders. But he placed greater emphasis on support from appropriate character traits, because,

> political checks will no more act of themselves than a bridle will direct a horse without a rider. If the checking functionaries are as corrupt or as negligent as those whom they ought to check ... little benefit will be derived ... from the best constructed constitutions.[122]

Paradoxically, leadership, which is neither essentially liberal nor democratic, seems to be necessary for liberal democracy to prosper.

---

122 John Stuart Mill, *Considerations on Representative Government*, pp. 26–7

Raia Prokhovnik

Political Leadership and Sovereignty

This chapter makes the case that clarifying the relation between leadership and sovereignty is central to understanding the role of political leadership in politics, and to comprehending the lack of attention given to the question of leadership in mainstream strands of democratic theory. Specifically, the underexplored political property of sovereignty[1] enables us to highlight the value and operation of leadership to politics, and to illuminate what sovereignty does in establishing the context in which questions about leadership are asked. The final section of the chapter discusses the impact of the political property of sovereignty on political leadership.

Political Leadership and Democratic Theory

The idea of political leadership can be conceptualized as having at least three faces. The first is concerned with the conduct of elected governments within the state structures (including all the phases of policy-making from initiatives to delivery and rethinking policy) which provide governments with a framework of continuity. The second is concerned with party politics, electoral competition and appeal to the electorate. Leadership here refers to the outcome of differentiating between candidates. The third face relates to the exercise of leadership on the world stage. In all three faces it is important to distinguish statesmanship, the exercise of headship, from political leaders who manage day-to-day governing.

While questioning of the idea of political leadership in all three of its faces is nothing new, recent challenges seem particularly acute. The notion of a positive bond between leaders and led has traditionally been thought to give legitimacy to political leaders, especially in the first and

---

[1] Raia Prokhovnik, *Sovereignties: Contemporary Theory and Practice* (Basingstoke: Macmillan, 2007). Raia Prokhovnik, *Sovereignty: History and Theory* (Exeter: Imprint Academic, 2008).

second faces. The idea of legitimacy provided the warrant for modern democratic governments' policy-making programmes and the sanction for the indirect nature of representative democratic processes. The continuing credibility of this bond in relation to the first face is thrown into doubt by high levels of citizen cynicism about neo-liberal economics and politics in modern states which prioritise profit and efficiency over social responsibility. In addition, forms of privatization and public/private partnership blur the scope for government accountability.

Political leadership is also questioned in relation to the second face, by voter disaffection in the light of unease about domination by political elites and the mediatisation of politics. One important discourse which has been used to capture these issues centres on the role of charisma in political leadership. Charisma is now best conceived not as just about personal traits or attributes but about power, the type of authority such politicians wield. Charisma is thus regarded as an idea that belongs under the rubric of power, and political leaders are recognized as cognitively perceived as individuals but as socially defined. This discourse also points to the limits of the explanatory force of charisma, to its instability, its ephemeral quality, to the way it cannot be classified in a non-controversial way, and to attempts in politics to routinise it, to entrench it in institutions of administration, so that it becomes bureaucratic.

But the most crucial aspect of the discourse of charisma for this chapter is the idea that the growing standardization of leadership in modern societies leaves less room for charisma. Television and other electronic media have changed the nature of the relationship between leaders and led. According to this line of argument there is a need to move from the study of charisma to the study of mediatised political leaders, such a shift having the benefit of demystifying political leaders. The idea of charisma as an object of study has been overtaken by the sense that what is now required of political leaders is a telegenic ordinariness, informality, a seeming approachability, the capacity to frame soundbites, and an ability to enact consensual decision-making rather than being a charismatic leader whose effect is divisive in the political field.[2] Television and the other electronic media have fostered a politics which is at once spectacle and banality. In addition, the whole process of political selection and electoral contest has seen the adjustment of governing to modern modes of campaigning, through the images projected by the media which blur the line between governing and campaigning. The ability of a leader in governing is confused with the ability of a campaigner.[3] For instance, Gordon

---

2 Mauro Barisione, *L'immagine del leader* (Bologna:, Il Mulino, 2006).
3 Sidney Blumenthal, *The Permanent Campaign* (New York: Touchstone books, 1982).

Brown's performance in the economic downturn in late 2008 was feted in the media as showing a much-needed decisive leadership, but there was a distinct sense that his leadership was thought to be impressive because it represented a political campaign and not just because it was taken to express effective governing.

With respect to the third face the notions have gained popularity over recent years (although clear evidence has yet to support them) that the theory and practices of disaggregated transnational networks of anti-capitalist social movements effectively challenge the model of traditional top-down nation-state based politics and political leadership with an ensemble of popular protest, while economic 'globalisation' curtails the role of statesmen in international politics by reducing the power of the states they represent.

In sum, traditional ideas of political leadership are under threat, in the first face through the challenge to the identity of the state, in the second through the challenge to the identity of the political process, and in the third through the challenge to the identity of international politics. More generally, the idea of politics as occurring in autonomous spaces and practices outside mainstream formal channels, of alternative forms of mobilization, and of post-representational forms of resistance, struggle and self-definition, challenges formal politics inside and outside the state of which political leadership is a key part.

The democratic tradition largely fails to integrate the concept of leadership into its theory. Since Locke, liberal political theory has primarily exhibited a lack of trust in politics, the political process, and in politicians, and advocates instead the implementation of liberal moral principles, while at the same time seeking to efface the conditionality of those principles. More recently, the erasure of politics by liberal political theory since the abstract turn with the early Rawls is not just an oversight but a direct consequence of the approach taken by the liberal tradition.[4] The distrust of politics and its abstract approach render the liberal tradition unable to recognize in an effective manner that leadership (the real focus of attention, rather than the qualities of individual leaders) is a contingent and historically-embedded practice. Machiavelli and Weber are among the key sources to turn to for insights into the way leadership is not about managerial activity, and is not primarily normative, but is about the judgment, craft, and skill of statecraft.[5] The liberal democratic tradition and liberal theory struggle to embrace such concerns, in the light of the prior-

---

4   Bonnie Honig, *Political Theory and the Displacement of Politics* (Ithaca: Yale University Press, 1993).
5   Timothy Fuller (ed.), *Leading and Leadership* (Notre Dame: University of Notre Dame Press, 2000).

ity given to limiting the role of government and replacing the rule of men with the rule of law.

Democratic theory more broadly has been concerned with theorizing the relationship between leaders and led, if not leadership itself. In the first face, democratic theorists have discussed accountability and scrutiny, in the second face in terms of questions of participation and representation, and in the third face through notions of cosmopolitan political institutions, international justice and a human rights regime. It is the second face of political leadership which is primarily at issue here, although the idea of the political property of sovereignty could also be discussed in relation to the first and third faces. What counts as adequate accountability and scrutiny of leaders, how definitions of these concepts change over time within a polity, and how those values are weighed against other values such as government efficiency and success could also be discussed. Political leadership in the third face could also be considered, for instance in relation to the tension for political leaders between domestic and international agendas, or debates about Blair's role in supporting US policy over Iraq.

Electoral competition in the second face of leadership in modern democracies involves a potentially volatile and dynamic process, in terms of concrete and/or symbolic governance, characterised by the contingency of voter preferences, uncertainty over electoral outcomes, and the risk of a government with unpalatable views. The commitment to pluralism which multi-party politics involves also contains dangers in striking an ever-tenuous balance between incommensurable positions and negotiating intractable differences. At stake here is a wider understanding of politics than simply governing. These features of volatility and uncertainty and their limits are figured differently in different polities.

Many theories of democratic politics are unable to account for these aspects of politics. The appeal to an overly-narrow and supposedly 'neutral' reason and a seemingly depoliticised standpoint are, to a greater or lesser degree, features of liberal representative, deliberative, aggregative, and participative models. Democratic theorists (for instance in both the Rawlsian and Habermasian traditions) also tend to operate according to an abstract form of reasoning which leads only to universalized normative theorizing of ideal principles or to a retreat into proceduralism. Their ahistorical approaches fail to take account of the impact of cultural values, social norms and political conventions in shaping the way politics is done in a specific polity. Many such theories are also often intent upon containing or constraining the way in which politics operates. Most forms of democratic theory have little to contribute to the meaning and understanding of the second face of political leadership. Some theories of deliberative democracy are more innovative in seeking to engage with political contestation and local political conditions but such ideas rely on a much-criticised notion of what counts as a consensus over 'reasonable' outcomes, and they do not supplant the problems associated with the mainstream representative system. The discourse on democratic theory is also in general reluctant to theorise political leadership in a positive sense, in part due to a predisposition toward promoting more effective bottom-up participation, citizen involvement and popular sovereignty, and resisting the claims of top-down schemes.

The Political Dimension of Sovereignty

A.V. Dicey's influential 1885 distinction between legal and political sovereignty laid the groundwork for the received modern view about the meaning of these terms but also opens up an interpretive field of debate about the meaning of the categories. Dicey is primarily concerned to elucidate the meaning of legal sovereignty in the British constitution, and his key contention is that legal sovereignty resides in 'the ready admission of the doctrine that Parliament is, under the British constitution, an absolutely sovereign legislature', and that the sovereignty of Parliament is 'the dominant characteristic of our political institutions',[6] that Parliament 'constitutes the legally supreme power in the state'.[7] At the same time he allows that, 'the electorate constitutes politically the true sovereign power',[8] for 'the people of the country, or to speak more accurately the electorate, are politically sovereign',[9] because 'the will of the electorate...is sure ultimately to prevail on all subjects to be determined by the British government'.[10] However, Dicey emphasizes, 'this is a political, not a legal fact', for 'the Courts will take no notice of the will of the electors', except insofar as 'that will is expressed by an Act of Parliament'.[11] Moreover, while Dicey concedes that the 'political sense of the word "sovereignty" is, it is true, fully as important as the legal sense or more so' but that 'the two significations, though intimately connected together, are essentially different',[12] he is also very keen to underline that Parliament holds a crucial trump card in being solely capable of enacting a sovereignty which holds the status of legality and thus legitimacy. In other

---

6   A.V. Dicey, *Introduction to the Study of the Law of the Constitution* (Indianapolis: Liberty Fund Inc, 1982), p. 71.
7   *Ibid.*, p. 81.
8   *Ibid.*, p. 26.
9   *Ibid.*, p. 88.
10   *Ibid.*, p. 87.
11   *Ibid.*, p. 88.
12   *Ibid.*

words, from the perspective of ultimate law-making ability and legitimacy, Parliament holds sovereignty, while the voting public can claim the ultimate sovereign ability to bring down the government. As Dicey argues, the 'external limit to the real power of a sovereign consists in the possibility or certainty that his subjects, or a large number of them, will disobey or resist his laws'.[13]

Dicey's statement is fascinating in making the key distinction that between law-making power and the will of the people, between lawful and popular sovereignty, and in positing a complete disjunction between them. Legal and political sovereignty refer to quite different and separate things, for Dicey. However, traditionally since Dicey and exhibiting an important shift from his statements, legal or *de jure* sovereignty is said to correlate to the idea of authority and is based on the right to command, while political or *de facto* sovereignty corresponds to the idea of power and rests on the power to ensure compliance. Dicey's sense of political sovereignty equated with the will of the people has been channeled into liberal democratic procedures and political sovereignty has become focused on the power of *governments*. In the mainstream discourse, then, legal sovereignty is said to reside in the supreme law-making body, and is sometimes exemplified with quotations from Bodin,[14] while political sovereignty identifies the holder/s of political authority and capacity to govern, has to do with force, and is sometimes elucidated with quotations from Hobbes,[15] with great weight given to his view that the sovereign has the monopoly of coercive power.

In this complex way, the differentiation between legal and political sovereignty is one of the central dichotomies through which sovereignty is discussed in the mainstream discourse (along with internal and external sovereignty and constituent and ordinary power). However, the distinction is only a very narrow one since both sides of it now concern what we can call 'ruler sovereignty', in the context of a *Rechtstaat* understood as a modern state based on law as a moral principle. The term 'ruler sovereignty' sums up the two sides of the traditional legal and political sovereignty instead of effecting a meaningful difference, since it concerns the identification of the ultimate authority to make law, subject to no higher authority, and coincides with the conventional idea of internal sovereignty in terms of the competence and capacity, authority and power to govern. The key point is that the ruler sovereignty invested in the legal

---

13 *Ibid.*, p. 89.
14 Jean Bodin, *On Sovereignty. Four Chapters from 'The Six Books of the Commonwealth'*, ed. J Franklin (Cambridge: Cambridge University Press, 1992).
15 Particularly from Thomas Hobbes, *Leviathan*, ed. M Oakeshott (Oxford, Blackwell, 1946).

and political sovereignty formula, leaves unaccounted for the political properties of sovereignty. It is these qualities which enable us to highlight the value and operation of leadership to politics.

This chapter thus contends that the traditional legal/political sovereignty dualism overlooks an important political dimension of the concept which captures contemporary political experiences including leadership. For alongside the orthodox meanings focused on a narrow view of politics as ruling and governing, the idea of sovereignty also operates within a broader understanding of politics to provide the conditional settlement of the content, parameters and limits for the conduct of politics within a political community, and the boundary between the political and unpolitical. The mainstream notion of sovereignty focuses on the creation of order through law- and rule-making within a modern state in the *Rechtstaat* tradition, while this political dimension of sovereignty is about how the negotiation of a space for politics—which cannot be taken for granted[16]—is organised in the circumstances of a particular political society. It is the repository of political values that underlie traditional legal and political sovereignty—about the nature, scope and limits of politics, about what constitute legitimate questions and answers—which are expressed in laws, rules and policy orientations, as well as in social values and norms. The content of this political dimension of sovereignty, expressing a background condition for political action to take place, is culture-specific. In this light we can see that, whatever the differences between Dicey and later received meanings of the terms legal and political sovereignty and their relationship, sovereignty understood in these orthodox terms does not have much to offer the renewal of discussion about political leadership.

Sovereignty in this sense is a practice and an idea which conditionally sets out the conditions of the existence of politics, and a concept for establishing the legitimacy or otherwise of challenges within politics. It is taken as standing above the fray, above particular ideological positions and interests. It is invested with establishing the rules of political engagement and the conventions of oratory, for instance what counts as responsive leadership in the sense of accountability after the fact. As a system of meaning it is open to interpretive but not causal explanation, and it represents a balance of tensions within stretchy boundaries. The system of meaning is successful when, instrumentally, it upholds and so protects the commonwealth. In this way, sovereignty is successful when it is

---

16 Richard Ashley and R.B.J. Walker, 'Reading Dissidence/Writing the Discipline: Crisis and the Question of Sovereignty in International Studies', *International Studies Quarterly*, Vol.34 (3) (1990), p. 381.

depoliticized and naturalized, but it is also open to interrogation based on the imperative that its meaning is not natural after all.

This idea argues that the political nature of the concept of sovereignty has also been obscured in the modern state conception by the division of labour between internal and external dimensions. In the 'internal' discourse on modern sovereignty the emphasis has been either on analysing a depoliticised notion of authority or on prioritising legal over political sovereignty and promoting the *Rechtstaat*. The 'external' discourse has largely fixed upon political sovereignty very narrowly in terms of the agency of the sovereign body through its executive acting as an autonomous individual in relation to other states. In consequence, full recognition of the political work of sovereignty has fallen between the legal and international relations discourses.

The political dimension of sovereignty, alongside sovereignty referring to the highest authority to make law and to ruler sovereignty, comprehends then another, profoundly political task that we ask sovereignty to perform. Sovereignty is necessarily outside politics but it also establishes the sphere and condition of politics itself, the boundaries and limits of politics, and so the identity of the political unit. At the same time the settlement that sovereignty establishes is conditional and these functions are politically negotiable. The idea calls attention to the way the concept of sovereignty is at the same time both political and unpolitical in this fashion. At a conceptual level the political and unpolitical functions of sovereignty are clearly separated while at the political level, as Ashley and Walker argue, 'sovereignty emerges as an intrinsically problematical construct'.[17] It is also clear that the political property of sovereignty described here is a feature of both legal and political sovereignty and of the field of politics overlooked by that dichotomy, and so is a condition of the concept rather than a new conception of sovereignty.

Seeing one thing in terms of another, or understanding a thing by mapping it onto an already familiar pattern of meaning, is central to the work of metaphor in our lives. To add a level of complexity we can recognise that all metaphors play with the boundary metaphor, for the boundary between the two things metaphorically related is being disrupted. To add another level of complexity sovereignty is a metaphorical concept *par excellence*, because its meaning is constituted in a complex mapping process which conditionally establishes boundaries. The potency of the concept of sovereignty lies in part in its metaphorical potential. Black describes how '[t]hose metaphors which turn out to be successful establish a privileged perspective on an object or constitute "the" object and by

---

17 *Ibid.*, p. 403.

doing so, disappear as metaphors'.[18] This process whereby the metaphorical dimension of a meaning becomes invisible and naturalised accurately expresses the way that we expect sovereignty to establish the content and limits of politics as unpolitical.

Sovereignty provides the architecture, the 'supporting structure' and 'fund of authority',[19] within which other political concepts operate and so works as a master concept in this sense. The cluster of concepts involved in the meaning of sovereignty includes authority, legitimacy, and power; politics, law, economics, government, a constitution, social values; democracy, participation, citizenship; rule of law; freedom, equality, individuals; choice, respect, autonomy, independence. Sovereignty also relies on recognition in a more complex way than other political concepts do. The successful working of sovereignty depends on the recognition of its distribution, coordination, allocation, and architecture functions, as well as on the recognition that the meaning of sovereignty is also constituted by the meaning of the things that make it up. It also depends on the recognition that all of this *does* define the political architecture. The role of recognition here also leads to sovereignty's function in forming the identity of the 'whole' to a greater or lesser extent. Order, cohesion, and stability also follow from a successful setting up of sovereignty's properties and conditions within the polity.

The idea that sovereignty is exercised through claims to sovereignty points to the way that sovereignty is not just a discursive practice rather than an institutional 'fact', and is not just about the importance in authority relationships of making claims rather than asserting power. The idea of sovereignty as a claim also spells out the political nature of sovereignty, the way a claim is tentative, can be made against the grain of the dominant order, may be a point of contestation, a demand to be heard, or an assertion for inclusion.

One perception that arises from such observations is that different conceptions of sovereignty shape political reality very differently and that sovereignty has a massive effect on the way we conceive politics in the broader sense. An important attribute at the core of the concept of sovereignty follows from the manner in which the category of sovereignty occupies a 'neutral' position outside of politics and would be invalidated if thought to be partial to or captured by particular interests, and yet it is also deeply political in regulating the negotiation of the norms and processes of political life in a particular society through a claim that is condi-

---

18 Max Black, *Models and Metaphors. Studies in Language and Philosophy* (Ithaca: Cornell University Press, 1995), p. 15.
19 Ashley and Walker (1990), p. 382.

tionally-stable. As a result, all 'lived' conceptions of sovereignty, because they are maintained by the fragile mechanism of recognition and because they are political, are immanent, on-going and highly charged. The fragility of sovereignty inheres in the tentativeness of reliance on recognition, in the way recognition is not given once and for all but needs regular reaffirmation, in the job we give politics to negotiate indeterminacy, the way politics is conducted within rules and parameters which are partly tacit, as well as in the shadowy, not fully acknowledged meaning that sovereignty must have on a day-to-day basis.

We can use a transcendental argument to derive this characteristic of sovereignty from the character of politics itself. If we can take politics reasonably unproblematically to be among other things the use of power in the search for social cooperation, the articulation and negotiation of contestation and difference, and the designation of political identity, then sovereignty is a condition of and for politics, in two ways. We use sovereignty to specify the boundaries of politics, for instance in the end or limits to politics in Schmitt, the condition of politics in Spinoza and Rousseau, the elimination of politics in Hobbes. In addition sovereignty helps to define (the nature of) politics and political practice in any particular society, through its links with a constitution, the kind of law and the importance given to it, the dominant political mentality, where the boundary between participation and dissent is set, customary ways of doing politics, and the sense of political identity. It also regulates norms, in social values, rules regarded as obligatory and habitually practised, customary conduct, moral beliefs, standards that constitute the identities of actors, as well as in patterns of behaviour that arise from fear of sanctions.[20]

Definitions of sovereignty which highlight 'supreme authority' only point to the extreme case, and so can only be partial understandings. On a day-to-day basis sovereignty is much more importantly the repository of political values. The view that sovereignty involves a legal face in laws and a political face in the system of party politics and government, leaves out of the equation the crucial glue provided by background social norms and values which in a sense express the constituent power of the people.

In practical terms the conventional meaning of political sovereignty designates a very limited and constrained notion of politics. It is a politics in terms of a given set of liberal democratic institutions and procedures (contested elections, a multi-party system, a free press, the rule of law, religion located in the private realm, a neutral public realm, liberal plural-

---

20 Daniel Philpott, 'Westphalia, Authority, and International Society', *Political Studies*, Vol. 47 (1999), p. 573.

ism), focused on the legitimacy of the supreme law-making body. This narrow conception of politics leaves out of the picture of the political the still-active context out of which these institutions and processes have congealed, the changing patterns and changing impact of social values and norms that sustain it (for well or ill—look for instance at the debate about voter disenchantment and the erosion of support for political parties), the volatile forms of popular energy and social movement (such as disability politics and pro-hunt campaigns in Britain) for contesting the settled channels in which established politics is conducted, and the issue of the political identity of the polity. Furthermore, just as the different theorists in the canon on sovereignty allow different roles and meanings for politics,[21] so different political societies have different approaches. Polities and theorists may enable and facilitate politics, prevent and erase popular politics, rein in and control politics in particular ways, align politics with the identity of the nation state, reduce political questions to ones about economics, technology, morality or religion, or critique and dismiss the value of politics. The narrow conception of politics also sidesteps the way in which politics is the business of negotiating indeterminacy, and about making decisions about what counts as politics, the conditions under which politics operates, and the terms in which it is performed. The political property of sovereignty highlighted here is about the overlooked but crucial importance of these kinds of background and second-order factors.

In this way, then, we expect sovereignty to be a key means of setting out the degree of space allotted to politics (how much participation, dissent, contestation), as well as the ways in which politics is habitually expressed (the formal institutions and informal forms it habitually takes, what kind of 'street' politics is tolerated, and politics at national, regional, local, and international levels). This political property of sovereignty sums up the normative purpose and identity of the political form. It is also a power, in Morganthau's sense, the power of meaning imposition. Part of the meaning of the political property of sovereignty here is that, in establishing the boundary between the political and the unpolitical, sovereignty functions as the principle beyond which there is no appeal to a more ultimate set of rules, and yet that boundary is only conditional, 'unstable and tentative',[22] and can be contested and re-formed.

Specifying the political property of sovereignty in this way and postulating narrow and broad ideas of politics raises the question of what more precisely is meant by 'the political' here. This question can be answered

---

21 Prokhovnik, *Sovereignty: History and Theory* (2008).
22 Ashley and Walker (1990), pp. 382–3.

through a brief outline of key affinities with and differences from Chantal Mouffe's still fresh ideas in her influential 1993 book, *The Return of the Political*.[23] For the purposes of this chapter, the points that are most valuable in Mouffe's work are her insights that 'the political' expresses the positive role of contestation and debate between a plurality of views in a political community, and so the contribution of 'agonistic pluralism' to a flourishing political system; her recognition that all identities 'are relational', since the 'condition of existence of every identity is the affirmation of a difference';[24] and her elucidation of 'the incapacity of liberal thought to grasp' the nature of the political and 'the irreducible character of antagonism'.[25] She argues that a 'great deal of democratic thinking today' is informed by a conception of politics as 'rationalist, universalist and individualist'. It cannot 'but remain blind to the specificity of the political in its dimension of conflict/decision', and it cannot 'perceive the constitutive role of antagonism in social life'.[26] In contrast, Mouffe proposes conceptions of rationality, individuality and universality which affirm 'that they are necessarily plural, discursively constructed and entangled with power relations'.[27] Also useful is Mouffe's skepticism towards the communitarian valorizing of the idea of the common good, with 'politics as the realm where we can recognize ourselves as participants in a political community'.[28]

Less convincing is Mouffe's commitment to the Schmittian friend/enemy distinction to formulate these insights, the 'dimension of the political that is linked to the existence of an element of hostility among human beings',[29] even though she modifies Schmitt's meaning. The justification of agonistic pluralism requires only the recognition of politics as a field wherein intractable and incommensurable differences are negotiated, and not the greater commitment to a friend/enemy distinction. Also less persuasive are her enthusiasm to valorise 'democratic political struggles',[30] an unfounded faith in democracy, in particular in the idea that a 'project of radical and plural democracy'[31] within an ongoing 'democratic revolution'[32] is required and involves 'the creation of a chain of equiva-

---

23 Chantal Mouffe, *The Return of the Political* (London: Verso, 1993).
24 Ibid., p. 2.
25 Ibid., p. 1.
26 Ibid., p. 2.
27 Ibid., p. 7.
28 Ibid., p. 61.
29 Ibid., p. 2.
30 Ibid., p. 6.
31 Ibid., p. 152.
32 Ibid., p. 153.

lence among democratic struggles, and therefore the creation of a common political identity among democratic subjects'.[33] Furthermore, the book sidesteps the question of whether pluralism is to involve the value pluralist belief that all comprehensive ways of life are to be valued, or only the much less exhaustive claim, as found in Rawls's reasonable pluralism, which commits one only to the fact that people differ.

Whether the location of the sovereign is a prince, a queen, a parliament, an expression of the general will, the state, a constitution, a set of powers distributed to different institutions which check and balance each other, Stalin, or Leviathan, what they all do, behind the particulars of what they do, is establish (by word or deed or both) the content, character and limits of politics, and in doing so they are both unpolitical and political. This is so for both ancient and modern conceptions of sovereignty. Sovereignty is an important feature of politics itself. It is because sovereignty performs this role that we can then go on to say, for instance, that sovereignty is about establishing the relation between ruler and ruled. We have lost sight of this link between sovereignty and politics because in studying political concepts in political theory, we rarely talk about politics and the political. We take politics as a given and it gets erased. Moreover, there is a strong case for arguing that sovereignty changed in the modern period, not just because of the rise of the modern sovereign state, but also because of a change in how politics was done. Sovereignty is an effect of politics as well as acting to regulate politics. Starting with politics makes sovereignty look much more comprehensible.

With this view of 'the political' in mind and encompassing a broader rather than narrower understanding of politics, then, we can see that both of the ways in which sovereignty is a condition of and for politics set out sovereignty as unpolitical. Where a conception of sovereignty is generally accepted within a political society, its definition of the political/unpolitical boundary will be unpolitical and its specification of the definition and scope of politics within the polity is unpolitical. Moreover, the specific content of both these settlements will vary considerably from one polity to another across time and space. One of the things we ask sovereignty to enable, through a conditionally-settled claim, is the establishment of a stable link between rulers and ruled, and among the ruled, and it can do this precisely because it offers a settlement of what can and cannot be done by politics in a particular society. However, as well as functioning to specify politics, the limits of politics and the unpolitical, it is clear from history and from the history of political thought that conceptions of sovereignty and the effects of sovereignty will at times be contested and are chal-

---

33 *Ibid.*, p. 60.

lenged, and so become political. As Schmitt recognized (and his valuable insight into the political stands, without the added freight of the friend/enemy distinction), 'we know that any decision about whether something is *unpolitical* is always a *political* decision, irrespective of who decides and what reasons are advanced.[34] By 'political' Schmitt means that this is the realm of intractability and conflict, and priority over the legal. This point deserves to be underlined in a culture in which the meaning of sovereignty in particular is taken by many political actors and academic writers alike to have a wholly 'off-limits', fixed and universal meaning which ignores 'empirical tendencies',[35] and which in practice acts to sustain patterns of privilege and exclusion.

Like Schmitt's theory, this notion emphasises the political nature of sovereignty and sees both the political and unpolitical aspects of sovereignty as central to its meaning. Strong highlights this aspect of Schmitt's work. He notes that sovereignty 'is what Schmitt calls a *Grenzbegriff*, a "limiting" or "border" concept'. In other words, sovereignty for Schmitt 'thus looks in two directions, marking the line between that which is subject to law—where sovereignty reigns—and that which is not—potentially the space of the exception'. As Strong underlines, according to Schmitt, to 'look only to the rule of law would be to misunderstand the nature and place of sovereignty'.[36] Like Schmitt, the performative character of the meaning of the political property of sovereignty is seen as important, though here the performativity lies in the way sovereignty is a process, constructed through specific forms of politics, rather than resting in the decisionist act of the sovereign President.

However, this notion differs from Schmitt's theory in several key respects. Schmitt is committed to a state conception of sovereignty, places great weight on a dichotomous friend/enemy distinction, and regards the nub of politics as contestation. In contrast, the political property of sovereignty outlined here is compatible with a relational conception involving a variety of polity forms and interrelations, and with politics understood as being as much about social cooperation as about conflict. Moreover, the key to sovereignty for Schmitt lies in identifying he who decides on the exception in the context of the threat of social disintegration. The proposal put forward here sees sovereignty more broadly, and post-theologically, and focuses primarily on challenges (such as from feminism or anti-racist

---

34 Carl Schmitt, *Political Theology. Four Chapters on the Concept of Sovereignty* (Cambridge MA.: MIT Press, 1985), p. 2, emphasis in original.
35 R.B.J. Walker, *Inside/Outside. International Relations as Political Theory* (Cambridge: Cambridge University Press, 1993).
36 Tracy Strong, 'Forward', in Carl Schmitt, *Political Theology*, trans. G. Schwab (Chicago: University of Chicago Press, 2005), pp. xx–xxi.

politics) that fall short of the kind of political crisis experienced in Germany under the Weimar Republic. The notion developed here is also political in a more thoroughgoing way, in contrast with the perspective of Schmitt which keeps at the forefront the inadequacies of the legal order. At the same time the current proposal does not valorise liberal constitutionalism, so despised by Schmitt. As a result, the characterisation of sovereignty sketched here has the capacity to move beyond Schmitt's problematisation of sovereignty.

Sovereignty is political and unpolitical at the same time, which seems contradictory but isn't. It is one of the functions of sovereignty to stabilize the meaning and content of politics, where that meaning and content are always to be invented in any particular polity, and yet sovereignty settlements are necessarily formal, fixed, bloodless. The way in which sovereignty is both political and unpolitical renders its definitive meaning elusive and mysterious. Fassbender[37] refers to the way that sovereignty, over 'the centuries...has acquired an almost mythical quality', and this is not just the cloaking of power that Foucault draws attention to. However, this mystery is not one that can or even needs to be solved. Rather the political property of sovereignty is a settled and stable condition at the core of the constitution of the meaning of sovereignty (although also one which needs regular reaffirmation or reform and one which is precariously dependent on recognition, as described earlier), and it can be either (or both) benign and put to malign use in domination. It is part of the very concept of sovereignty itself to hold together that sovereignty is political but also outside politics. At the same time, identifying this attribute of sovereignty discloses a fugitive and transgressive quality in the meaning of the concept. As Brown notes, sovereignty contains 'multiple yet incommensurable truths' and 'challenges received authority — goes against the *doxa*'.[38] We take it for granted that sovereignty at some abstract level functions to regulate politics but we also forget its own link to the political realm.

It is useful to take a step back from questions of who has the power to act in the name of the collectivity, who has the ultimate legal authority, who has the power to coerce on behalf of the whole (the questions into which discussions of sovereignty are often immediately reduced), and to consider the habitual and conventional procedures and rules through which politics is conducted and which define its limits, and to note the political character of those things. By identifying how sovereignty is both

---

37 Bardo Fassbender, 'Sovereignty and Constitutionalism in International Law', in N. Walker (ed.), *Sovereignty in Transition* (Oxford: Hart, 2003), p. 115.
38 Chris Brown, *Sovereignty, Rights and Justice. International Political Theory Today* (Cambridge: Polity, 2002), p. 238.

unpolitical and political, it then makes sense that at the level of these questions of the locus of effective power, legal authority, and power to coerce, there can be very different conceptualisations of sovereignty, the coupling of state sovereignty with the dominant liberal popular sovereignty being only one.

The spectre and long shadow of ruler sovereignty figures strongly in writers who see the state as dangerous and all-powerful and is taken up by Foucault in his conception of sovereignty as allowing a form of oppressive power relations. The idea of popular sovereignty has not banished the association of sovereignty with overpowering and tyrannical government. This notion of ruler sovereignty remains a powerful threat, from James II to Louis XIV to Napoleon to dictators of the twentieth century. The idea of the political property of sovereignty focuses on something very different. Rather than aligning sovereignty with one side of the dichotomy formed by the burden of unjust and burdensome government against the political power inhering in 'the people', the political dimension of sovereignty calls attention to the implicit but ongoing work that is done in shaping the parameters of political debate in all polities.

This property of sovereignty goes to the heart of the sovereignty concept. It fills in the meaning behind the definition of sovereignty as supreme authority, or as Bellamy puts it, 'some ultimate adjudicator of all conflict in a world where consensual agreement on the right and the good cannot be counted on'.[39] Bellamy's conception, like the one put forward here, sees sovereignty as something we ask to perform a political function for us. This idea of the function of sovereignty in designating the meaning and limits of politics thus gets behind the definition of sovereignty in terms of questions about 'the proper exercise of power'. It also provides a way of getting beyond the fixation with the state as the concept that presupposes 'that central authority is a necessary condition for the existence of political order'.[40]

The content, parameters and limits of the political that the political property of sovereignty provides covers both of Chryssochoou's constitutive principles, namely the 'conditions of shared rule', and the normative commitments in the 'search for the common good'.[41] The condition for sovereignty outlined here also resembles in some ways the idea of 'normative order' that Neil Walker uses in his distinction between 'ruler sov-

---

39 Richard Bellamy, 'Sovereignty, Post-Sovereignty and Pre-Sovereignty: Three Models of the State, Democracy and Rights within the EU', in N Walker (ed.), *Sovereignty in Transition* (Oxford: Hart, 2003), p. 171.
40 Jens Bartelson, *The Critique of the State* (Cambridge: Cambridge University Press, 2001), p. 171.
41 Dimitris Chryssochoou, 'Europe's Republican Moment', *European Integration*, Vol. 24 (2002), pp. 343.

ereignty...the will to power as the source of normative order', and 'rule sovereignty...normative order as the source of power'.[42] It also represents one way of spelling out Neil Walker's contention that the different ways in which sovereignty can be operationalised (for instance identified by Krasner as domestic sovereignty, interdependence sovereignty, international legal sovereignty, and Westphalian sovereignty) gain their coherence from a 'common derivation from a deep core claim to know and order the world in a particular way'.[43]

The political meaning of sovereignty developed here also throws light on the question of the division of labour in a modern polity between sovereignty and a constitution. Although sovereignty and constitutionalism are closely aligned concepts, it is sovereignty which we invest with the function of deciding what is political and the boundary with the unpolitical. Rob Walker rightly insists that sovereignty is 'a highly complex and variable practice' rather than being just 'an inert constitutional principle'.[44] We use a principle of sovereignty, expressed in the idea of a formal constitution, to effect a distribution of powers, a coordination of institutions and processes, an assignment of entitlements, and an allocation of values. Bellamy and Castiglione note Jon Elster's definition of the functions of constitutions, and this list reinforces the sense of the closeness or overlap between the two concepts. From 'a purely technical point of view written constitutions have three main functions: (1) to define and protect rights; (2) to establish a map of political powers; and (3) to fix the procedures for constitutional revision'.[45]

However, while sovereignty and constitutionalism are contiguous and in some sense overlapping political concepts, a constitution does not account for all the work that we ask the political property of sovereignty to do for us. A constitution does not have to have, in itself, a guiding principle — it is the political dimension of sovereignty which provides this. It is the political property of sovereignty which sums up and provides the conditionally settled political identity of a polity as a whole, and without this support a constitution will be a dead letter. Moreover, while some theorists of cosmopolitanism put forward the idea of replacing sovereignty with constitutionalism, the problem with this proposal, as Schmitt understood, is that jurisdictional bodies are precisely not in a position to

---

42 Neil Walker, 'Preface', in N Walker (ed.), *Sovereignty in Transition* (Oxford: Hart, 2003a), p. vii.
43 Neil Walker, 'Late Sovereignty in the European Union', in N Walker (ed.), *Sovereignty in Transition* (Oxford: Hart, 2003b), p. 8.
44 R.B.J. Walker, 'Forward', in J Edkins, N Persram and V Pin-Fat (eds.), *Sovereignty and Subjectivity* (Boulder, CO: Lynne Rienner, 1999), pp. xiii.
45 Richard Bellamy and Dario Castiglione, 'Constitutionalism and Democracy — Political Theory and the American Constitution', *British Journal of Political Science*, Vol. 27 (1997), pp. 597.

offer a decision in problematic cases that the law cannot adjudicate on. Where the problem is political, legal instruments (legal process, laws, the constitution) are impotent.

To conclude this section, we can see that the political property of sovereignty has links with and differences from the notion of political culture. There has in recent years been a resurgence of interest in the study of political culture[46] but at the same time there has been a very marked fragmentation of the field, in terms of subject-matter, methodology, and normative commitments. Indeed there is ground for holding that the field as a whole now lacks even a minimal coherence. The original specification by Almond and Verba[47] of political culture as an area of study does not show a strong association with the idea of the political property of sovereignty, focusing as it does on the aggregation of individual political preferences as expressed in periodic political participation in voting. As Sidney Verba describes, their cross-national comparative political science method used 'survey techniques and values within a set of quite varied nations to deal with the macropolitical problem of democratic stability'.[48] Gabriel Almond identifies the categories with consequences for political behaviour through preference formation which interest them as 'subculture, elite political culture, political socialization, and culture change'.[49] The 'civic culture' project also has a clear ideological agenda with which this theory of the political property of sovereignty is not in sympathy, to promote a particular ideal of liberal democracy.

'Political culture' now ranges across investigations which draw on ethnographic methodologies from anthropology, the hermeneutic method of Clifford Geertz, the cultural theory approach of Mary Douglas, to studies of political domination and the contestation of power within the Foucauldian context of power in institutional discourses and the cultural definitions of politics. Also included under the term 'political culture' is Samuel Huntington's specification of group behaviour in terms of distinct civilisational identities reproduced through socialization, and the ubiquity of a psychological disposition to conflict between them. Building on Almond and Verba's project, the term also covers statistical investigations into national culture, the interaction between personality and cul-

---

46 Richard Wilson, 'The Many Voices of Political Culture', *World Politics*, Vol. 52 (2000), p. 246.
47 Gabriel Almond and Sidney Verba, *The Civic Culture: Political Attitudes and Democracy in Five Nations* (Princeton: Princeton University Press, 1963). See also Dennis Kavanagh, *Political Culture* (London: Macmillan, 1972).
48 Sidney Verba, 'On Revisiting the Civic Culture: A Personal postscript', in G .Almond and S. Verba (eds.), *The Civic Culture Revisited* (Boston: Little, Brown and Co., 1980), p. 397.
49 Gabriel Almond, 'The Intellectual History of the Civic Culture Concept', in G Almond and S Verba (eds.), *The Civic Culture Revisited* (Boston: Little, Brown and Co., 1980), p. 1.

ture, and rational choice and game theory cognitive methods of social psychology. Political culture also embraces the social psychology approach using Piaget which correlates political preferences to one's level of moral reasoning and development, and now also evolutionary psychology with memes as social instructional codes.[50]

The field thus encompasses—non-exhaustively—investigations as diverse as the context of normative patterning in which politics operates, how socially constructed shared meanings are accepted and questioned, how the rules of the political game are fashioned and refashioned, how political knowledge and values are reproduced and why they are queried, how rhetorical strategies such as metaphors, symbols, myths and rituals carry emotional resonance to represent the set of salient themes about values and aims in political rules and norms, and how they are expressed in socially valued political action, how the political legitimacy of political institutions, offices and leaders is established, how traditions of political practice are maintained and challenged, an explanation of 'preference orientations', the kind and degree of 'civic culture' present in different democracies, the role of ideologies as shared social and political understandings, the relationship between elites and masses, the peripheral or key positions of various groups within society, modernization theory, the study of political communication, how power is transformed into authority and authority disputed, and the factors involved in social cohesion and social solidarity that make political societies stable while tenuous or unstable and self-destructive.

Nevertheless, within this diffuse field there are some valuable insights to be gained for the character of politics and the political dimension of sovereignty. For instance the focus of the field of political culture is useful in understanding the culturally specific 'social glue' that is experienced by members of political societies, the idea of 'the embedding of political systems in sets of meanings and purposes',[51] the dynamic range of subjective and intersubjective 'meanings attributed to politics',[52] and the social construction of social norms and knowledge. One of the concerns of the field of political culture which overlaps with the concerns of this chapter is 'the legitimate boundaries of collective identity', and 'what constitutes or determines the boundaries of the political'.[53] The idea of the political property of sovereignty also shares with one strand of the political culture discourse an emphasis on the historical perspective of a political society's

---

50 Wilson (2000), p. 272.
51 Ibid., p. 246.
52 Myron Aronoff, 'Political Culture', in Neil Smelser and Paul Baltes (eds.), *International Encyclopedia of the Social and Behavioural Sciences* (Oxford: Elsevier, 2002), p. 11640.
53 Ibid.

processes and values. The political culture discourse also enriches our understanding of how in mainstream political theory, the criteria of reasoning and persuasiveness are taken to be supplied by narrowly rational abstract argument.

However, the key strength of the theory of the political dimension of sovereignty offered here derives not from commonalities with some of the central perceptions about politics which the political culture debate brings to light, but from the starting point of conceptual analysis of political concepts.

To start with, even the broadly interpretive areas of the 'political culture' field, where resemblances with the present enterprise are greatest, already render a set of assumptions (for instance about the role of emotion in political ideas, the potency of myths, the way social inter-relationships operate in the formation, reinforcement, and challenging of norms and values) as unproblematic ideas, whereas starting from the political theory analysis of political concepts sees such assumptions as precisely needing explanation and justification. Furthermore, proponents of political culture use a variety of descriptive, normative, and causal quantitative and qualitative methods, and the areas of the political culture field which rely on statistical and behavioural models in particular are at variance with the interpretive approach associated with the political dimension of sovereignty developed here. But most importantly, the political culture field—whether interested in the politics of culture or the culture of politics[54]—primarily takes its bearings from a sociological rather than a political level of attention, with the consequence that political values and norms are largely regarded as just another kind of values and norms. The distinctiveness of the political is easily dissipated there. The case for the political dimension of sovereignty relies very heavily on an understanding of politics as a distinct field of enquiry and one which differs from and is not reducible to sociology, cultural studies, anthropology, or social psychology. In addition, this theory of the political property of sovereignty encompasses a much broader and richer notion of what politics is, as not just about institutions and procedures, ruling and governing, and not just a matter of contestation and conflict.

The Political Dimension of Sovereignty and Political Leadership

Clarifying the relation between leadership and sovereignty is central to understanding the role of political leadership in politics, and to redressesing the neglect of political leadership in mainstream strands of

[54] *Ibid.*, p. 11641.

democratic theory. The mainstream notion of sovereignty as ruler sovereignty has little to offer the understanding and rethinking of political leadership. Ruler sovereignty, while paying lip service to the role of the people as *pouvoir constituent*, accents a hierarchy of law-making and the top-down authority by elites to govern in *pouvoir constitué*. The effectiveness of political leadership in all its faces can be enhanced by recognizing the way the political property of sovereignty operates.

One example of a polity in which there was a robust consciousness of, though not necessarily reflection upon, the role of the political dimension of sovereignty in defending a specific way of conducting politics is found in the United Provinces in the seventeenth century.[55] The Dutch defended their notion of the complex autonomy of the different provinces, their loose polycentric confederal system, and their mode of consensual politics, and as a result had a clear and successful sense of political leadership, particularly under the De Witt government.

The political property of sovereignty has a range of practical consequences for the second face of political leadership. The political dimension of sovereignty throws into perspective the depleted agency of current political leadership practices and a way to reinvigorate that agency. Reflection on the meaning of political leadership is enriched by considering how sovereignty regulates politics and casts the conditional boundary between the political and the unpolitical. It promotes debate about the conceptual vocabulary of politics, enriches the business of governing, gives greater meaning to elections, and highlights government misreadings of citizens' political values. It enriches the understanding and so the practice of politics, decreases the tension between government desire to suppress dissent and citizens' (or subjects') desire to participate in political decision-making. It revitalizes the bond between leaders and led, elite and masses, re-energises the notion of legitimacy, and underlines the normative aspect of politics. It restores the importance of constituent power to the conduct of ordinary power, and demonstrates how this distinction plays a key role in conditionally settling the boundary between what counts as political and what is regarded as unpolitical. The rest of the chapter briefly outlines these points.

Articulating the role of sovereignty in establishing the architecture of the content of politics and boundaries of the political promotes reflection on politics within a political society, prompted by political leaders. In most modern western societies such a level of reflection is lacking, political debate nearly always revolving around specific policies, cases, events, and figures. Explicit awareness of the role of the political property of sov-

---

55 Raia Prokhovnik, *Spinoza and Republicanism* (Basingstoke: Macmillan, 2004).

ereignty could lead to a reflexive valuing of politics as political and of the specificity of political leadership. Such a proposal marks a course between rationalist social engineering and Oakeshottian conservatism. It encourages a more open and critical appreciation of the political while also acknowledging the profound importance of custom, tradition and conventional practices in shaping the conduct of politics in a particular polity.

There is a dialectical relationship between leaders and political institutions, and between political processes and the conditional sovereignty settlement. Political leaders help to articulate and shape, and at times contest, the values and ideas about the boundaries of the political which are central to the political property of sovereignty. We noted above that a useful aspect of the idea of charisma was that it places leadership under the rubric of power, and that while political leaders are cognitively perceived as individuals, they are socially defined. Decisions which renegotiate this political property of sovereignty require a special type of leadership, since the boundary between normalcy and emergency is blurred. The study of charisma and of mediatised politics seek to explain political allegiance less through an individualized approach to politics and more through something like the conditional sovereignty settlement which finds room for particular kinds of leaders or which is being contested by such leaders.

Reflection on the nature of political leadership within a specific polity, brought about through utilising the political property of sovereignty, also refers to the sharpening up of the conceptual vocabulary of politics and so of political debate. For instance, what kind of gender values political leaders tap into in the context of a particular polity can be pinpointed, and the gendered dimension of political leadership more generally comes into focus. How 'the people' are conceptualized, whether 'the people' are regarded as homogeneous, and how 'the people' differs from 'the masses' can be evaluated more accurately. The relationship between 'the people' and the political elite, how that distinction aligns with the one between rulers and ruled, whether it is only the elite who take effective part in politics, whether they exercise a monopoly of power, and how the elite is constructed can be analysed more clearly. What counts as good leadership in a prime minister or president (taking a firm line, being conciliatory, forming a united front within the governing party, having spokespersons act on your behalf or making a personal intervention), and what counts as leadership in a leader of the opposition (setting out a distinctively different agenda, copying the governing party's agenda, claiming to be more youthful, or more wise) can be more effectively gauged. What counts as innovation in political leadership and what is simply a development of previous practice can be distinguished. What role is accorded to 'public opinion' and how it operates can be highlighted. What kind of relationship between leaders and led is most successful (patriarchal and hierarchical, empowering and populist, distant or hands-on) and how leaders take decisions on behalf of the led can be assessed. How the boundary is constituted and understood between compliance, obedience and acts made through voluntary obligation on the one hand, and oppression, coercion and domination on the other, can be explicated. How the difference between fair and unfair taxes is accounted for, can be explored. The roles of and balance between symbolic and concrete political action can be studied. The levels, and limits, that are tolerated of disenchantment, cynicism, apathy, and low voter turnout can be considered.

The political reading of sovereignty advanced here articulates the contexts in which decisions are taken on the nature and scope of the political (where those things are not naturally or neutrally given), and as providing a certain latitude for the expression of difference as well as of a sphere of commonality and equality. The active side of this is, as Fassbender notes, that sovereignty is invoked in practice most often in a political rather than legal fashion, when claims are being made 'for a change of the *status quo*, or claims to power', and the 'clearest manifestation' of the 'impulse to power' is still war.[56] Sovereignty is in this sense a threshold concept, invoked when claims are being made on it or in its name. Fassbender attests to the political, 'untamed', character of sovereignty, notwithstanding the efforts of 'legal science to domesticate the notion and define it as the legal autonomy of a state under international law'.[57]

Focusing on the under-acknowledged political property of sovereignty throws light on the way the conduct of government business as well as contests for leadership take place within (largely tacit) rules and understandings about how politics is done, what counts as political, and what is beyond the political. Also, governments are not in control of the political dimension of sovereignty and can misread what counts as political. Governments are constantly testing out, stretching, or reinforcing the tacit conventions and values about how politics is done, and the boundary between the political and unpolitical. Issues in British politics in recent years all confirm this, such as the Commons vote over renewing the Trident nuclear deterrent, the long process under the Blair Government considering options for the reform of the House of Lords, the revelation of the major political parties being financed through secret loans as well as from registered donations and the cash for honours affair, government

---

56 Fassbender (2003), p. 141.
57 *Ibid.*, p. 142.

responses to fuel protests, pro-hunting protests, and Fathers for Justice protests, and the restrictions placed on street protest against the new animal testing laboratory at Oxford University.

One effect of this political function that we ask sovereignty to perform for the polity is to provide legitimisation for the polity. The way in which legitimacy is granted or achieved is often shrouded. We see the performativity of the election, the coronation, the popular assembly, but there remains a gap between such acts and the polity they are said to legitimise. With the political property of sovereignty analysed here the gap is narrowed or eliminated for we can see the correspondence between the dominant or commonly-understood (if not universally agreed) norms and values about the conduct of politics and the settlement about the content and parameters of the political, the agreed area of (even if ever more symbolic) contestation and political negotiation.

Leadership contests, paradigmatically in the form of general elections, can be seen as periods of collective drama when the political dimension of sovereignty is critical and is invoked (either explicitly or implicitly) in two ways. The legitimacy of political leaders to represent constituent power, and the move from politician to leader, derive in part from the recognition and sanction by voters and elites that such persons can be authorised to perform the roles of ruler sovereignty. Leadership contests are also concentrated periods when politicians either make claims to best reflect the settled conventions governing political debate and action, or claims that those conventions need to be challenged and redrawn and that a particular potential leader is best able to perform this task. The important process of articulating such claims, which plays a crucial role in the creation of political leaders, concerns the affirmation or contestation of the conditional sovereignty settlement. Governments can also misread what counts as political, for instance when the French government initially dismissed rioters in the *banlieue* of Paris in 2005 as mere criminals and trouble-makers, and when Thatcher sought to impose the poll tax in Britain in the late 1980s.

The political property of the concept of sovereignty provides a deeper understanding of the distinction about sovereignty highlighted for instance by Franklin[58] in relation to Locke, between constituent power and ordinary power. The meaningfulness of the link between the power of the people as the ultimate lawmaking authority on the one hand and the legislative, executive and judicial branches of government on the other, depends precisely upon the successful conditional settlement hold-

---

58 Julian Franklin, *John Locke and the Theory of Sovereignty* (Cambridge: Cambridge University Press, 1981).

ing the specific content given to politics and the border between what is political and what is unpolitical. This is a key function we ask sovereignty to perform.

One practical consequence that follows from the way the ordinary and constituent power distinction is made in modern polities is the decision in democracies about whether that distinction and connection is expressed in direct or representative form. Neil Walker also notes illuminatingly that, in Foucault's terms, 'sovereignty expresses both the power that enacts law and the law that restrains power—(political) ruler sovereignty and (legal) rule sovereignty—*pouvoir constituant* and *pouvoir constitué*'. Walker makes the case that for 'many, including Foucault, this double claim is testimony to the conceptual incoherence of sovereignty'. However, as Walker argues, it can also be viewed more constructively, as the 'conceptual key to sovereignty as a dynamic process of mutual constitution and mutual containment of law and politics'. If the term sovereignty is taken as 'expressive reminder'[59] of the interdependence and mutual underpinning of law and politics, then the paradox dissolves.

Finally, while the political property of sovereignty outlined here has a clear functionalist element, it much more importantly has a strong normative dimension. Determining the notional content of politics and placing the boundaries of politics at a certain point are outcomes of normative thinking about relations amongst individuals and groups within the polity, participation and dissent, equality, democracy, multi-party electoral contestation, and politics as progressive and transformative or conservative and constrained in the liberal sense. Answers to all such questions are the upshot of political debate within a larger or smaller group and are expressed in a dominant set of values, either open to further contestation or exercising an oppressive hegemony.

---

[59] Neil Walker (2003b), pp. 19–20.

Gábor G. Fodor

The Two 'Faces' of Political Creativity
Two Paradigms of Political Leadership[1]

This paper clarifies the relationship between leadership and creativity which is central to understanding the role of governance in politics, and increases comprehension of the lack of attention given to the question of leadership in the mainstream of governance theory. The 'new fashions', the primary contemporary approaches to the nature of governance[2] — the idea of 'good government', 'governance without government', 'joined-up governance', 'New Public Management' (NPM) or 'Post-NPM', and the 'multi-dimensional concept of governance' — seem to undermine the so-far axiomatic premise according to which governance is mainly a political activity. The mainstream endeavours of governance theory suppose that the matter of governance is not the central issue of political science, *but* rather that of public administration. These new, trendy ideas do not concern the old question: the problem of political leadership.

Paradoxically, the separation of the problems of governance from political science is crucially determined by new theories of governance. The

---

1 My research has been supported by OTKA F-68112.
2 See, for example, Michael Barzelay, *The New Public Management. Improving Research and Policy Dialogue* (California: University of California Press, 2001); Stephen Goldsmith, William D. Eggers, *Governing by Network. The New Shape of the Public Sector* (Washington D.C.: Brookings Institutions Press, 2004); Martin Minogue, Charles Polidano, David Hulme (eds.), *Beyond the New Public Management. Changing Ideas and Practices in Governance* (Cheltenham: Edwar Elgar, 2000); Jon Pierre, Guy B. Peters, *Governance, Politics and the State* (New York, 2000); Jon Pierre, *Debating Governance. Authority, Steering, and Democracy* (Oxford: Oxford University Press, 2000); Christopher Pollit & Geert Bouckaert, *Public Management Reform. A Comparative Analysis* (2nd edn.) (Oxford: Oxford University Press, 2004); Pierre Calame, *La démocratie en miettes. Pour une révolution de la gouvernance* (Paris: Descartes &Cie, 2003); Guy Hermet, Ali Kazancigil & Jean-François Prud'homme, *La gouvernance. Un concept et ses applications* (Paris: Karthala, 2005); Julia von Blumenthal, *Governance-eine kritische Zwischenbilanz, Zeitschrift für Politikwissenschaft* (Heft 4, 2005), pp. 1149–80 and Renate Mayntz, 'Governance-Theory als fortentwickelte Steuerungstheorie', in Gunnar Folke Schuppert (Hrsg.), *Governance-Forschung. Vergewisserung über Stand und Entwicklungslinien* (Baden-Baden, 2005), pp. 11–20.

newly fashionable approaches—by combining aspects of public management and leadership—instead deal primarily with managerial questions of administration and organisation instead of political conduct. They are mainly interested in the organisational structure and the decision making procedures of the modern democratic state. Practitioners of these approaches are also interested in the operation of governance as an executive power, and focus on the administrative, technical, economic, and efficiency issues of leadership. This view of governance mostly concentrates on structures, procedures, and normative frames, so it abandons and empties aspects of actual exercise of power.

This study attempts to reinvent the political content or political core of governance by saying that the *coincidentia oppositorium*[3] (the unity or coincidence of opposing parts) in politics, and, therefore, in political science (and *not* in public administration), is the question of governance. This chapter argues that the problem of governance primarily can be comprehended through the phenomenon of political leadership; the focal point of political leadership is creativity. Political creativity is like *'virtu'* controlling the power of *'fortuna'*: political cleverness, a special manner of relating to and dealing with power, and the ability to rise above contingent circumstances. We simultaneously state that governance is primarily a political process that obtains momentum from political leaders and the way that they exercise power creatively. This first idea reflects the uneasy comprehension of political creativity. So, in order to grasp the gist of its meaning we propose observing how creativity works. In my opinion, this angle of examination makes it possible to recognise the Janus-face of political creativity.

The 'creativity thesis' proposes that the core of understanding governance is the exercise of power, and this has to be a *creative* exercise that contributes to the *organization* and the *operation* of political power, too. Therefore, the concept of political leadership as a creative force can be conceptualized as having two faces. The first is concerned with the *organization of power*, and investigates the creativity that creates the scope of power. This kind of creativity is concealed, and remains unseen to the public. The second face concerns the actual representation of governance, and concentrates on the actively presented view of creativity that relates to the visible operation of power.

The first, hidden 'face' of creativity refers to political leadership as a way of thinking and an arsenal of tools of which the foundation was laid

---

3 The term of Nicholas Cusanus. See Nicholas Cusanus, *Of Learned Ignorance* (Wipf & Stock Publishers, 2007).

by Tilo Schabert.[4] This concept emphasizes princely figures in politics belonging to human societies in an essential way. They have appeared at all times and at all places, and they represent in one person the classical features of political leadership. As Schabert argues, what modern leaders have in common is that they govern modern democracies in the way of the classical prince.[5] This paradigm relates to the 'concealed' scope of politics in which creativity is related to *organising the conditions of governance*.

The latter face of creativity, the open face, is the aesthetic paradigm that emphasizes the aesthetic connotations of the term 'representation' and talks about leadership as representation by the government. Accepting Frank Ankersmit's view,[6] the second concept describes the nature of modern democracy as a problem of mediatisation, and as the result of mediatisation, politics is personalized. According to Ankersmit's thesis, we may say that persons represent politics for the audience day after day and governance will be only a mockery of the activity: pantomime.[7] This paradigm deals with the 'public face' of political power, and thus focuses on *the exercise of power* and on the problem of governmental capacity.

This chapter also makes an attempt to analyse the components and character of leadership in modern democracies with the help of two theoretical approaches. As political creativity is Janus-faced, my present study is also two-faced. One part is about the knowledge of governance which is complemented by the other part, i.e. the knowledge needed for governance. In this respect, my sentences can be read as an introduction to the world of politics and political leadership, but at the same time, they can be applied as a 'cheat' to political activity or a textual guidance addressed to unskilled emperors (in this latter case, an ironic reading of my study also works).

As a consequence, this study implicitly separates two different types of knowledge from each other.[8] The first is knowledge *about* governance, while the other is knowledge *of* governance. There is no doubt that these differing kinds of knowledge can be examined together, however, the mutual and parallel investigations of these do not mean a fusion of the differing sorts of knowledge or a mixture of their incompatible aspects.

---

[4] Tilo Schabert, *Boston Politics: The Creativity of Power* (Berlin/New York: Walter de Gruyter 1989); Tilo Schabert, 'A Classical Prince: The Style of François Mitterand', *Philosophy, Literature and Politics: Essays Honory Ellis Sandoz*, Cooper, Embry (eds.) (Columbia/London: University of Missouri Press, 2005), pp. 234–57.

[5] Schabert, *A Classical Prince*, pp. 234–57.

[6] Frank R. Ankersmit, *Aesthetic Politics. Political Philosophy Beyond Fact and Value* (Stanford, CA: Stanford University Press, 1996).

[7] See G. Fodor Gábor, 'A kormányzás-tudás válsága. A pantomime-kormányzás természetrajza', *Kommentár*, no. 1. (2007), pp. 61–76.

[8] See G. Fodor Gábor, *Kormányzás/tudás* (Budapest: Századvég, 2008).

The study distinguishes the two types of knowledge via the consistent usage of different fonts and letter sizes. As a result, some ironic 'decalogues' are going to be deployed separately in the body of the text, which at the same time are to follow the schemes of 'political mirrors'. Anyone who is a politician and seeks for readily available and quick knowledge about governance has to scan through only the framed, text-boxed guidance. Nevertheless, those who quest for knowledge of governance have to find cohesion and a relationship between the different texts on dissimilar creativity. I would like to highlight some crucial aspects to demonstrate the differences and emphasise the conclusion that one can lean on each concept at the same time in this essay.

The First Face of Creativity: The Conditions for Governance

One side of creativity refers to the hidden world of politics, from this perspective, creativity contributes to organising the conditions for exercising political power. Tilo Schabert argues that politics and governance constitute power. A government that possesses power is unimaginable without a governor who is not able to organise the conditions of power in a creative manner, moreover, organising the conditions of power is more significant than the content of actual governance. Therefore the core of understanding politics is '*follow the leader*'. Schabert's concept emphasizes a princely figure in politics belonging to human societies as an essential element. They have appeared at all times and at all places, and they represent in one person the classical features of political leadership. As Schabert argues, what modern leaders have in common is that they govern modern democracies in the manner of the classical prince.[9]

1. First and foremost: *divide et impera*.
2. Divide and isolate people by a proliferation of commissions, advisory groups, task forces. If the complexity of the governmental apparatus is critized, propose the creation of a commision for the study of governmental reform.
3. Do not establish precise lines of authority. Keep responsibilities blurred. Make overlapping assignments.
4. Give your associates and aides some lattitude for running their affairs. Foment competition. Reward the winner.
5. Engage several agencies in projects on similar turf. Make them jockey for position.
6. Distribute from time to time chips of influence among your aides and subordinates. They tantalize their yearning for power.

---

9   See Schabert, *Boston Politics*, pp. 41–2.

7. Launch periodically into a shake-up of the governmental apparatus. Shuffle the personnel.
8. Create two layers of government, a visible and an invisible one, by splitting governmental positions into nominal and real functions.
9. Become an expert in substituting a web of personal relationships for the system of government.
10. If you steadily apply these methods, you will erect a chaotic but powerful rule of which you will be the sole master. The manipulation of governmental chaos is the source of your personal power.

To Schabert, the question of political leadership is the core of political science. As Schabert argues, in politics the few represent the many. The notion of 'executive power' implies a moment of creativity: 'the Many emerge as the One'. Also somewhere in politics acts of transformation occur: acts which make the multitude appear as a body politic. The notion of 'executive power' implies a moment of transfiguration. 'The moment of creativity, the moment of transfiguration — the current vocabulary of political science does not feature such expressions. We are offered the term "political leadership"'.[10]

While the science of politics continues to consider as governmental 'reality' what its symbols and concepts evoke, governmental politics has been moving beyond the known institutions of government towards quite another reality of governing. According to this concept, space and time are not homogeneous, but plural and multitudinous.[11] The phenomena of politics should be studied in the context of their history and space. First, behind the scenes of the public institutions there is a 'second government', the 'Court', which tends to supersede the public world, that is, the formally instituted government. The Court is the crucible of politics and the locus of creativity. Second, to apperceive the Court, one must comprehend its history, that is the history of its manifestations and transformations. Schabert argues, 'time' occurs in manifold ways: as a 'time of advance' or as a 'time of renaissance', as a 'time of ruptures and discontinuities' or as a 'time of parallel and corresponding events'. 'The city dwells in the age of television when it elects its governor and it appears to be a medieval city-state considering the fabric of its government'.[12] Also a present-day state or city the government of which is headed by a 'classical prince' is a *contemporaneous* for example with Rome's late Republic or Machiavelli's Italy. Political practice rests on the plurality of space and

---

10 Ibid., pp. 50-1.
11 Ibid., pp. 4-5., 45-95., 99-109, 112-17.
12 Ibid., p. 100.

time. Moreover, the assumption of temporal parallelism substantiates the idea that the nature of governing is perennial.

The hypothesis of plurality allows of the utterance that Kevin White (ex-mayor of Boston), Roosevelt, Truman, Eisenhower, Johnson, Adenauer, Helmuth Kohl, and François Mitterand (and naturally Blair, Sarkozy, Merkel, or the Hungarian Prime Minister Ferenc Gyurcsány) have in common that each govern in the manner of the classical prince, and each is for that reason original. For instance

> Mitterand did not govern in a way similar to Roosevelt because he may have wished to imitate the latter. The astounding similarity came from another source. Mitterand attained in his practice of governing a classicism in the art of government to which Roosevelt had come by his practice of governing [...] Viewed from the perspective of this classical understanding of the *Prince*, however, they were similar to each other: in Mitterand's conduct of government we find Roosevelt's art of governing, and in Rossevelt's conduct of government we find Mitterand's art of governing.[13] Namely to govern is to govern *within* the classical structure. The problems of governing are solved in similar ways: although by different people in different times under different circumstances.[14]

The prince can evoke the classical structure by means of imitation of laws of creativity. Princes actualize patterns of examples and follow such examples. But then, 'to follow' 'would not mean simply to imitate, to continue, or to join. Rather, it would have to be understood by way of a law of structural similarity'. The prince does not follow examples, but he follows a general paradigm of governmental creativity that others before him had followed. The similarity emerges from a similar practice of governing. 'Each prince thus created in this general, paradigmatic form his own form of governing and became, in his following the paradigm, similar to others who followed it as well.'[15]

The actualization of classical patterns is suited for creating *the conditions for governing* and not only *the tasks of governing*. As Schabert argues, organizing a creative powerful government is of greater importance than the process of governing itself.[16] And the prince can ensure the conditions for governing by the help of creating a chaotic government.[17] The autocrat deliberately keeps his government in a state of confusion throwing it again and again into a whirl of shuffles and commutations. By creating confusion the prince's exclusive knowledge as to the current configura-

---

13 Schabert, *A Classical Prince*, p. 237.
14 See Schabert, *Boston Politics*, pp. 21–2.
15 Schabert, *A Classical Prince*, p. 239.
16 Schabert, *Boston Politics*, p. 24.
17 Schabert, *A Classical Prince*, pp. 236–7.

tion of organizational strings makes him superior to anyone: Whoever becomes involved in the process of governing could hardly ignore his wishes, intentions, and plans. The reading of those is at least as important as any technical comptence or practical knowledge.[18]

The instrument of creating a chaotic goverment is that the prince shifts the lines and constructs a flexible net of configurations.' by the help of producing overlapping circles of authority. He ensures the predominance of policy over insitutions by the means of evoking the primacy of persons and creating a second government, a Court. To Schabert the field of political creativity is a phenomenon to be seen by the second government that is formed by the Court. 'The Court defines the area of political reality where the representative acts are performed through which a multitude of people becomes the one people acting as a body politic. The Court is the crucible of politics.'[19]

Also the paradigm of creativity focuses on the personality of the political leader and the relation between the prince and his environment. Between the two sides exists a dynamic connection. The leader has great, autonomous acting-sphere, but this autonomy is not by far absolute.[20] As Schabert argues, constitutional government is a 'miraculous' mechanism: it produces political authority by denying it. Schabert asks: How can the prince gain the power to govern and still remain the head of a constitutional government?[21] The answer: the logic of creativity in politics induces princes to create a party of friends and the para-governmental configurations of a second government, a Court. Thus the leader becomes the master of the paradox of power by creating within the framework of constitutional government, a para-institutional configuration of personal power. Against the shattered pieces of constitutional government he sets off monocratic powers—an autocracy with the help of the power of friends. The primacy of persons is the foundation of 'personal machine-government'.

---

18 Schabert, *Boston Politics*, p. 27.
19 *Ibid.*, p. 54.
20 See Ervin Csizmadia, 'A politikai vezetők és a politikai környezet I.', *Politikatudományi Szemle*, no. 2–3 (2006), pp. 25–52., Fred Greenstein, Can Personality and Politics be Studied Systematically? *Political Psychology*, Vol. 13. No. 1 (1992), pp. 105–28. and Robert Elgie, *Political Leadership in Liberal Democracies* (Basingstoke and London: MacMillan Press, 1995).
21 Schabert, *Boston Politics*, p. 11.

The Distortion and the Limits of the Paradigm

To govern means to create power, through persons, on the one hand, and through forms of power — 'court politics'[22] — on the other hand, that allow creativity for the prince to break the institutional resistance encountered in the formation of power.[23] The constitutional system produces political authority by denying it. It deliberately weakens the political executive in the name of liberty. However, not even a constutional government can exist without power; so political power is necessary: 'Yet, it should be the power of liberty'.[24] The core of the creativity, the second government, the Court, emerges from the government and the government is shaped by the Court. This is the foundation of autocratic power in a constitutional system. Authority is exercised *within* the governement and *by* the government, but not *outside* the government. The greatest danger for the autocracy is the autocracy itself: democracy cannot become an autocracy: it has to respect liberty (the object of a constitutional system.)

In this regard, the creative organisation of power (e.g.: centralized bureaucracy, reward positions for the loyal, a set of overlapping scopes of authorities, unaccountability, faded responsibilities, staff member fluctuations, customary structural changes, the establishment of different advisory and professional committees and boards, the creation of parallelism in formal and informal governmental operations, and corruption[25]) reinforces the position of the governor in the government who follows the behavioural pattern of the emperor, though it also makes the governor's supremacy vulnerable in times of crises. By the singular control of different decision-making competencies, the emperor degrades all of the policy- makers in his cabinet to mere executors, and by doing so, political conflicts will accumulate around the person of the emperor as well. Since the governor embodies the government, the weakening of his position affects the performance, effectiveness, and the operation of the whole government; hence each member of the cabinet shares the governor's fate. Owing to the concentration of power, the governor can easily change his cabinet, but paradoxically, it is indeed the growing insignificance of the cabinet that contributes to the diminishing importance of these changes. In parallel, those private staff members who are drawn into real deci-

---

22 See G. Fodor Gábor, 'A paradigmákba zárt miniszterelnök. A politikai vezetés három paradigmája a modern demokráciákban', Gazsó Tibor, G. Fodor Gábor, Stumpf István (eds.), *Őszöd árnyékában. A 2. Gyurcsány kormány első éve* (Budapest: Századvég, 2007), pp. 45–99, and Dennis Kavanagh, 'The Blair Premiership', in Anthony Seldon, Dennis Kavanagh (eds.), *The Blair Effect 2001–5* (Cambridge: Cambridge University Press, 2005), pp. 3–20.
23 Schabert, *A Classical Prince*, p. 251.
24 Schabert, *Boston Politics*, p 11.
25 '...an autocracy is prone to corruption'.*Ibid.*, p. 19.

sion-making processes can hardly be replaced because the loyal, politically confident people are always personally connected to the governor. These people cannot be removed without the weakening the governor's position. The possible outcome of this vicious circle is that the substantive contents of governance become slowly subordinated to the technical matters of political authority. By this, not only the organisation, but also the operation of political power might turn autocratic. Hidden creativity that serves autocratic governance alienates its own scope of existence, the artistic side of creativity. In other words, the governor who is the head of politics in the court can be easily imprisoned by the logic of his own court. However, governance that is proactive, stable, and capable of action cannot be imagined without representative creativity. Sufficient governance is partly supported by the constitution and the rule of law, yet, there is another, less tangible precondition. Beyond the written code of legality there is another set of political factors needed for creative governance to at least the same extent - this precondition is legitimacy. In political science legitimacy refers to the aspects of the relationship between the governor and the governed that describe to what measure, and on what grounds the governed accept the governor to be an authority. Legitimacy might be based on legality as well, but in fact, the real capacity for governmental action that truly influences the circumstances of governance, is determined by such social admittance that can be independent from judgements of legality. Hence, legitimacy is always the fundament of exercise of political power. When legitimacy decreases, the capability of governance will inevitably scale down as well. When the latter melts away, the governor—if he wants to avoid resigning—has to favour his supporters (voters or party members), in other words, he has to buy their support. This is the way the uncontrolled improvement of creativity building autocracy leads to the disappearance of other types of creativity, the representative interpretation of capable governance, and, therefore, to arbitrary and impotent politics.

Another Face of Creativity:
(Re)Presentation as the Facility of Governance

The aesthetic paradigm of political leadership emphasizes the aesthetic connotations of the term 'representation' and talks about leadership as representation by the government. We may say that this concept describes the nature of modern democracy as a problem of mediatisation, and as the result of mediatisation, politics is personalized. To Frank R. Ankersmit representation can be seen as the heart of politics, because all politics presuppose the self-awareness of the political collectivity that is paradigmatically exemplified by political representation.[26] Indeed, Ankersmit uses the term representation both in the strict sense and figuratively. The term of representation means both political and artistic representation in making something present that is absent. On the one hand, the government is the agent of representation (accordingly political representation means the political act of governing), on the other hand the government is the subject of governing. Inasmuch as a substantive problem of governing is finding out and manipulating what constituents think of the government, the government must also represent the illusions of governing toward the people.

As artistic representation is making something present that is absent, there is an intimate relationship between artistic and political representation.[27] As Ankersmit argues, aesthetics will be able to make our insight into aesthetic political representation more precise.[28] The key to artistic representation is a substitution for reality, a substitution that admittedly evokes an illusion of reality, but which nevertheless remains distuinguishable from reality itself.[29] The difference between the representation and what is represented is the source of and condition for all aesthetic pleasure. 'Aesthetic pleasure is not possible until we have learned to accept the radical rift between the real world and the world of artistic representation'.[30] As Ankersmit argues, we can only talk about representation when there is a difference — and not an identity — between the representative and the person represented. Moreover, political reality only comes into being after and due to representation (also, according to Ankersmit, there is no *objective* political reality). Therefore, political representation is nothing else but creativity that proposes and sustains the scope of an aesthetic gap - this is called by Ankersmit 'aesthetic representation'. The political reality created by aesthetic representation is therefore essentially political power.[31] Even as aesthetic representation creates a 'gap' or difference to allow the action of governance, mimetic representation eliminates this 'gap'. The key to mimetic representation is the thesis of identity. There is an identity between thought and act, similarly between the representative and the person represented.[32] For the mimetic

---

26 Ankersmit, *Aesthetic Politics*, p. 23.
27 See Edmund Burke, 'A Philosphical Inquiry into the Origin of our Ideas of Sublime and Beautiful', *Edmund Burke. Pre-Revolutionary Writtings,* Ian Harris (ed.) (Cambridge: Cambrige University Press, 1993), pp. 58–78.
28 Ankersmit, *Aesthetic Politics*, p. 45.
29 *Ibid.*, pp. 45–6.
30 *Ibid.*, p. 46.
31 *Ibid.*, p. 49.
32 *Ibid.*, pp. 25–6.

theory there are two situations only: 'either the representative is a correct representation of the represented (but is, in that case, superfluous) or he or she is not and in that case the representative's power is, according to the logic of the mimetic theory, illegitimate'.[33] Also the mimetic practice will be forced either to deny the existence of political power or to declare all political power intrinsically illegitimate. In this respect, aesthetic representation creates and maintains the creativity needed for political action, whereas the mimetic one annihilates that.

Ankersmit simultaneously claims that representation is not identical to mimetic practice but representation organizes knowledge.[34] Representation is selective: it proposes that we see the world from a certain perspective and we arrange it to be seen in a specific way. And obviously such preferences cannot be decided in terms of differences between truth and falsehood. As artistic representation organizes knowledge in a specific way, in the same manner political practice arranges preferences and demands, together with the maintenance of illusions.

In an autocracy, the paradigm of hidden creativity[35] focuses on the conditions of governance, and another face of creativity emphasises governance as both presentation and representation. Governance relates not only to fulfilling or refusing requirements. It does not merely reform expectations relevant to governance, but also wants to (re)present these expectations. The hypothesis of this concept articulates[36] that political reality exists only through representation. Much like in aesthetic representation in arts, politics strives for display and preservation of the gap between reality and its representation. Representation finds its purpose and meaning in the indeterminable and interpretable character of the 'reality' that is to be represented. Political representation indeed strongly resembles historical representation: we cannot properly speak about historical reality outside or apart from its historical representation. Historical and political realities are always realities that are given to us through and by representation. In addition, it is not the representation that organizes knowledge, however political knowledge organizes representation.

According to Ankersmit's thesis, we may say that the classic branch of aesthetic representation is *heresthetics*,[37] more specifically: the art of manipulation. In the age of modern politics, the seriousness of herestetic

---

33 Ibid., p. 49.
34 Ibid., p. 39.
35 'Every autocracy tends naturally to be secretive its inner workings', Schabert, *Boston Politics*, p. 22.
36 See Ankersmit, *Aesthetic Politics*, pp. 50–1.
37 About heresthetic see William H. Riker, *The Art of Manipulation* (New Haven: Yale University Press, 1986).

proficiency is relieved and partly replaced by the job of spin doctors, who, in this respect, submit political marketing into the service of governance. However Ankersmit does not write about that concretely, as a presumption, his approach implies that heresthetics and spin doctors have different methods for cultivating knowledge. Since spin doctoral formulas alleviate the intellectual burden of inventiveness on politicians, the knowledge of governance eventually dwindles to political dexterity based on sheer practical wisdom and technical expertise. While the instructions of PR-governance are dedicated to the inexperienced prince, and the recipes actually guarantee success, as for heresthetics, the free individual is enabled to make a decision by following his own judgements in a situation the outcomes of which are quite uncertain. According to the self-proclamation of spin doctors, they do not only supplement, but replace classic political knowledge (and by this they devalue it at the same time), seeing that a modern mediatized democracy needs fewer deeds and more imitation; (re)presentation is more significant than reality, and the image becomes a crucial point in governing instead of classic political knowledge. Devaluation which entails arrogance does not lead to superiority as a direct consequence. The fall of pantomime-governance sheds light on the timelessness of Seneca, Thucydides, and Montesquieu, contrary to the guidelines of those concise 'know-how bibles' which are considered to be radically reforming nowadays.

The purpose of the exploitation of political knowledge is to deploy a leeway of creativity which ensures the capacity for governing and which, at the same time, also makes a place for deliberation and political bargaining. Because this leeway is the precondition for creative measures and governance, political power can be possessed neither by the represented, nor by he who represents. The reason for this is that if any of the two expropriated authority the system would fall back into the mimetic tradition.

In order to avoid this, we need the aesthetic approach of representation.[38] Political representation makes such things present that are absent. A crucial point is that artistic representation does not offer a mimetic likeness of what is represented, but a substitute for it. A substitute admittedly evokes an 'illusion' of reality, but it remains distinguishable from reality itself. Ankersmith says: 'this difference between representation and what is represented, which is the source of and condition for all aesthehtic pleasure [...] Aesthetic pleasure is possible until we have learned to accept the radical rift between the real world and the world of artisitic representa-

---

38 See Ankersmit, *Aesthetic Politics*, pp. 45–51.

tion.'³⁹ The preconditioning of political actions is one such free leeway where creative and innovative steps can be taken. Correspondingly, good or at least successful governance cannot be accomplished without similar aesthetic representation, which establishes the leeway of creativity. Hence, power has an aesthetic rather than an ethical nature. The aesthetic difference or gap between the represented and its representation is the origin of legitimate political power. Political power has its origin neither in the people represented nor in their representative, but in the process of representation itself. Political power is not the possession of anyone; it is a result of the relationship between the representative and the represented, which is unconcealed to the public sphere. In addition, Ankersmit primarily concentrates on the representational view of creativity that relates to the visible operation of power. This creativity is the face of power that appears publicly, and underlies the fact that without a necessary aesthetic gap or capacity the creative exercise of power is hardly imaginable.

In fact, the government is not just the agent of representation, but is also the subject of representation (as visualisation) as well.⁴⁰ We cannot imagine governance without reckoning with what the governed think about the governors. Governments have to unravel themselves, representing the mood of governance is compulsory for them; but during this, they do not have to destroy some agreeable illusions about themselves—without illusions nobody can cope with the task of governance. Consequently, while aesthetics makes the state capable of functioning appropriately, with a radical geometry, there is a danger of overestimating the power of human rationality which would diminish the illusions necessary for governance.

In the first place, dramaturgy is considered to be part of theatrical terminology. It is the particular technique of generating tension; it is the mechanism of producing and easing conflicts. A good dramaturge intends to involve the audience into the story he/she tells by using affective methods so that the plot can sustain the spectators' attention up to the end of the narration. The dramaturge's role, in this respect, can be grasped through the way he/she creates tension by the gradual and proportional withholding or allocation of information (essential for understanding the happenings), the way he/she plays with the expectations of the audience, and the way he constructs and dissolves the conflicts of the plot. In the world of politics, the dramaturge is the main character of representative governance, because he is the person to focus on increasing the inclina-

---

39 *Ibid.*, p. 46.
40 See András Körösényi, 'Political Representation in Leader Democracy', *Government and Opposition*, vol 4, no 3 (Summer 2005), pp. 358–78.

tions of the governed to follow the governors. As a consequence, the character of the governor is not something omnipresent, given to anyone and anytime: the leader becomes inaugurated to be a real emperor through a certain sequence of situations and through his personal ability to create and manage these situations. As Murray Edelman puts it, the highest possible level of politics is rather a question of dramaturgy than that of decision-making.[41] The key to political success is not whether the political decisions are good or bad, but it is rather the fact of whether the prince is able to render a constant image of his competency and appropriateness or not.

1. Be creative.
2. Create the expectations you can meet. Take the lead.
3. Sustain the illusion that planning the future and its consequences is absolutely possible.
4. Do not hesitate. Hesitation is enormously dangerous for the emperor. Your actions can secure your popularity.
5. Dramatize crises and your influence in developing their solutions.
6. Create your dramaturgy so that you can come out with an easily identifiable, palpable enemy at any place and time. Your enemy has to be something or somebody that you can struggle with effectively, and that you can signify as the cause of all problems.
7. The crucial point of your creativity is recognizing the limits of your actions. Do not want to save the world just form it. Do not expropriate but get use of your authority.
8. Confine your ambitions. The fall of the Tsin and Sui dynasty was caused by the emperors' ambitions. Instead of being satisfied with a general authority of supervision, the emperors desired for over-centralisation, and they wanted to manage everything directly on their own.
9. Sustain illusions. If the emperor deprives his people of illusions, the irrationality of governance can be enlightened immediately. Because of this, vulnerability might become evident for the governed.
10. If you do not want to share the wealth of the state with people, then explain that the state itself is the most appropriate manager of that. Explaining means that you can share the experience of enjoying wealth virtually instead of doing so in effect.[42]

---

41 See Murray Edelman, *The Symbolic Uses of Politics* (University of Ilinois Press, 1985), pp. 73–95.
42 See to points 1–6 Edelman, *The Symbolic Uses of Politics*, pp. 73–95., and to points 7–10 Charles de Secondat, baron de Montesquieu, *The Spirit of Laws*, Book VIII, XIX.

The Distortion and the Limits of the Paradigm

As far as the terminology is concerned, by applying the two meanings of representation (representation is the act of representing people, and at the same time, the act of presenting that which is not seen) we might state that governance is something that is seen as the actor of political representation. In other words, political representation (in term of substantive deeds) is primarily a political action, meaning governance. The precondition of the political action is the free scope of innovation and creativity. The government that thinks of representation to be an absolute mimesis becomes pretentious when launching reforms, puts chaos in the institutional system, and generates dissatisfaction, so this government creates havoc. However, at this point, we have to make a distinction. On the one hand, *chaotic governance* is the modus of governance (see Schabert) and, as a procedure, it targets the establishment of governmental conditions, whereas, *the chaos of governance* is rather the consequential crises of the course, actions (governance as political action), and mindset entailed (the ability to govern).

While the representative 'gap' is the origin of (legitimate) political power, without that, mimetic government brings about proto-totalitarian tendencies in our democracies.[43] Mimetic political power tends to become invisible and paralyzes political control. Because mimetic power rests not on the presumption of difference but identity, its aim is the liquidation of plurality. The mimetic government is out to transform the old world and create a new one, but this tyrannic aim results only in the impotence of the government. The mimetic practice produces a paradoxical combination of tyranny (because the government wants to gain its ability) and impotence (because this practice is incapable of gaining mastery over its own incarceratedness).[44]

Summary

We attempted to restore the question of political leadership from the viewpoint of political science. Our hypothesis was that the problem of governance is not primarily connected to governance theories and public management literature, but rather to political science and political theory. We argued that scaling the issue of leadership down to administrative, organisational, economic, and managerial matters cannot be fully justified. The new theories of governance focus on premises and concepts like public management, the logic of bureaucracy, the 'vacuous centre', social

---

43 Ankersmit, *Aesthetic Politics*, p. 53.
44 Ibid., pp. 50-1.

self-regulation, horizontal coordination, economic functioning, transparency, etc.; however, political leadership as creativity rather concentrates on the political leader, political power, the arrangement of the centre via vertical and chaotic coordination, autocracy, corruption, the importance of the hidden or concealed, mockery, governance through sustaining illusions, manipulation, and dramaturgy. The new theories of governance strive to depoliticise the issue of political leadership and political conduct. The perspective of political theory, however, underlines that, originally, governance is a political activity, a process the dynamistic factor of which is the political leader him/herself, the concept of power which stands in its centre, and the fact that this power should be exercised in a creative way. This means that conditions for exercising power should be established; this is the autocratic face of creativity hidden to the public. On the other hand, this means that power has to be operated creatively; this representative face of creativity is in connection with the public workings of political power. We attempted to characterise the hidden face of creativity according to Tilo Schabert, while we applied Frank Ankersmit's conception to explore and describe its public face.

In conclusion, one can embrace each concept simultaneously, and both conceptions share the presupposition that power is the fundament of politics. Consequently, politics cannot be 'civilised' — it can be only restricted or disciplined. This is what the system of institutions and norms serve for in a democracy. As a result, in modern democracies neither face of creativity can function without restrictions (that is to say, neither organising nor exercising power can be unlimited). Ignoring restrictions, however, leads to distortion: the 'hidden power' may be distorted to be an autocracy exceeding its own limits, while the 'public power' may become a paradoxical combination of impotence and tyranny. Being distorted, the two faces of creativity show clearly that there are two sides to creativity, not two different types of creativity. On the one hand: the creativity serving the autocratic governance eliminates the scope needed for the operation of creative power; on the other hand: the tyranny and the impotence, limiting its own ability to act, make the creative organisation of power difficult. In this way, the creativity needed for the organisation and operation of power is not only the centre where every possible opposition coincides ('*coincidentia oppositorum*'), but also a vicious circle ('*circulus vitiosus*'), which allows an open path to an uncivilised power exceeding (eliminating) democratic conditions.

Index

Achen, Christopher 70
Adenauer, Konrad 182
Almond, Gabriel 168
Ancient Greece 49-50, 68, 102, 135
Ankersmit, Frank 9, 179, 185-9, 191-2
Arendt, Hannah 47
Aristotle 49-50, 88-9, 135-40, 142-4
Arrow, Kenneth 91, 99
Ashley, Richard 157-9, 161
Augustine 50

Babouvian 107
Bakunin, Mikhail 102-3
Barber, Benjamin 11, 25, 129, 146
Barry, Brian 5, 11-12, 15, 17
Baumeister, Roy F. 74
Bellamy, Richard 166-7
Berlin, Isaiah 5-6, 33, 42-7, 85, 179
Bernstein, Eduard 114, 123
Bishop, George 70
Bismarck 37, 46
Blair, Tony 15, 154, 173, 182, 184
Blanqui, August 102-3, 116
Bobbio, Norberto 83, 95
Bodin, Jean 50, 60-2, 65, 156
Britain 15, 23, 83, 126, 141, 155, 161, 173-4
Brown, Chris 165
Brown, Gordon 145, 152-3
Burns, James M. 128
Bush, George W. 15, 154

Caesarism 37-40
Carlyle, Thomas 131
Castiglione, Dario 167
Cavour, Camillo Benso 46
Christianity 25, 135
Chryssochoou, Dimitris 166
Churchill, Winston 43-4
Civil Rights 32
Cohen, Joshua 68, 96

Communist League 103, 108
Communist Manifesto 104, 107-8, 123
Confucianism 14
Converse, Philip 69-70

Dahl, Robert 81-2, 85-99, 141
Dante 50
De Gaulle, Charles 43, 129
De Jouvenel, Bertrand 92
De Tocqueville, Alexis 33, 73
Deleuze, Gilles 120
Demagogues 37-8, 40, 68, 147
Derrida, Jacques 120, 123
Deutsch, M. 73-4
Dicey, Albert Venn 155-7
Dionysus of Halicarnassus 50
Douglas, Mary 168
Downs, Anthony 92, 99
Durkheim, Emile 132
Dworkin, Ronald 5, 11, 26

Edelman, Murray 148, 190
Eisenhower, President Dwight 182
Elster, Jon 68, 71, 75, 167
England 107
Enlightenment, The 134, 150
Erikson, Robert S. 70, 134
Europe 3-4, 17, 71, 98, 112, 114-17, 123, 143, 145, 166-7

Fassbender, Bardo 165, 173
Faust 4
Femia, Joseph 3, 6-7, 30, 80, 91, 93, 99, 101-2
Festinger, L. 73
Fodor, Gabor G. 9
Foucault, Michel 165-6, 175
France 102-6, 109-10, 112, 121, 127, 174
Franklin, Benjamin 135
French Revolution 102-5, 121
Freud, Sigmund 1

Friedrich, Carl J. 84, 94

Galston, William 8, 17, 126, 130, 133, 135, 137, 141-3, 148
Garibaldi 43
Gauthier, David 59
Geertz, Clifford 168
Gerard, H. B. 73-4
Germany 38, 105, 107-9, 112-14, 118, 131, 165
Goethe 4
Gomard, Sebastien 127
Gramsci, Antonio 70-1, 102, 112, 117-24
Gray, John 5, 28
Guattari 120
Gulag 102
Gyurcsany, Ferenc 182, 184

Habermas, Jurgen 4, 36, 68, 73, 120-1, 143, 154
Hague Congress 107
Hamilton, Alexander 54, 125, 131, 134, 136, 138-42, 147
Harding, Neil 115
Hegel, Georg Wilhelm Friedrich 105-6, 110, 115, 132
Held, David 80
Heller, Agnes 120-1
Heraclitus 49
Herzl, Theodor 45
Higley, John 130
Hitler, Adolf. 1, 43, 46-7, 50, 52
Hobbes, Thomas 6, 50, 57-66, 156, 160
Holdon, Barry 129
Holland/Dutch 107, 171
Horton, John 5-6
Hume, David 134
Hunt, Richard N. 102, 106, 108
Huntington, Samuel 95, 168
Hyndman 109

Industrial Revolution 105, 115, 126
International Working Men's Association 108
Iraq 154

Jacobins 21, 102, 106, 108, 111-15, 119, 121, 123
James II 166
Jay, John 54, 125, 131, 134, 136, 138-42, 147
Jefferson, Thomas 54
Johnson, President L.B. 182

Kant, Immanuel 32, 50, 134
Kautsky, Karl 102, 112-19, 123-4
King, Martin Luther 24-5, 32
Klosko, George 21

Kohl, Helmuth 182
Körösényi, András 7, 31, 49, 64, 77, 125, 130, 189
Kruglanski, Arie W. 143

Lacan, Jacques 122
Laclau, Ernesto 120-2
Lassman, Peter 5-6, 93
Lasswell, Harold 138
League of the Just 108
Leary, M. R. 74
LeBon, Gustave 1
Lenin 7, 46-7, 102, 106, 112, 115-19, 122-4, 131
Leviathan 58, 61-2, 66, 156, 163
Lincoln, Abraham 32, 43, 46
Lloyd George, David 46
Locke, John 6, 54-5, 60, 62-6, 153, 174
Lord, Carnes 14, 52
Louis XIV 166
Lyotard, Jean-Francois 120

Machiavelli 2-3, 6, 14, 50, 52-7, 59-66, 136, 145, 147, 153, 181
MacIntyre, Alasdair 135-6, 140, 148
Madison, James 54, 125, 130-1, 134, 136, 138-142, 147, 150
Mandevillean 134
Marsilius 50
Marx, Karl 7-8, 33, 101-24, 132
Marxism 7-8, 13, 33, 70-2, 101-24
May, John D. 82
Merkel, Angela 182
Michels, Robert 78, 130, 134
Mill, John Stuart 14, 94, 130-3, 137-144, 146, 150
Mitterand, Francois 179, 182
Modernists 50
Montesquieu 54, 188, 190
Morganthau, Hans 161
Mosca, Gaetano 14, 130
Mouffe, Chantal 33, 120-2, 162
Mussolini, Benito 1, 50, 52

Napoleon 37, 43, 46, 166
Nazism 36
Newey, Glen 17-8
Nietzsche, Friedrich 1, 13
Nirvana Fallacy 77

Oakeshott, Michael 76, 172
Ockham 50
Olson, Mancur 91, 99

Pareto, Vilfredo 14, 78, 130
Paris Commune 106, 110
Pateman, Carole 80, 109

Pericles 68
Piaget, Jean 169
Pitkin, Hanna 27, 82, 84, 86
Plamenatz, John 79-80, 83, 94
Plato 5-6, 14, 33, 41, 49-53, 57, 60, 64-5, 68-9, 88, 136
Polybius 50
Popper, Karl R. 49, 51-2, 66
Primordialists 50
Prokhovnik, Raia 8-9
Przeworski, Adam 71, 83, 89
Puritans 46

Rawls, John 4-5, 11-12, 17-19, 22, 24, 26, 32, 35, 54, 130, 153-4
Reagan, President Ronald 6, 52
Renaissance, The 3, 181
Riker, William 91, 187
Robespierre 46, 102-5, 121
Rokeach, Milton 141, 143
Roosevelt, Franklin D. 43-6, 129, 182
Rousseau, J. J. 1, 27, 160
Ruge, Arnold 103
Ruscio, Kenneth 6, 52-9, 62, 64-6
Russia 114-17

Sarkozy, Nicolas 182
Saward, Michael 67, 78, 87-8, 90, 96, 97
Schabert, Tilo 9, 179-84, 187, 191-2
Schmitt, Carl 6, 14, 33, 36, 60-6, 85, 93, 160, 162, 164-5
Schumpeter, Joseph 5, 14, 77, 79-81, 85, 89-90, 92, 94-9, 130
Scoccia, D. 76
Searing, Donald D. 8-9
Seneca 188
Shklar, Judith 5, 28
Slomp, Gabriella 6
Smith, Adam 134
Social Democratic Party 112-14
Sorell, Tom 61
SPD 112-4

Spinoza 160, 171
Steenbergen, Marco R. 8-9
Strong, Tracy 164
Sunstein, Cass 76

Tetlock, Philip 140, 142
Thatcher, Margaret 6, 52, 174
Thompson, Dennis F. 52, 137, 145
Thucydides 188
Totalitarianism 47, 102, 191
Townshend, Jules 7-8
Trotsky 43
Truman, President 182
Turin Factory Councils 118-19, 123

Ulpian 50
United States of America 3, 15, 26, 33, 36, 38, 70-2, 107, 135
Utopia(n) 21, 35, 43, 45-7, 75, 108, 122, 124

Verba, Sidney 168
Verrier, Marie-Claude 127
Voegelin, Eric 49
Voltaire 24

Walker, Neil 165-7, 175
Walker, Robin B.J. 157-9, 161, 164, 167
Weale, Albert 129
Weber, Max 1-2, 5-7, 14, 33-42, 47, 81, 85, 93-4, 112, 114, 123, 130, 132, 153
Weimar Republic 165
Weitling, Wilhelm 102
Weizmann, Chaim 43-5
White, Kevin 182
Williams, Bernard 4, 7, 17, 22-3, 28-9
World War I 112-116
World War II 2

Zaller, John R. 69-72
Zolo, Danilo 79-80, 99